# SEAWARD

# SEAWARD

## Chasing Master Mariners in the Golden Age of Sail

## HAROLD BRADLEY

LUMINARE PRESS
WWW.LUMINAREPRESS.COM

## SEAWARD
### Chasing Master Mariners in the Golden Age of Sail
Copyright © 2023 by Harold Bradley

All rights reserved. This book or any portion thereof may not be reproduced or used in any manner whatsoever without the express written permission of the publisher, except for the use of brief quotations in a book review.

Printed-on-Demand in Australia, the United Kingdom, and the United States of America

10 9 8 7 6 5 4 3 2

Luminare Press
442 Charnelton St.
Eugene, OR 97401
www.luminarepress.com

LCCN: 2022914338
ISBN: 978-1-64388-630-5

---

Title page illustration: Ship *Epaminondas* (Official Number 15388). John Kelly served as first mate on this ship in 1859 to 1860. Image credit: Dean Daniels, whose great-great-grandparents arrived at New York from Prussia via Rotterdam on the *Epaminondas* in the summer of 1858. They eventually settled in Minnesota. According to the Daniels family, this rendering of the ship is a charcoal tracing of the original image, which once hung in the Belfast office of David Grainger & Co.

Dedicated to the memory of my parents
who always nurtured interest in
our family lineage and heritage

# Contents

*Illustrations* ........ ix
*A Note to Readers* ........ xi
*Acknowledgments* ........ xv

INTRODUCTION
On the Shores of Lough Neagh ........ 1

CHAPTER ONE
Down to the Sea in Ships ........ 13

CHAPTER TWO
William Kelly and the *Miles Barton* ........ 64

CHAPTER THREE
William Kelly and the *Merrie England* ........ 109

CHAPTER FOUR
John Kelly's Last Voyages ........ 136

CHAPTER FIVE
Conflagration and Destruction ........ 142

CHAPTER SIX
Swallowing the Anchor ........ 149

CHAPTER SEVEN
Standing Over ........ 192

CHAPTER EIGHT
Trail's End ........ 240

*Sources* ........ 252
*Bibliography* ........ 256
*Notes* ........ 261
*Index* ........ 288
*About the Author* ........ 317

# Illustrations

## Family Tree

Family Tree: Kelly, Moore, and Wallace Families, xx

## Figures

Frontispiece: Captain William Kelly (1811–1877), xviii

Fig. 2: The packet ship *Margaret Johnson* approaching Liverpool, 15

Fig. 3: Scatarie, a flying island with tattered wings, 45

Fig. 4: William Thompson Bartoll, *The Great Gale of 1846*, fireboard, 48

Fig. 5: William Kelly's master's certificate, 61

Fig. 6: A wooden model of the clipper ship *Miles Barton*, 65

Fig. 7: *Miles Barton*, voyage 3, option A—Eastern Passage, 96

Fig. 8: *Miles Barton*, voyage 3, option B—Torres Strait Passage, 97

Fig. 9: William Kelly's percussion revolver, 101

Fig. 10: John Kelly's master's certificate, 107

Fig. 11: John Kelly's Claim for Certificate of Service, 108

Fig. 12: *Merrie England*, voyage 1, 122

Fig. 13: *Merrie England*, voyage 4, 132

Fig. 14: Report of John Kelly's death by drowning in the sinking of the ship *Hilton*, 141

Fig. 15: John Kelly's gravestone inscription, Muckamore burial ground, 141

Fig. 16: Approximate location of the *Miles Barton* wreck site, 146

Fig. 17: The ship *Princess Alexandra*, watercolor on paper, 188

Fig. 18: William Kelly's home at 6 Richmond Cres., Belfast, 193

Fig. 19: The first page of William Kelly's letter to Elizabeth McFerran, 199

Fig. 20: The glittering McFerran sisters, 202

Fig. 21: Mary (Kelly) McFerran (c.1813–1895), 210

Fig. 22: The back garden at 6 Richmond Crescent, Belfast, 225

Fig. 23: The Kelly plot at Muckamore burial ground, 230

Fig. 24: The barque *Bankfields* moored at Port Pirie, South Australia, 233

Fig. 25: The *Bankfields*'s last passage to the Ships' Graveyard, 234

Fig. 26: Captain William Kelly (1811–1877), 239

Fig. 27: Artist's concept of LightSail 2 in Earth orbit, 247

Fig. 28: Trail's End, The Sea Ranch, Sonoma County, California, 251

## Tables

Table 1: Workhouse emigrants transported to Quebec via the ship *Belinda* (1846), 34

Table 2: 1861 UK Census, 18 Upper Parliament Street, 133

Table 3: William Kelly's career as a ship's master at sea (1836-1863), 158-160

# A Note to Readers

Like a square-rigged sailing ship emerging from impenetrable fog into a sun-splashed sea, this book reveals the comings and goings of Captain William Kelly, a nineteenth-century master mariner from Antrim, Northern Ireland. As my paternal great-great-granduncle, he occupies a twig of some significance in my family tree. His younger brother, Captain John Kelly, is just the shadow of a twig. Both have been lost to history until now.

Fortunately, once I discovered how and where to look for them, they began to appear with some regularity. The marine news sections of historic newspapers at ports around the world announced when they had arrived and departed—although every now and then they would slip surreptitiously into or out of port with no one the wiser, especially William. Sometimes the papers noted their cargoes and passengers. Occasionally there were reports indicating that they had "spoken to" (hailed) other ships at sea, or they had "been spoken to." The questions remain: Why research these men now when they are so remote from us and the likelihood of getting their stories right is so small? Indeed, are they even relevant today?

Initially the challenge alone was incentive enough. The exercise of looking for them generally resulted in the thrill of finding them. This nourished the urge to look again and dig deeper into where they had been, what they had done, and where they were going next.

The project expanded in breadth and depth. As the brothers crisscrossed the vast oceans that constitute over 70 percent of our planet's surface, they left wakes to trace and history to plumb. William participated in the great Irish migrations to Canada, the United States, and Australia; the German exodus to the United States; and the transport of plantation workers from India to the West Indies. Both men carried people with high hopes and scant possessions to far-flung outposts of the known world. They also moved timber, cotton, tobacco, salt, wheat, rice, guano, and manufactured goods of all kinds around the globe.

This is why the title of the book is a simple directive—*Seaward*—signifying the direction taken. Water was their medium and the sky their motive force, filling their sails with the winds that drove them forward. And when the winds did not oblige, there were tricks of the trade. *The Oxford Companion to Ships and the Sea* defines ghosting as "the art of making headway in a sailing ship without any apparent wind to fill her sails." The entry goes on to say, "By taking advantage of such breaths of wind as may occur, a well-trimmed sailing vessel can often make quite an appreciable way through the water, appearing to move, or ghost, even in a flat calm."

Researching and writing this book has been an exercise in historical and genealogical ghosting. Navigating across a sea of questions, I have gratefully received whatever answers have come my way to arrive at a remarkable place—a greater understanding and appreciation of the lives and times of master mariners William and John Kelly of Antrim Town.

My only regret is that I cannot share these discoveries with others, now also long gone, who wished to know more about these men. For example, in a 1928 letter to *Sea Breezes* magazine, William Kelly's grandson wrote of him and one of his ships: "I wonder if there is anyone alive today who remembers him or anyone who can tell me what the end of the *Miles Barton* was?" This book answers that question and many more like it. Remarkable portraits of William and John Kelly have emerged from surviving fragmentary records. These scraps of the past do not constitute the whole story by any means, but they do offer intriguing glimpses into two representative seafaring lives during the golden age of sail—lives that still resonate today.

# Acknowledgments

My father, Wilfred, told us about William Kelly with obvious delight. When flipping through our family albums, he would always tap our two photographs of Kelly and tell us never to lose them, declaring, "He was an important man, an Irish sea captain. Imagine the tales he would have told." I am grateful to my father for drawing our attention to Kelly. I am also indebted to my brother, Richard, for beginning our Kelly research, for conserving our memorabilia from this branch of our extended family, and for encouraging my efforts to find and pass on some fascinating stories from our family's nineteenth-century past.

Thanks to Dr. Bob Foy, whose book *Dear Uncle: Immigrant Letters to Antrim from the USA, 1843–1852* contains the remarkable letter William Kelly wrote in 1871 recounting the murder of his brother-in-law in Reconstruction-era New Orleans. Another of Bob's books, *Remembering All the Orrs*, speaks of John Orr, the grandfather of Sarah Orr, who married William Kelly's brother, John, in 1845. Bob has been an enthusiastic and highly valued resource for Antrim history, advice, photographs, inspiration, and manuscript review over many years.

Crew agreements listing the seamen who sailed on Kelly ships and their ports of call have been very useful in reconstructing some of the brothers' voyages. Thanks to the staff at the Maritime History Archive (MHA), Memorial University of Newfoundland, for researching and forwarding the MHA crew agreements pertinent to my interests.

Surviving ships' logs are rare. As a result, I have relied principally on two sources for piecing together the likely routes sailed by William and John Kelly. These are *Ocean Passages for the World* (1895), compiled by Captain Robert Jackson, R.N., and various other nineteenth-century publications of the British Admiralty's Hydrographic Office, such as *The Australia Pilot*, *The Red Sea and Gulf of Aden Pilot*, and *The China Sea Directory*, to name a few.

I am grateful to Patricia Stavely Baird for sharing her great-grandfather's diary of his 1853 trip from County Down to Melbourne, Australia, as a passenger on the *Miles Barton*. David Stavely's journal brings us about as close to experiencing a nineteenth-century sea voyage as is possible today.

Thanks to the RootsWeb Mariners Mailing List (now no longer hosted by RootsWeb). Piers Smith-Creswell and other members of this group provided many useful answers and suggestions in response to my numerous twenty-first-century "landsman" questions. Another list member, Clare Abbott (author of *Faithful of Days: The Story of Robert Crighton, Master Mariner*), generously researched crew agreements at the National Archives (UK), where she discovered and passed on to me many fascinating details of individual Kelly voyages.

Thanks to the staff at the Royal Museums Greenwich, and to Lorna Hyland of the Merseyside Maritime Museum, Kevin Johnson of the Penobscot Marine Museum, and Jason Davis of the Planetary Society. Thanks to David and Anne Burton of Wolfville, Nova Scotia, for kindly allowing me to include their painting of the ship *Princess Alexandra* in the book.

# Acknowledgments

I am grateful to my cousins Bill and Ian Bradley for supporting and supplementing my research during their tours of South Africa and Northern Ireland, respectively. I also greatly appreciate Ian's (and my brother's) expertise in preparing many of the book's images for publication.

I wish to thank Kristen Brack, Kim Harper-Kennedy, Nina Leis, Patricia Marshall, Caitlin McCrum, Melissa Thomas, and Sallie Vandagrift of Luminare Press for preparing *Seaward* for publication—and Linda Christian for creating the index. Many thanks as well to Sarah Currin, Kristen Hall-Geisler, Jennifer Kepler, and Ali Shaw at Indigo Editing for copyediting and proofreading the manuscript. Thanks also to Kit Foster of Edinburgh, Scotland and Nina Leis at Luminare Press for their assistance with *Seaward*'s cover design.

Additionally, I am most grateful to Patricia Nasko Smith who has given me free rein to chase my mariners over many years. Pat has also provided valuable suggestions and advice as the manuscript evolved.

Finally, I must acknowledge William and John Kelly for their seafaring travels, travails, and triumphs. Piecing their stories together has transcended a learning experience. It has been a journey and an adventure in its own right. To those who read this book, I hope you enjoy the lives and voyages recounted here, wherever they may take you.

# Frontispiece

Captain William Kelly (1811–1877).
Image credit: Bradley archive/undated.

*No creation man ever achieved was more in the hands of its master than the ocean-going sailing-ship. He was more than her brains. He was her character, her resolution, her hope of integrity. If he failed, she failed. If he did not know his business, it was no use giving him the best ship in the world. If he had a defect of character, in the long run that would affect his ship and the men in her. The big square-rigged ship can be compared to a great orchestra, needing an inspired conductor really to bring it to full life. Lesser conductors might do something, of course, but with a real master the performance could be magnificent.*

—Alan Villiers, *The Way of a Ship* (1970), 45

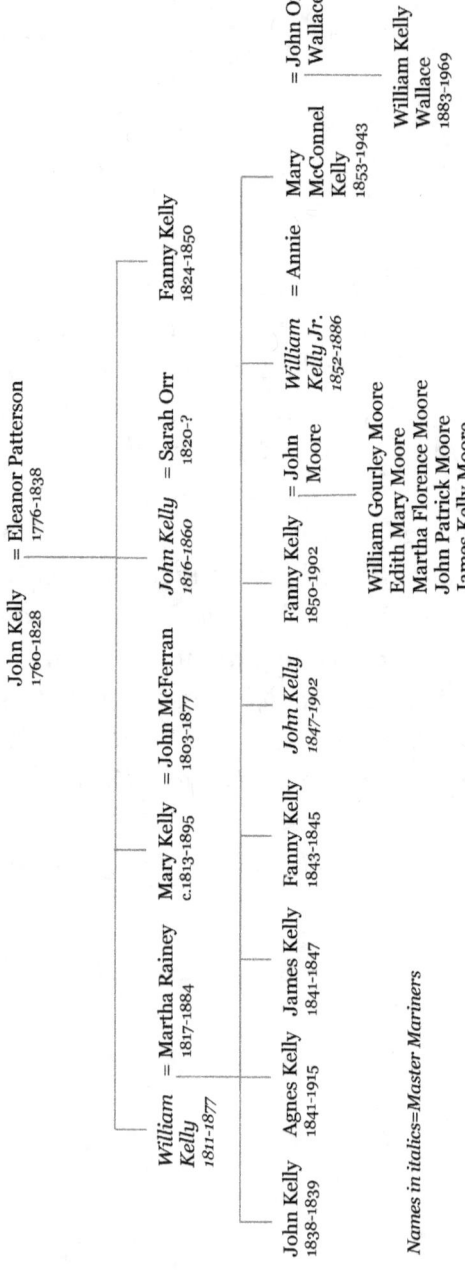

INTRODUCTION

# On the Shores of Lough Neagh

(1811–1830)

This is the story of two lives in windswept motion during the so-called golden age of sail when oceans were the lifeblood, sea lanes the arteries, ships the muscle, and mariners the heartbeat of a global impulse to move people and goods around the world. The people were immigrants looking for better lives in new places. The goods were agricultural produce and timber flowing from the New World to the Old with manufactured products returning from the Old World to the New.

This circular exchange enabled some in the working class to earn a living, others in the middle class to prosper, and a few wealthy people to get wealthier (or go bust!) during the unprecedented churn of populations, products, and possibilities that characterized the Victorian age. In an elegant and lucrative *pas de deux*, this complementary rotation of people and goods was driven by the circular movement of the trade, monsoon, and variable winds that deep-sea mariners harnessed to move passengers and cargoes seaward, wherever they had to go.

Brothers William and John Kelly of Antrim Town were players in this demographic and economic outburst of escape and trade. They sailed then-well-known British ships ranging from sturdy wooden packet boats plying the UK coastal and trans-Atlantic routes to speedy, far-ranging, state-of-the-art clipper ships billowing out to India, Australia, and China under clouds of sail.

## William Kelly (1811–1877)

As a shipmaster sailing out of Belfast, Liverpool, and London, Captain William Kelly crisscrossed the Atlantic and Indian Oceans and the Arabian, Philippine, and China Seas, plunging before the wind to Quebec, New York, New Orleans, and Mobile in North America; to Lima and Demerara (now part of Guyana in South America); to Bremen and Rotterdam in Europe; to Cape Town, Calcutta (now Kolkata), Melbourne, and Aden; and all the way to Ceylon (now Sri Lanka), Burma (now Myanmar), the Philippines, Indonesia, Hong Kong, Singapore, and Shanghai—and he brought his ships home safely, with only one mishap along the way. The 1850s were the pinnacle of his career when he traveled the greatest distances, carried the largest loads, and affirmed his reputation for fast, well-managed trips under a steady hand.

William never circled Earth in a single voyage, but in a career just shy of thirty years at sea, he traveled more than 400,000 nautical miles on approximately thirty round trips from UK ports. This equates to roughly eighteen circumnavigations of the globe at the equator. He and his wife, Martha, had eight children, with five surviving to adulthood. His sons, John and William Jr., also became master mariners in both sail and steam. They staked their own claim to the inscription from Psalm 107 that is incised in the base of the Kelly family monument in Muckamore graveyard,[1] southeast of Antrim Town: "They that go down to the sea in ships, that do business in great waters, these see the works of the Lord and his wonders in the deep."

## John Kelly (1816–1860)

Like his older brother, John Kelly went to sea at an early age and worked his way up to master mariner. His early career sailing out of Belfast and London took him to Quebec, Saint John (New Brunswick), New Orleans, Charleston, Mobile, Savannah, Philadelphia, and Sierra Leone in the early and mid-1840s. His later career, after he apparently decamped to California for a time in 1848, is murkier. During these years he slips out of focus, perhaps with his wife, Sarah, by his side, possibly moving to the booming settlement of Yerba Buena, the forerunner of today's San Francisco. This was the jumping-off point for the California gold rush that drew men, women, and the seamen who transported them in droves to America's West Coast in the late 1840s.

After his mysterious California adventure, the next evidence of John's career emerges from the particulars of service he filed when renewing his master's certificate in 1856. This was immediately prior to a momentous joint undertaking with William that constitutes perhaps the best part of their shared narrative. Then follow two shadowy years when John appears to descend a rung in his career, remaining at sea but not as master. The Kelly monument at Muckamore commemorates his last voyage as follows: "Captain John Kelly…lost in a hurricane off Mauritius, January 1860, aged 45 years." The unraveling of the circumstances surrounding John's death, especially determining the year and month in which he died, was a particularly challenging task in piecing together his story.

But the Kelly monument is the end of this story, and we seek its beginning. This means starting in Antrim and following the brothers across surging, white-capped seas, through lashing winds, towering waves, contrary currents, and stifling doldrums to far-away ports of call. Both men experienced the bracing freshness and tug of the open ocean—the freedom to go anywhere in a rapidly unfurling world—until time and the unfathomable led William inexorably back to Antrim and the Kelly family plot at Muckamore, home to firm ground.

John never returned to Muckamore, but his fate is carved in stone there. I can only speculate about his final resting place, somewhere off the plangent, white-sand beaches of Mauritius beneath a wind-whipped shipping lane in the Indian Ocean.

To begin with the first piercing squalls, the Kelly brothers were born in a public house, the sons of John and Eleanor Kelly, innkeepers of the Head Inn at Antrim Town. Their home was approximately twenty miles northwest of Belfast on Lough Neagh, the largest lake by area in the British Isles. William was born on Tuesday, July 16, 1811.

The Head Inn was located at the top of the town's main street. It was a good-sized coach and wagon stop, often referred to in those days as a carman's inn. Deeds in the Public Record Office of Northern Ireland (PRONI, Belfast) show that up to about the late 1790s, before John Kelly Sr. took over the Head Inn, the family had been handloom linen weavers in Islandreagh, a townland near Muckamore, about two and a half miles east of Antrim Town.[2]

To set William's birth in its astronomical context, he was born in the same year as the Great Comet of 1811. This impressive celestial visitor was visible like a bright eyelash in the night sky over the British Isles for 260 days—a record length of time until Comet Hale-Bopp's eighteen-month flyby in 1997–1998. The French astronomer Honoré Flaugergues first discovered the Great Comet in March 1811 in the neighborhood of three constellations in the southern sky: Carina (the hull), Puppis (the poop deck), and Vela (the sails), all parts of a previous larger constellation called Argo Navis (the Ship Argo). I do not mean to imply that William's seaward disposition was in any way predetermined by the stars. This is just an interesting coincidence.

The 1811 comet was also known as Napoleon's Comet because it was thought to have heralded the French emperor's unsuccessful invasion of Russia as well as the War of 1812. In other Napoleonic engagements, British, Spanish, and Portuguese forces were playing cat and mouse with the French army on the Spanish peninsula. It was the Regency period in England when King George III, declared unfit to rule with the symptoms of what many suspect was porphyria, was replaced by his son George, the Prince of Wales. In what was then called the Far East, an English expeditionary force was poised to conquer the Dutch East Indies. In my own vicinity, Russian settlers had just established a seaside trading post at Fort Ross in what is now Sonoma County, ninety miles north of San Francisco

Bay—a particularly beautiful area where I enjoy hiking the rugged coastal bluffs of The Sea Ranch community.

In the world of letters, Oxford University had expelled Percy Bysshe Shelley for printing "The Necessity of Atheism," and Jane Austen was poised to publish *Sense and Sensibility*. Other notables born in 1811 include English poet Arthur Hallam, American journalist and publisher Horace Greeley, Hungarian composer and pianist Franz Liszt, French writer Théophile Gautier, British novelist William Makepeace Thackeray, and the British maritime painter Samuel Walters, who would in due course celebrate Kelly's ship the *Merrie England* in oils.

John Kelly's birth five years after William, on Saturday, June 1, 1816, occurred against the backdrop of the "Year Without a Summer" when climate abnormalities caused by the 1815 eruption of Mount Tambora in the Dutch East Indies dropped temperatures worldwide, triggering crop failures and food shortages across the northern hemisphere. As a result, a foot of snow blanketed Quebec City in early June, and a typhus epidemic triggered by famine swept Ireland from 1816 to 1819. Approximately 100,000 Irish people perished during this period. John was lucky to survive the year of his birth.

In 1816, King George III's health was continuing its downhill slide, but probably not for lack of nutrition. Napoleon had been banished to Saint Helena after (literally) meeting his Waterloo the previous year. In the give-and-take of international realpolitik, the British handed the East Indies back to the Dutch. A Russian expedition led by Captain Otto von Kotzebue was continuing to explore the coastal terraces around Fort Ross with their billowing, grass-covered hills and steeply wooded slopes.

Charlotte Brontë was born on April 21, 1816; Irish playwright Richard Brinsley Sheridan died on July 7. Also in 1816, Samuel Taylor Coleridge published "Kubla Khan," his vision in a dream with a sacred river running down to a sunless sea, and John Keats penned his sonnet "On First Looking into Chapman's Homer," with its allusion to traveling in the realms of gold. Thirty-three years later, it might have been something like the anticipation of discovery in this well-known sonnet that drew John Kelly "with wild surmise" to the American Gold Coast.

## The Queen of Antrim Town

Antrim's Head Inn might itself have been a bit of a literary hothouse. A highly prized family heirloom has survived for over 190 years. It is an acrostic verse in which the first letter of each line spells out "Miss Fanny Kelly." Fanny was the Kelly brothers' youngest sister, just two years old when a Kelly family member penned this admiring poem, possibly in honor of her birthday, perhaps also in hopeful anticipation of the child's future promise.[3]

## An Acrostic

>Matchless praise bears on thy soaring Wings
>Import her name whose Fame a Kelly sings
>Sweet is the maid both beautiful and gay
>Sweet as the primrose in the month of May
>Fairest of Maidens, Pride of every Eye
>Angelic Dame whose fame shall never die
>Nature has framed thee with the utmost care

> Not Hebe self so beautiful and fair
> Youth wit and beauty in her face combine
> Kind heaven protect this favorite of the nine
> Expressive sweetness in her face behold
> Like Per[s]ian Marble set in Indian gold
> Look for the Fair whom all the graces crown
> You'll nominate her Queen of Antrim Town

"Kind heaven protect this favorite of the nine" implies that there were nine children in the Kelly family, but only four are currently accounted for—my great-great-grandmother, Mary (c.1813–1895); my seafaring great-great-granduncles, William (1811–1877) and John (1816–1860); and their youngest sister, the incomparable Fanny (1824–1850), whose future promise would sadly not be of long duration.

In my admittedly overheated imagination, I picture the Head Inn as a boisterous place in the 1820s, with assorted visitors coming and going and a brood of gifted children conversing in trochees and iambs. With its classical allusions, careful metrical line, and meticulous rhymes, Fanny's acrostic and William Kelly's fluent letter writing later in life suggest that the Kelly children might have received a better-than-average education, at least by the standards of the day. John and Eleanor Kelly might have been relatively well-to-do and able to send the children to schools that offered more than just reading and writing. Navigating ships across oceans later in life (without today's ubiquitous Global Positioning System) would have required agile young minds capable of grasping geometry, mathematics, and astronomy, as their education progressed.

## A Dispute with Mrs. Frizell

The sudden death of innkeeper John Kelly at age sixty-eight on September 16, 1828 marks the end of the line for the Kelly family at the Head Inn.[4] Most importantly, William Kelly, the seventeen-year-old eldest son of the family, would not take on his father's role as a publican. Instead, he would look elsewhere for a career—but not before tangling with an intriguing woman over the disposition of the Head Inn. This dispute comes to light in two newspaper articles from 1829 and one from 1830.

The woman in question is Mrs. Eleanor Frizell (also variously spelled Frizel, Frizzel, and Frizzle), who claimed to have in her possession the last will and testament of innkeeper John Kelly naming *her* as the heir to the inn. On December 14, 1829, she placed the following advertisement in the *Belfast Commercial Chronicle*, offering the property for sale:

> TO INNKEEPERS. To be sold for the purposes of the will of the late John Kelly, deceased. That well-known tenement in the town of Antrim late the property of the deceased, and which has been for upwards of twenty years established—and in the very best trade and situation as a CARMAN'S INN, having every requisite accommodation for the business. The house is roomy, the offices and stabling extensive, and the entire concern in excellent order. This property is held for a long unexpired term of years, at the trifling rent of £3 per Ann. And the stock, etc. may be had at a valuation. To a person intending to carry on the business, a better situation, or more complete concern,

may not readily offer. Apply to Mrs. FRIZELL on the property; or to Mr. Fred. Wm. Macauley, solicitor. Antrim, 10th December, 1829.[5]

Eight days later, on December 22, 1829, William Kelly responded to Mrs. Frizell with the following admonitory announcement placed in the *Belfast News-Letter*:

CAUTION: Having seen an Advertisement in the Belfast Commercial Chronicle of the 14th inst. headed "TO INNKEEPERS," offering for Sale that TENEMENT in the Town of Antrim, late the property of JOHN KELLY, DECEASED; I HEREBY CAUTION ANY Person from treating with Mrs. FRIZZEL for the purchase thereof, inasmuch as it is my intention to set aside the alleged will of the said John Kelly, and I have already commenced proceedings for such purpose, he having died intestate—Dated this 18th day of Dec., 1829.

> Wm. Kelly, Son and Heir at Law
> of the late John Kelly of Antrim[6]

After this clash, the newspapers were silent for ten months until Mrs. Frizell returned to the fray. On October 15, 1830, she placed the following advertisement in the *Belfast News-Letter*, this time offering the Head Inn for rent:

TO BE LET: For such term of years as may be agreed upon, and possession given upon the first day of November next—THAT HOUSE and PREMISES, long established an INN, in ANTRIM, formerly in the occupation of the late JOHN KELLY, deceased. There is a large and commodious HOUSE in front, and a large YARD, enclosed by Stabling, Cowhouse, Barn, etc. all lofted, in the rear. There is also a BAKE-HOUSE on the premises, in complete working order, and a good KITCHEN GARDEN in the rear. The tenant can be accommodated with the License; the place will be found on inspection the most commodious as an INN of any on the same line of road. For terms, apply on the Premises to ELEANOR FRIZEL.

ANTRIM, Oct. 4, 1830[7]

This 1830 clipping, with its detailed description of the Kelly property, implies that Mrs. Frizell might have prevailed in her dispute with William Kelly. The question remains: Did this real estate quarrel drive William and John Kelly to sea? With the Head Inn no longer in the cards for them, did a complete break with their native town appeal to them as the best way forward?

As a sidebar to this discussion, John Kelly Sr. owned other properties in Antrim. A subsequent newspaper announcement refers to the auction at the Head Inn of "Matson's Tenement, situated on the North side of street, near the Town Head-well; on part of which the capital DWELLING-HOUSE and OFFICES demised to John Kelly (in September 1806 for 61 years at £3, 5s per annum) are built."[8] If the owner of this tenement was Mrs. Frizell, she might have been liquidating her assets for some new venture. If the owner was the twenty-two-year-old William Kelly, he might have also needed ready cash to fund an undertaking of his own—perhaps a foray into shipping, possibly to buy shares in a ship or otherwise launch or advance a seafaring career?

William and John Kelly might first have imagined the great wooden ships that they would subsequently sail across oceans far and wide in the intertwining hedges and woodlots of Antrim's green glens. Here W. S. Smith observed: "Beeches, horse-chestnuts, Scotch firs, alders, sycamores, larches, ashes, wild cherries, hazel and hawthorn bushes intermingle and constitute generally a soft, varied, luxuriant scene, truly delightful to look upon."[9]

Many of the ships they sailed were Canadian-built, largely softwood vessels that combined a variety of timber. In Wallace's deconstruction, we read: "19th-century shipbuilders used tamarack (also known as hackmatack) for ships' timbers and planking; black birch for keels, floor timbers and lower planking; white oak for stems, stern posts, keelsons and beams; yellow pine for decking; red pine for ceilings and planking; white pine for cabins, interior finishing and masts; black spruce for yards and top masts; beech for ships' bottoms; white elm for under-water planking and blocks; and white cedar for top timbers."[10]

The Kelly brothers' early vessels were built in Quebec and New Brunswick, where seemingly limitless timber resources fed Britain's inexhaustible appetite for wood, wood products, and wooden sailing ships sliding down the slipways of saw-biting, hammer-ringing shipyards at home and abroad.

CHAPTER ONE

# Down to the Sea in Ships

(1836–1852)

I know nothing about William Kelly's earliest experiences at sea. Did he begin as a ship's boy? Did he serve as an apprentice groomed from an early age to be an officer, or did he rise from ordinary seaman to able seaman to third, then second, then first mate, steadily working his way up the chain of command to becoming a captain of square-riggers? I would love to know the details of his early career, but they are lost and likely irretrievable now. All I can say is that he took to the sea early[11] and might have cut his teeth as a ship's master in the UK coastal trade, possibly crisscrossing the Irish Sea between Belfast and Liverpool in the mid-1830s transporting oats, potatoes, salt, and other sundries on Belfast ships like the *Hillsborough* and the *Success*.[12]

The first mention I have found of William Kelly as a ship's captain appears in an advertisement in the *Belfast Commercial Chronicle* of Wednesday, August 17, 1836.[13] Here the twenty-five-year-old seaman is listed as commander of the barque *Margaret Johnson* (366 tons, built in 1825 in Nova Scotia), which subsequently departed

Belfast for New Orleans on August 23 with a cargo of slates, railroad iron, crockery, coal, and dry goods. She arrived at New Orleans on October 26, eventually departing on December 9 carrying 1,150 bales of cotton and arriving safely back at Liverpool toward the end of January 1837 with William still in command. Interestingly, his brother, John, appears to have been with him on this voyage, serving as a twenty-year-old apprentice seaman.[14]

The Penobscot Marine Museum's (PMM's) object record for the painting shown in Figure 2 describes the two code flags flying from her mizzen mast as representing the numbers 9 and 3. This code confirms that she is the *Margaret Johnson*, according to the Liverpool or Watson's Code of Signals (1826–1843). The vessel has a figurehead and a beakhead bow, a style that went out of fashion in the 1850s.[15] Why is she flying the American flag? The PMM record suggests this might have been an artistic flourish added by the painter, Joseph Heard, possibly for an American customer.[16]

The *Margaret Johnson* had been newly coppered and rebuilt with a new pitch pine top and sides and new standing rigging in 1835, which means that Kelly had essentially a new vessel of 437 tons for the voyage to New Orleans. The vessel would remain registered at Belfast under the ownership of David Grainger and the command of various captains including Peter McIntyre, Neil McCauley, and William Groom for another decade. On March 15, 1845, she was abandoned at sea in the North Atlantic while bound from Ichaboe Island (off the coast of Namibia today) to Liverpool with a load of guano. Captain Groom and the rest of his crew were rescued by the ship *South Stockton* and taken to London. In noting her loss, one newspaper described the *Margaret Johnson* as "one of the prettiest and fastest-sailing vessels" then registered at Belfast.[17]

Figure 2: The packet ship *Margaret Johnson* off the south stack light approaching Liverpool; Joseph Heard (signed), oil on canvas, c. 1835. Image credit: Penobscot Marine Museum, Image ID 1970.23.

William next appears in the *Belfast News-Letter* of Tuesday, February 14, 1837, listed as commander of the barque *Rowena* (314 tons, built in 1826 in Nova Scotia). She was preparing to sail for New York and Quebec with goods and passengers, thereafter returning to Belfast with a cargo of timber. However, when the *Rowena* departed on March 29, she was under the command of Captain Stewart Edington of Greenock, Scotland—not Kelly.

Why did William not follow through with the *Rowena* trip? A subsequent *Belfast News-Letter* article answers this question. On March 16, 1837, at Craigmore Presbyterian Church near Randalstown, Antrim, Mr. William Kelly married Miss Martha Rainey, the youngest daughter of the late John Rainey of Ballydunmaul.[18] The tiny church at Craigmore is still there, perched on a hill overlooking Lough Neagh.[19] William was twenty-six and Martha twenty; instead of a trip to New York, William had embarked on the voyage of a lifetime.

Also of interest, the *Rowena*'s passenger list shows that one of the passengers stepping off the barque into a new life in the New World on May 15, 1837 was none other than Eleanor Frizzle, a forty-five-year-old woman from Belfast. Of course, I wonder if this was the same Eleanor Frizell who had tussled with William Kelly over ownership of the Head Inn seven years earlier (and perhaps taken it from him).I cannot be sure about the identity of this single traveling woman. However, if she was the Eleanor Frizell who had an interest in the Head Inn, her all-consuming hunt for cash in the early 1830s might have been motivated by the need to pay for her passage to America and set aside a lump sum to help her get established there. It would be hard to imagine the dynamics aboard the barque *Rowena* if William Kelly had remained her master as advertised. Putting these two rivals together on a one-month ocean crossing staggers the mind, especially with Kelly responsible for the safety and well-being of the adversarial Mrs. Frizell. There might have been a story there.

Returning to William and Martha, they were married just three months before Queen Victoria's coronation at Westminster Abbey. William Kelly had launched his own career around the same time as his sovereign began hers. However, he and Martha were poised to forsake queen and country for a different place an ocean away, where the Mississippi River cradled what many considered to be the fairest city of the American South.

## William and Martha in New Orleans

Martha Kelly's family probably played a role in the couple's decision to relocate to New Orleans. Her brother James was already there, working in the booming cotton industry and laying down roots in the city. New Orleans would have beckoned seductively to a young mariner looking to start over again in a different, perhaps more promising place on the edge of the New World. In 1832, pioneer and author Timothy Flint commented, "No place in the United States has so much activity and bustle of commerce crowded into so small a space in the months of February and March. During the season of bringing in the cotton crop, whole streets are barricaded with cotton bales. The amount of domestic export from the city exceeds $12,000,000.00 a year, being greater than that of any other city of the Union, except New York, and nearly equaling that. The greatest items that make this amount are sugar and cotton."[20]

These and other agricultural products had to be transported out of New Orleans, up the Eastern Seaboard to the northern states, and across the Atlantic to Liverpool, Le Havre, and other ports for processing in the UK and Europe. As a master mariner, William Kelly would have been able to carve out a lucrative future for himself, his new wife, and his family in the booming Crescent City. He had already tasted something of the forbidden fruit when he sailed the *Margaret Johnson* there in 1836. In addition, his wife's brothers lived there, and his mother, Eleanor, had died in Antrim in 1838. With no remaining parental ties to his homeland, it was a propitious time for William and Martha to move on.

I do not know when or how they arrived in New Orleans, but William and Martha were there in 1838 when Martha gave birth to their first child—a son they named John. This child died just twenty months later on September 5, 1839, possibly succumbing to one of the virulent yellow fever outbreaks that were endemic to the city.[21] Their next children, Agnes and James (probably twins), were born in New Orleans in 1841.

Many men named Kelly sailed brigs and schooners into and out of New Orleans between 1838 and 1840, but there is nothing to tie my William Kelly definitively to any of these men or ships. Some of the schooners under command of a Kelly (e.g., *Amazon* and *Emeline*) sailed primarily west from New Orleans to Galveston, Matagorda, and Lamar, Texas. Other schooners under a Kelly (e.g., *William Archer, Drusilla,* and *Berry*) sailed east and north from New Orleans to Mobile, Apalachicola, and up the Eastern Seaboard to Charleston, Philadelphia, New York, and Boston. The brigs *Baltimore* (Captain Kelley) and *R. W. Brown* (Captain Kelly) both sailed between New Orleans and Mobile in 1839. I suspect William Kelly might have commanded vessels sailing east and north up the coast, bringing him closer to the next major port of call to figure in his career—Quebec.

I can definitely connect one New Orleans ship to William Kelly because he mentions it himself in a letter. In this ship, the now twenty-nine-year-old seaman would solidify his reputation as a reliable skipper of oceangoing vessels.

## William Kelly and the *Ambassador*

When I commanded the Ambassador twenty-eight years ago, I took out a boy a son of Jack Boyd's, he was with Gwynn of Antrim. James Rainey took him into his house and in his service he is now a rich man.

William Kelly to James Graham,<br>
July 28, 1871[22]

The ship *Ambassador* had arrived in New Orleans from Liverpool on May 26, 1840, under Captain Wade, but when she departed for her return trip to Liverpool on June 25 carrying 1,707 bales of cotton, 49 hogsheads of tobacco, and $1,100 in cash, William Kelly was at her helm. He brought her back to the Mersey in forty-nine days—not a particularly swift passage, but a serviceable effort.

Kelly subsequently sailed the *Ambassador* back to New Orleans in the fall of 1840 with a cargo of slates, coal, iron, firebricks, hardware, and whiskey; cabin passengers Mrs. Edgar and child, Miss Rogers, and Messrs. Edward Duncan, Sam Boyd, P. Carrolan, Haggerty, and Searight; and thirty steerage passengers.

Passenger Sam Boyd was the boy mentioned in William Kelly's above-quoted 1871 letter to James Graham, which is reprinted in its entirety in Chapter 6. Another native of County Antrim, Sam Boyd was only fifteen years old when he arrived in New Orleans on the *Ambassador* in 1840, and there he stayed, working in the cotton industry under the tutelage of James Rainey, Martha Kelly's older brother. Sam Boyd would ultimately far outpace his mentor—buying and selling cotton presses until he cornered the market in this lucrative sector of the cotton industry. In fact, New Orleans newspapermen dubbed Sam Boyd the "Cotton Press King" in the 1870s. As detailed in Chapter 6, Sam Boyd's relationship with James Rainey would be sorely tested in 1871 when two of Boyd's nephews, William and John Boyd of Ballymena, Antrim, murdered Samuel Rainey, the younger brother of James Rainey and Martha Kelly. This was the result of a bitter, prolonged, and ultimately tragic business dispute between three young Irishmen who had once been the best of friends. The remarkable chain of events was set in motion by the Ambassador's arrival at New Orleans in 1840, carrying the ambitious teenager, Sam Boyd of Antrim.

Kelly and the *Ambassador* next departed New Orleans on January 11, 1841, arriving back in Liverpool on February 19 with 682 bales of cotton—a respectable forty-day passage. On his third trip to New Orleans in May 1841, Kelly carried cabin passenger Augustine Fitzgerald (a merchant) and fifteen others in steerage. He then returned the *Ambassador* to London instead of Liverpool with 748 hogsheads of tobacco and other merchandise, arriving at Gravesend at the end of August.

On the *Ambassador*'s fourth and final trip to New Orleans in September 1841, Kelly made a speedy crossing, arriving on November 15, just thirty-eight days from London in ballast. According to the *New Orleans Commercial Bulletin*, she was brought up to the city from the Passes[23] by the steam tug *Swan* along with the steam barque *Clarion*. There she was moored three tiers above the New Orleans Cotton Press and offered for sale by Duncan S. McAlister & Co. The 'for sale' ad ran through December 16, and then on December 17 the *Bulletin*'s "Coastwise" shipping column listed the *Ambassador* as preparing to leave for Boston, still with Duncan McAlister as agent and Kelly as master. This notice ran through January 28, 1842, but there is no indication of the ship leaving for Boston or any other port. Thus Kelly's connection with the *Ambassador* in New Orleans peters out with no documented resolution as to what happened either to the ship or her master. This is one of many transitions in Kelly's career, a time of movement when the storyline blurs. All I can say for certain is that William and Martha Kelly, with children Agnes and James in tow, were once again on the cusp of a different place with another square-rigger on the horizon.

William's brother, John, also launched his career in the 1830s and '40s. John would follow in his older brother's footsteps, and the two would sail together on occasion, but John would shape his own unique career in the years to come.

## John Kelly's Early Career

John Kelly's application for his master's certificate in 1856 reveals something of his first sixteen years in the foreign trades sector of the British mercantile marine service. At the beginning of his career, between the ages of sixteen and twenty (from 1832 to 1836), he served as an apprentice on the brig *Jessie* (335 tons) and on the barque *Margaret Johnson* (366 tons), probably under the command of his brother, William, during this ship's 1836 voyage to New Orleans. Both vessels were owned by David Grainger of Belfast.

The apprenticeship system was the minor league for officer training in the nineteenth-century British merchant service, the place where young men expecting to rise in the ranks learned the ropes. As such, masters and mates often took a personal interest in the apprentices on their crew rosters. According to Bullen, the apprentice "lives in the cabin, eats at the cabin table, associates with the officers, and breathes the air of authority."[24]

John Kelly's on-the-job training continued into 1837, when he served as a seaman on the Sunderland barque *William Herdman* (345 tons) under Captain J. Sweeting. John was likely a member of this crew in July 1837 when the *Herdman* sailed from Sierra Leone in West Africa to Sunderland, England, with the governor of the colony, Major General Henry Dundas Campbell, and his entourage aboard. They were fleeing a devastating yellow fever outbreak that had claimed upward of 40,000 victims, including many British and European residents.

While his older brother, William, was residing in New Orleans, John Kelly was climbing his own career ladder. Between 1839 and 1842, he served as chief mate on the new ship *Lord Seaton* (713 tons, Captains Skeoch and Fitzsimons), sailing on possibly half a dozen round trips primarily from Belfast to Quebec and New Orleans. With this experience under his belt, John was ready to assume his first command: the London-registered barque *Clio* (383 tons, built in 1824 in Nova Scotia and owned by H. C. Bowden of 24 Donegal Quay, Belfast).

## John Kelly and the *Clio*

John took command of the *Clio* in the summer of 1843, sailing her from London to Quebec in July and London to Bridgewater, Nova Scotia, in the fall. There was another trip to Saint John, New Brunswick and then Quebec in the late summer and fall of 1844, with a return to London in January 1845. The *Clio* was then cleared for Savannah, Georgia, in February 1845. It was on this passage that John came to grief while attempting to pass a sandy barrier island east of Beaufort, South Carolina, on the night of Friday, April 11, 1845.

> Shipwreck.—The Savannah Republican of Tuesday morning says: The Br. Barque Clio, Capt. Kelly, from London, sailed 17th February, in ballast, bound to this port, went ashore on the Hunting Islands, on Friday night last, and will be a total loss. She was consigned to Messrs. Harper & Stuart, of this city, who have sent a schooner to the wreck to bring to town such portions of the rigging, sails, &c., as may have been saved.[25]

The *Liverpool Mercury* stated that the *Clio*'s crew and part of her materials were saved; the *New York Herald* confessed ignorance as to whether she was insured; the *New York Commercial Advertiser* subsequently reported that the schooner *Joseph* arrived at Savannah on April 22 from the wreck of the *Clio* with rigging, sails, anchors, and chains. As she had been sailing in ballast, there may not have been much cost associated with this mishap beyond the loss of a twenty-year-old barque.

Undeterred by this setback, John returned to Antrim, where he quickly rebounded from adversity. Two and a half months after the wreck of the *Clio*, and one month after celebrating his twenty-ninth birthday, John married a local twenty-five-year-old woman who had grown up less than a mile from the Kelly's inn at Antrim: Miss

Sarah Orr, the fourth daughter of James Orr, Esq., of The Folly, South Antrim.[26]

Here we leave John and Sarah Kelly's wedding to pick up William and Martha Kelly's trail. It appears that they had returned from New Orleans to Northern Ireland sometime around 1841 or 1842, because this is where they next appear.

## William Kelly and the *Dumfriesshire*

Back in Belfast, William Kelly took another step in his career, assuming command of the ship *Dumfriesshire* (built in 1837 in Portland, New Brunswick; 873 registered tons; 1,500 tons carrying capacity; owned by David Grainger & Co. of Belfast and others). Between July and October 1843, Kelly sailed the *Dumfriesshire* from Liverpool to Quebec in a relatively quick thirty-four days and brought her back to Belfast with the requisite load of timber. The *Belfast Mercantile Register and Weekly Advertiser* of October 10, 1843, notes the *Dumfriesshire*'s return from Quebec with an extraordinary detail: "This fine vessel was only 19 days on her passage." If this crossing time is correct, Kelly had cut the typical number of days for the return passage in half. Either this was a typo, or wind and wave had smiled upon him. In point of fact, his breakneck return to Belfast was a good thing. Upon arriving home, he discovered that Martha had given birth to a daughter. They named her Fanny, after William's sister, the former "Queen of Antrim Town."

The *Dumfriesshire* was a Belfast ship, and here William settled for the next few years. He was back in the commercial and industrial heart of County Antrim, with his family lodged at 21 Pilot Street, just steps from the River Lagan, and his ship snugly berthed at the recently opened Dunbar's Dock.[27]

The Belfast Seamen's Friend Society conducted religious services for seamen in a chapel not far from Pilot Street. This society's chaplain visited vessels in port and the families of those connected with the sea. However, Kelly's closest denominational allegiance might have been nearer to his ancestral home. At the end of September 1843, the Rev. Thomas Magee Morrow gratefully acknowledged Captain Kelly's contribution of five shillings toward the completion of a new Presbyterian church in Dunadry near Muckamore on the outskirts of Antrim Town. Several weeks later, with the winter freeze putting Quebec out of reach, Kelly prepared the *Dumfriesshire* for departure to a sunnier and more easily accessible destination: the booming cotton port of Mobile, Alabama.

After sailing early from Belfast on November 14, 1843, the *Dumfriesshire* arrived in Mobile Bay around the middle of January 1844. This was a somewhat extended voyage that might have involved stops at intermediate ports that were not noted in the newspapers. In the early 1840s, Mobile was second only to New Orleans in US cotton exports; accordingly, Kelly returned to Liverpool with a load of cotton, making "a remarkably quick passage."[28] He then returned to Belfast to await the first fair wind for the rapidly thawing port of Quebec where 'les habitants' eagerly awaited sails on the Saint Lawrence River again.

Following a quick sidetrip to Liverpool to load a cargo of salt, the *Dumfriesshire* departed Belfast again on May 20, 1844, with 460 passengers for Quebec. They arrived at Jones Wharf on the left bank of the Saint Charles River on June

28, "having made the quickest passage out this year—passengers and crew all well."[29] Here George H. Parke & Co., the consignee of the vessel, took her passengers and cargo in hand, and William Kelly entered yet another transition in his career.

When the *Dumfriesshire* left for Belfast on July 30, 1844, Kelly had been replaced by his first mate, Alexander Davis. The man from Antrim fades once again into the fog of uncertainty that so often accompanied his movement from one ship to another. Did William remain in Quebec or return to Belfast? His movements are unknown for the next year and a bit, but I hope he did find his way back to Belfast in March 1845 to be with his wife and family at a time of shared sorrow.

> DIED.—On the 26th ult. at the house of her father, Dublin-bridge, Fanny, youngest daughter of Captain William Kelly, late of the Dumfriesshire.[30]

According to the inscription on the family monument at Muckamore, Fanny was only a year and a half old when she died of unknown cause at the same age as William and Martha's firstborn John had died seven years earlier in New Orleans. The devastating infant mortality of the nineteenth century had left Agnes and James, both age four, the two surviving children in a saddened Kelly household reduced by one more.

## William Kelly and the *Belinda*

Launched on Monday, May 5, 1845, at John James Nesbitt's Saint-Roch shipyard in Quebec, the *Belinda* (138 feet long × 27 feet beam × 20 feet deep hold and 750 registered tons) was built for George H. Parke & Co. in Quebec and David Grainger in Belfast.[31] She was a single-decked ship with a square stern and passenger accommodations that included a private room for a family. She was likely named for David Grainger's wife, Maria Belinda Grainger.

Three days later Nesbitt launched another new vessel for Parke and Grainger, the 700-ton *Arethusa*. On May 16, the *Quebec Gazette* announced that the *Arethusa* would depart for Liverpool on May 28 under the command of William Kelly. This implies that William was in Quebec at the time, or he was expected there. As it turned out, however, it was not William who took the *Arethusa* out on her maiden voyage. Instead, the command fell to a man named Lepan, who sailed her out of Quebec for Liverpool on June 10, 1845.[32]

The *Belinda* had already left for Liverpool and Belfast a week earlier on May 31 under the command of Captain Peter McIntyre, a well-known forty-nine-year-old Belfast mariner. Her maiden voyage carrying the predictable cargo of timber was not auspicious for two reasons. First, the ship lost two masts in a sudden squall downstream of the Île d'Orléans in the Saint Lawrence River. McIntyre had to return to Quebec and hire a steamer to carry two new topmasts back to his stranded ship, wasting precious time and effort in getting underway. Second, the captain probably should not even have attempted the voyage. Sick with consumption, McIntyre died on June 27 somewhere in the middle of the Atlantic Ocean, and here William Kelly surprisingly reappears to take control of McIntyre's leaderless ship, literally out of the blue.

The *Belinda*'s official crew agreement shows William Kelly's name appended as follows: "William Kelly,

34, Antrim, Master; Ship in which he last served: Dumfriesshire; Date of joining this ship: 27 June, 1845; Place where—at sea [signed: William Kelly]."[33]

How Kelly happened to be in the same patch of ocean as the *Belinda* at the same time that her captain died is open to conjecture. Two possibilities come to mind. Kelly might already have been on the *Belinda* traveling as a backup for her ailing captain and ready to take command should the sick man succumb to his illness (although the first mate would typically have assumed this responsibility).

Alternatively, Kelly might have been hitching a ride back to Belfast with Captain Lepan on the *Arethusa*, and the two vessels ended up sailing in tandem after the *Belinda*'s time-consuming overhaul in the Saint Lawrence River. This would have required a treacherous ship-to-ship transfer at sea, swinging out the longboat and rowing Kelly and his trunk across to his new assignment. I think this is the most likely possibility, as the crew agreement states that Kelly joined the ship "at sea." From the point of view of a good story, this would certainly have been the more cinematic of the two options.

When Kelly took command of the *Belinda* to see her safely through to the United Kingdom, he had no notion that his tour of duty on this fine new ship, which began with the death at sea of Captain Peter McIntyre, would end four years later with yet another regrettable turn of events, while Kelly was still at the helm.

The *Belinda*'s return trip to George H. Parke & Co. at Quebec was a quick and uneventful passage of thirty-one days in ballast. As it was summer, Kelly likely took the

*Belinda* through the North Channel around the top of Ireland, then headed west across the Atlantic and entered the Gulf of Saint Lawrence via the Strait of Belle Isle between Labrador and Newfoundland. On August 26, some two hundred miles below Quebec, the *Belinda* passed another Grainger ship, the *Conqueror* (Captain McCauley), en route to Liverpool. Upon arriving at Quebec on September 1, 1845, the *Belinda's* 123 passengers published an appreciative letter in the *Quebec Gazette*:

> CAPTAIN KELLY.
> SIR.—We, the passengers on board the ship BELINDA, from Belfast, feeling that we owe a debt of gratitude for your unwearied attention once we left our native land, do now before separating to our respective places of destination, return you our sincere thanks for your kind treatment during our pleasant and almost unprecedented short passage. We only feel sorry it is not in our power to do so in a more substantial manner, but we trust your unmerited kindness will not lose its reward. Signed on behalf of all the passengers,
>
> M. Walker, G. Agnew, James McMurry, James Carlisle, David Howard
> Quebec, 1st Sept., 1845[34]

William Kelly's three years as captain of the *Belinda* were tragic years for Ireland. It was the beginning of the potato blight that ravaged the island from 1845 to 1852. Approximately one million people died and another million emigrated, resulting in a population decline of 20–25 percent. The first fungus struck the potato harvest in the summer of 1845, destroying about a third of the crop. The disease reaped greater devastation in 1846, when three-quarters of the potato harvest were wiped out. In 1847 the crop was better but still greatly reduced, with many families forced to eat their seed potatoes. By 1848 the crops had returned to about two-thirds of normal, but the worst would not be over until 1850 to 1852. The Great Famine was a decisive moment in Irish history and for many Irish people. William Kelly would play an important role in the mass exodus that drew so many desperate Irish men, women, and children seaward to beckoning ports and new lives in North America and elsewhere.

After William completed his successful passage to Quebec, it took just three weeks to fill the *Belinda*'s hold with timber and provision her for return to Belfast. Then, on September 21, 1845, the ships *Belinda*, *Sea King*, and *Tom Moore* departed together, discharging their pilots fourteen hours later off Green Island in the Saint Lawrence River. On Wednesday, September 24, the *Belinda* passed the barque *Sir Henry Pottinger* of Belfast[35] while traversing the Gulf of Saint Lawrence between the Gaspé Peninsula and Anticosti Island. On Saturday, September 27, she hailed the barque *Prince Albert* bound to Miramichi, New Brunswick, off Saint Pierre and Miquelon, and on the same day she signaled the steamer *North America*, which was stalled with her machinery disabled on the way to Sydney, Nova Scotia. Kelly proposed to take the steamer's passengers on board, but the captain refused his offer. Finally, by hitching her keel to the Gulf

Stream and North Atlantic Drift, Kelly took the *Belinda* into the deep Atlantic and a quick passage of twenty-seven days to Belfast. Here he eased the ship into Dunbar's Dock on October 17, 1845. By the end of the month, David Grainger was auctioning off the *Belinda*'s load of timber while Kelly prepared for a Christmas return to his old stomping grounds in New Orleans.

The *Belinda* departed for Louisiana on December 14 with a cargo of general merchandise (typically abbreviated "mdz" in the newspaper ships lists) and only six passengers. Lee Simpson (age 27) and M. C. Birney (age 22), both clerks, occupied the cabin accommodations, while John Burke (age 25), Sarah Burke (age 14), William Lyle (age 22), and William Irvin (age 22), all laborers, had *Belinda*'s steerage all to themselves.

They sailed the southern route out of Belfast this time, down Saint George's Channel and around the bottom of Ireland, passing midway between Madeira and the Azores. Here they picked up the northeast trades and ran westward and south direct to the Gulf of Mexico. They arrived at the Crescent City on January 30, 1846, a passage of 48 days. There the stevedores on the levee proceeded to unload the *Belinda*'s merchandise, which was bewilderingly abbreviated in the *New Orleans Commercial Bulletin* (January 30, 1846) as "1 box mdz, R. Gamble—30 bales ditto, McDowell & Peck—6 boxes ditto, C. Barrier—20 ditto ditto O.B. Graham—3 ditto ditto, 7 bales ditto, T. Medley & Co.—12 boxes ditto to order."

The *Belinda* remained in New Orleans for about a month and a half, time enough for Grainger's agents to fill her hold with 1,739 bales of cotton, 1,500 barrels of flour, 471 barrels of beef, 100 barrels of grease, and 3,000 staves for her return to the United Kingdom. Five seamen and the cook deserted, and six replacements signed on in their place.[36] Clearing out of New Orleans on March 23, 1846, the *Belinda* arrived back in Liverpool on May 7 after a voyage of forty-six days.

## A Boatload of Emigrant Paupers

Kelly's next voyage with the *Belinda* was a return to Quebec during the height of that port's summer shipping season. It was a grueling experience that spotlights the challenges of moving large numbers of Irish emigrants to the colonies during the grim Potato Famine years. Compared with the *Belinda*'s previous trip to New Orleans when she carried only six passengers, her 1846 passage to Quebec was remarkable for its throng: 425 travelers, including approximately 100 workhouse emigrants from the Armagh, Coleraine, and Magherafelt Poor Law Unions of Northern Ireland, almost half of them children.[37]

As advertised, they sailed on June 3, 1846. Their forty-two-day crossing was more than two weeks longer than the *Belinda*'s previous trip to Quebec (although still faster than the average forty-six-day crossing from Ireland during the 1846 season). Seaman James Ward of Belfast, age twenty-six, died at sea on July 3, possibly struck down by the same sickness that swept through the ship's steerage passengers.[38] After arriving at Quebec on July 14, Mr. Alexander C. Buchanan, the chief agent for the Superintendence of Emigration at Quebec, touched on the difficulties of the voyage in his weekly return of vessels and official report to Governor General Charles Murray Cathcart in Montreal.

The passengers, per Belinda, from Belfast, 425 in number, are respectable looking people. There had been a good deal of sickness among them; 12 children had died during the passage of smallpox, and about 40 of the passengers were left at the Grosse Isle Hospital, where the ship was detained for six days. The passengers all speak in the kindest manner of the care and attention which Captain Kelly showed them during the passage and his unremitting attention to the sick. About 30 of the passengers are going to the States, the rest to the Newcastle, Home, and Simcoe Districts: 93 persons, by this vessel, were sent out by the following Unions, and received from Captain Kelly the sum of £37, 15 s. sterling, being at the rate of 10 s. to each adult, and 5 s. to children, viz., Coleraine Union, 61 adults and 40 children; Armagh Union, 15 adults, and 5 children; Magherafelt Union, 30 adults and 9 children. Those sent out by the Coleraine Union were mostly old and sickly people and helpless children, many of whom I fear will never be able to earn their support in this country. The others appear stout healthy men and women, all apparently willing to work.[39]

The Poor Law Commissioners in Ireland took issue with Mr. Buchanan's count of the workhouse passengers sent out under their sanction and especially with his observation that many in the Coleraine contingent would be unable to support themselves in Canada. It took a flurry of letters between G. Walcott, secretary of the Colonial Land and Emigration Commission, and E. Chadwick, secretary of the Poor Law Commission, to arrive at the following final tally of the workhouse emigrants transported to Quebec by the *Belinda* in the summer of 1846 (Table 1).

Table 1: Workhouse emigrants transported to Quebec via the ship *Belinda*, summer of 1846

|  | Under 5 | 6–15 | 15–20 | 30–40 | 40–50 | 50–55 | **TOTAL** |
|---|---|---|---|---|---|---|---|
| Armagh | 2 | 7 | 9 | 2 | 1 | 1 | 22 |
| Coleraine | 17 | 16 | 16 | 6 | 6 | 1 | 62 |
| Magherafelt | — | 7 | 2 | 1 | 2 | — | 12 |
| TOTAL | **19** | **30** | **27** | **9** | **9** | **2** | **96** |

*Source:* UK National Archives, Kew, Richmond, Surrey, Ref. HO 45/OS.1615

In due course (according to a letter dated January 1, 1847), Chadwick provided a complete list of the names and ages of all the passengers sent out under the auspices of the Poor Law Unions, concluding:

> From the above analysis, the Colonial Land and Emigration Commissioners will observe that the Poor Law Commissioners have not in any of those Unions sanctioned the Emigration of persons who could reasonably be expected from age to be incapable of earning their support in Canada, and it will be observed from the lists...that the young children would appear to have been for the most part the children of the Adult Emigrants. The Commissioners are unable to account for the discrepancy between Mr. Buchanan's Return and the number and description of persons whose Emigration was sanctioned by the Poor Law Commissioners.[40]

Kelly's 1846 voyage to Quebec provided an opportunity for Dr. George W. Douglas, the medical superintendent of the Grosse Isle Hospital, to write a perceptive report inveighing against the poor rations provided to passengers on Irish ships as compared with those on English and German ships.[41]

> A considerable number of pauper emigrants have been sent out this season from the Irish Poor Law Unions. Much sickness has prevailed among these, especially in those that arrived by the ship Belinda, from Belfast. It is to be regretted that it should not be found necessary to supply these people (many of whom had the appearance of having suffered long from misery) with any other provision for the voyage than a pound of meal per day. They contrast very unfavourably with those sent out under similar circumstances from England; these are generally sent in charge of a medical man, and are supplied with animal food, bread, flour, rice, and medical stores and comforts. In consequence, I rarely find sick among them, unless epidemic disease has been brought on board. I always understood the pound of biscuit, oatmeal, or Indian corn meal, which the vessel is bound by law to furnish daily to each adult, to be merely a guarantee against the starvation brought on formerly by the improvident use which the emigrant made of his own stores, and to be by no means intended to constitute his only support, as in the case of the Irish paupers in the Belinda and other vessels, to whom a pound of damaged Indian meal per day was their only food.

If necessary, I might here cite, as evidence, of the advantage of a liberal supply of wholesome food in warding off disease, even in a crowded emigrant vessel, the case of the German settlers who arrived this year; these people were supplied abundantly with animal food, bread, flour, lime juice, and beer; and though their voyages were longer than vessels coming from Great Britain (in the case of one vessel, extending to eleven weeks), yet out of eight vessels, having on board 902 passengers, I had only to admit seven to hospital.[42]

The Great Famine still stirs considerable debate in Northern Ireland, the Republic of Ireland, and the Irish diaspora today. There are some who accuse the British government of genocide in exploiting the famine to clear Ireland of unwanted people; others take a more neutral view of the Hunger and the exodus it instigated. Both sides acknowledge that overcrowded, disease-ridden "coffin ships," some with up to 30 percent mortality rates, plied the North Atlantic during these difficult years. The disaster peaked after the *Belinda*'s problematic crossing when, in 1847, a devastating typhus epidemic hit Grosse Isle and other Canadian quarantine stations at Montreal, Kingston, Toronto, and Saint John.

Dr. Douglas's report touts the importance of adequate, wholesome food in fending off disease even in overcrowded vessels and goes on to state that a pound of damaged Indian cornmeal per day was the only food provided for the *Belinda*'s steerage passengers. The doctor's protest against "yellow meal" is a recurring motif in the Famine debate. The Indian corn was unfamiliar to the Irish, and many ships' officers did not know how to store it correctly at sea. Few Irish would even have attempted to prepare and consume this unfamiliar, frequently mishandled, and therefore often moldy and unappetizing grain.

Because of their numbers, the Irish bore the brunt of the misery visited upon newcomers transiting to North America in the early years of settlement. According to government reports, some 32,500 persons immigrated to Canada in 1846 (approximately 21,000 from Ireland, 9,000 from England, 1,600 from Scotland, and 900 from Germany).[43] The *Belinda* was one of 146 vessels that sailed from Ireland to Canada that year with the entire Irish flotilla of 1846 carrying about 15,600 adults (15 years and up), 4,600 children (between 1 and 14 years), and 670 infants (under a year).[44]

While examining the list of workhouse emigrants sent on the *Belinda* in 1846, I was struck by the fact that twenty-one out of twenty-three apparent family groups were headed by a single woman with dependent children. Many of these women and children were likely joining husbands who had preceded them to Canada and already established themselves there.

When conditions are dire, it is the young and infirm who suffer most. Twelve children died of smallpox on the *Belinda* during her passage to Quebec. Upon arrival, an additional forty sick passengers were quarantined at the Grosse Isle Hospital, many of them likely children too. The hospital records report that some of these children died in the hospital under quarantine. These youngsters' names highlight the human stories over the cold numbers that populate the administrative accountings: James Campbell, 6 years old, died on July 27 of smallpox, and William

Campbell, 4 years old, died on July 29 of smallpox (the only children of Jane Campbell, 41 years old, of Aghadowey, Coleraine); William Connor, 8 months old, died on July 22 of debility (possibly the child of Rose Connery, 35 years old, of Magherafelt); Alexander Hunter, 3 years old, died on July 28 of smallpox, and Belinda Hunter, just 12 days old, died on July 20 of smallpox and debility.

Born at sea just five days before the *Belinda* arrived at Gross Isle, Belinda Hunter's parents likely named her after the ship that transported them, perhaps in a final, fraught gesture of hope tinged with despair. William Kelly, who had displayed "unremitting attention to the sick" while at sea, was likely touched by this acknowledgement on the part of Belinda's grieving parents. 45

Following this difficult crossing, the *Belinda* departed Quebec on September 12, 1846. The ship experienced fine weather until October 3, then heavy gales until they arrived at Liverpool on October 10. After this relatively quick return passage of twenty-nine days, the *Belinda* again made news, but this time in a happier context. The newspapers reported that she had brought across to Liverpool the largest shipment of Canadian flour received to date. The *Glasgow Herald* of Monday, October 26, 1846, stated, "A vessel named the Belinda, arrived at the port of Liverpool from Quebec, has brought, in addition to a quantity of wooden goods, the large number of 9,530 barrels of flour, of Canadian produce. So large an importation of flour from Canada, although arrivals to the same extent have, we believe, taken place from the United States of North America, has not before come under our notice, and therefore, the mention of it, especially at the present time, will, for various reasons, be interesting and of importance."

## Yellow Dust from Chincha

Following his established pattern of seasonally alternating trips to Quebec and New Orleans, Kelly and the *Belinda* squeezed in another excursion to the Gulf of Mexico in the winter of 1846–1847, returning to Liverpool in the spring with a mixed cargo of cotton, wheat, flour, hams, beef, Indian corn, soap, pork, and potatoes. Next, Kelly would vary the pattern and take the *Belinda* on a nine-month round trip from Liverpool into the South Atlantic, westward around Cape Horn via the treacherous Drake Passage, up the west coast of South America to the Chincha Islands north of Callao, Peru,[46] and back to London.

The Chinchas are a group of three small, granitic islands off the south coast of Peru where millions of seabirds have nested for millennia, depositing a tremendous amount of uric acid-, nitrogen-, and phosphate-rich bird droppings (guano) that make excellent fertilizer. With farmers around the world demanding Chincha guano, Peru began exporting it in 1840, creating the opportunity for the *Belinda* of Belfast to make this extended excursion to the Pacific coast of South America. After departing Liverpool on May 7, 1847, and hailing the ship *Ottawa* off Tuskar[47] on May 14, the *Belinda* dropped entirely out of sight until her arrival at the Chinchas in early fall. Here her crew waited their turn to fill their ship's belly with the fertile yellow dust excavated from the islands. This was a dirty, labor-intensive business requiring sailors to load sacks of dried bird droppings at exposed roadsteads off the forbidding rocks. The guano filtered into every part of the ship, emitting an ammonia stench that stung the nasal passages and eyes. Sailors could only stay below decks for short periods of time.

On October 14, 1847, at Callao, four seamen transferred from the *Belinda* to HMS *Grampus*, a fifty-gun, fourth-rate cruiser commanded by Captain H. B. Martin that had recently completed a year's tour of Hawaii, Tahiti, and the Society Islands.[48] At this time, it was common for crewmen to transfer back and forth between the Merchant Service and the Royal Navy. The Merchant Seamen's Act of 1844 allowed a mutual breach of the contract that a seaman signed when joining a merchant vessel (the crew agreement), enabling him to enlist for what was left of a naval ship's commission. The seaman would receive from the master of the merchant vessel his registration ticket, clothes, personal effects, and a prorated portion of the pay he had earned. The naval captain would then sign off on this, so there could be no future claims against the merchant vessel or her owners. A career in the Royal Navy became more of a lifelong commitment with the introduction of continuous service engagements in 1853, which also made it possible for naval retirees to receive pensions. These developments reduced the number of men who served in both the merchant marine and navy services, until the practice of moving between the two sectors ceased in the early 1870s.

Departing Callao on October 18, the *Belinda* retraced her long route home back around Cape Horn, eventually touching at Cork, Deal, and Gravesend before entering London's West India Dock on Friday, February 25, 1848—a moderately breezy and overcast day followed by a fine, clear evening.

After almost ten months at sea, Kelly was greeted by both heartening and devastating news. Martha had given birth to a boy on July 28, 1847 (around the time William had first arrived at Callao), but their six-year-old son, James, had died on November 13, 1847, of unknown cause while William was returning from Peru. Martha was racked by the extreme emotions of caring for one newborn child while mourning another. They named the new child John after William's father and brother (and after their own firstborn who had died in New Orleans eight years earlier).

The busy work of maritime port activities distracted Kelly at least somewhat from this family turmoil until his next trip loomed. However, before departing London again, he took the extraordinary step of sorting out an errant mattress.

## *Charlie Richmond's Mattress*

In an interesting postscript to the Chincha Islands voyage, William Kelly appeared at London's Old Bailey Central Criminal Court on April 3, 1848, just a month after returning from Peru. There he testified at the trial of Charles Richmond, a twenty-seven-year-old *Belinda* crewman who was accused of "stealing a mattress and other articles valued at 10 shillings, the goods of David Grainger, in a vessel at a port of entry and discharge." The case minutes, taken in shorthand by court clerks James Drover Barnett and Alexander Buckler, provide a verbatim transcript of the legal proceedings and a distant echo of Kelly's clipped and somewhat brisk Ulster English.[49]

> WILLIAM KELLY: I am master of the Belinda, lying in the West India Docks—I shipped the prisoner at Kallio [Callao, Peru], in America, and gave him the use of a bed on board—on 25th Feb. we arrived in

London—I discharged him on 14th March—on the 17th I missed a mattress which I had lent him, and a quilt, pillow-case, blanket and sheet—I did not give him any of them—they belong to the ship, and were not mine—these are them. (produced.)

PRISONER: I understood they were mine; I never made away with them; directly the captain missed them, he went into the Export Dock and got them; he had told me not to buy a bed, or I should have bought one.

WILLIAM KELLY: It is a rule at the Consul's establishment that no man is to have more than sixteen dollars at once—the prisoner said, unless he got another sixteen dollars he would not go—I advanced him eight dollars and a half—he said he had not got a bed; he had not the means of buying one—he had no shoes to his feet.

ALEXANDER BARR: I am mate of the Belinda. I shipped the prisoner at Kallio—he left on 16th March, and took his things away—I did not see him moving a bed—I missed it on the 17th—it was part of the furniture of a passenger's berth, which he used—he called me to look at his box, to see if everything was right—I did so—there was nothing belonging to the ship in it—it is usual for sailors to provide themselves with beds.

ROBERT TAYLOR: I am a constable of the East and West India Docks—I received information, and stopped the prisoner going into the Import-dock—I said he was charged with stealing a bed, and other things, from the Belinda—he said, "I did not steal them; when the captain comes, he will settle it"—I went with Barr to the forecastle of the Panama, and found these things—we got them out, and the ship sailed next day.

PRISONER'S DEFENCE: The captain gave me a bed, and I thought it was mine when I was paid off; I took it openly.

Charles Richmond was found guilty and sentenced to a month in jail. This episode suggests that Kelly was a considerate man. He advanced money to a destitute sailor and provided him with a bed. However, the incident also underscores Kelly's principled sense of right and wrong in charging the sailor for trying to keep the bed. With the matter settled, Kelly turned his attention to his next challenge—a boatload of German emigrants looking buoyantly westward.

## A Flying Island with Tattered Wings

On April 4, 1848, the day after his appearance at the Old Bailey, Kelly took the *Belinda* out of the West India Dock and down the Thames to Gravesend. One week later they sailed to the port of Bremerhaven on Germany's North Sea coast. There Kelly took on board 234 German emigrants, departing with them on April 27 for New York. On May 9, the *Belinda* hailed the ships *Elizabeth Hamilton* of Portsmouth and *Black Witch* of London and passed the ship *Apollo* of Warren—a collegial day in the mid-Atlantic. They arrived at New York on June 12, where they might have seen the British ship *Arethusa* commanded by William's brother, John. The *Arethusa* departed for Liverpool on the same day that the *Belinda* arrived from London.

Many of the *Belinda*'s passengers were Germans with liberal leanings fleeing the faltering 1848 democratic uprisings that were collapsing under reactionary pressure in the German Confederation and elsewhere in Europe. The failed German Revolution of 1848, which had aspired to constitutional government, brought thousands of highly educated men and women to North America. In all, the German states lost more than 1.5 million citizens to immigrant ships during the conservative-aristocratic reaction that crushed the Springtime of the Peoples. The Paris uprising of 1832 popularized in Victor Hugo's *Les Misérables* was an earlier iteration of these republican, antimonarchist insurrections.

Having played a role in the great European migration to America of the late 1840s, the *Belinda* departed New York on June 17, 1848. She was scheduled to sail north, up the east coast of America to Quebec. Here Kelly fully expected to fill the *Belinda*'s hold with timber before returning to Belfast. Indeed, the *Belfast News-Letter* was already advertising the ship's next voyage: a trip to New Orleans scheduled for early September. Regrettably, the *Belinda* would shortly find herself between a rock and a hard place on her way to the Gulf of Saint Lawrence.

Scatarie Island floats like a monstrous, tattered bat in the Atlantic Ocean off the remote northeastern tip of Cape Breton Island, Nova Scotia. As described by a knowledgeable local sea kayaker, the author of *Sea Kayaking in Nova Scotia*: "It is a raw world, and not a very pleasant landfall to many of the early visitors from across the sea. An ancient bedrock outcrop fringed by an irregular pattern of shoals, or "sunkers" as they were known in local parlance, guard its shores. Errant wooden ships split like fine tinder, spilling out goods and souls into the pitiless fray if they ventured too close. Only Sable Island and St. Paul's Island have claimed as many sailors in the Atlantic provinces. Sheltered harbours on Scatarie are non-existent, vegetation impoverished and the cold Atlantic fog and winds ever present."[50]

Kelly had to sail by this daunting obstacle to get around Cape Breton and into the Gulf of Saint Lawrence on his way to Quebec. There is a possibility that he had never approached the river from the south before and might not have been familiar with the treacherous currents and shallows surrounding this jagged barrier. I know nothing of what happened there on Thursday, June 22, 1848, beyond the following terse announcement that appeared in numerous newspapers.

> WRECK.—Ship Belinda, Kelly, from Belfast for Quebec, struck near Scaterie 22nd inst. and became a total wreck. Crew and materials saved.[51]

Figure 3: Scatarie, a flying island with tattered wings (© 2021 Google Earth, Image © 2021 CNES/Airbus, Image © 2021 Maxar Technologies, Data SIO, NOAA, US Navy, NGA, GEBCO).

By saving his crew and rallying them to recover his ship's valuable materials, possibly including her masts, sails, spars, rigging, sheets and ties, ropes, chain cables, anchors, brass fittings, boats, and tools, Kelly also salvaged his career as a master mariner. He might even have advanced it. This was his baptism by fire, and the thirty-seven-year-old skipper appears to have come through it well enough. The four redeeming words at the end of the newspaper announcement provide a clue to understanding where the *Belinda* might have met her fate. The fact that Kelly was able to save his crew and ship's materials implies that the *Belinda* did not sink at sea but was driven ashore, and this might have occurred somewhere along the dangerous Main-à-Dieu Passage[52] between Scatarie Island and Cape Breton—possibly near a promontory called Kellys Head (which is apparently spelled *without* an apostrophe). Of course, this place name might be just a coincidence; however, it is still a reminder that somewhere in this vicinity, William Kelly of Antrim faced one of the greatest challenges of his career and snatched a workmanlike achievement from the jaws of disaster. It would be fascinating to know more about this pivotal event in Kelly's career, but the full story with its high drama and adventure is well and truly lost—like the *Belinda* herself—somewhere among the hazardous, hidden shoals off Cape Breton's rocky coast.

As an interesting footnote to this calamity, three years earlier, in August 1845, William Kelly's previous ship, the *Dumfriesshire*, had itself gone ashore on the southwest point of Anticosti Island approximately 250 miles north of Scatarie with a cargo of salt. Captain Davis, who had succeeded Kelly as captain of the *Dumfriesshire*, also lost his ship but saved his crew.

## John Kelly and the *Arethusa*

Returning now to pick up John Kelly's trail, I found his career once again intersecting with William's. On May 25, 1846, the British ship *Arethusa* arrived at Wellington Wharf, port of Quebec, in ballast, from Savannah, Georgia, with Captain John Kelly in command. This was the same *Arethusa* that William Kelly might have sailed on in 1845 when he transferred to the *Belinda* at sea (as noted above, pages 27-28).

John Kelly's *Arethusa* opened her cavernous hold at Quebec to receive 15 tons of ash, 30 tons of elm, 40 tons of red pine, 45 tons of oak, and 825 tons of white pine along with a load of standard 3-inch pine deals, pipe staves, lath wood, and 194 barrels of flour. Thus laden, she departed Quebec on June 29 and arrived back in Liverpool on July 29 with the bulk of her cargo assigned to the merchant house of Wildes, Pickersgill & Co. of Rumford Street.[53]

The *Arethusa*'s next trip under John Kelly was a return to Quebec in ballast, departing later that summer on August 23, 1846. This turned into a longer trip than usual, as they encountered a powerful gale on the night of September 19 while crossing the Grand Banks of Newfoundland. According to the *Quebec Gazette*, many ships transiting to and from Quebec were severely damaged in this storm, and Kelly's *Arethusa* lost her sails. Providentially, the ship *Collins* of Gloucester, Massachusetts, which had also lost her canvas, had some left over to replace *Arethusa*'s sails, enabling the British ship to limp into Quebec, worn out and waterlogged, on October 11.

This mighty storm, which had likely been spawned by a hurricane, destroyed at least eleven vessels in a fishing fleet out of Marblehead, Massachusetts. The storm drowned sixty-five men and boys of the village, effectively ending the commercial fishing business there for many years. Captain John Proctor of Marblehead, skipper of the schooner *Samuel Knight*, which rode out the storm, commissioned a painted fireboard depicting the Great Gale of 1846.

Figure 4: William Thompson Bartoll, *The Great Gale of 1846*, fireboard, oil on wood panel, 36 × 57" (91.44 × 144.78 cm), deposited by Mr. Russell W. Knight, 1992, M23465. Image credit: Peabody Essex Museum; photo by Walter Silver.

This time upon arrival at Quebec, the *Arethusa* tied up at Martin's Wharf, where her hold's contents were consigned to Atkinson, Usborne & Co. of 38 Peter Street. Henry Atkinson and George William Usborne were wealthy lumber barons and shipping agents who probably lost vessels of their own in the Great Gale of 1846. This might have been why John Kelly found his hold laden with Atkinson & Usborne wood for *Arethusa*'s return to Liverpool—26 tons of elm, 73 tons of oak, and 746 tons of white pine, along with 7 cords of lath wood and 1,063 pine deals.

If there is a grain of truth to the tale of the "dripping sailor," John Kelly was fortunate to have made only one trip under the auspices of this firm (as far as is known).

## *The Dripping Sailor*

The story goes something like this.[54] Atkinson and Usborne had amassed a sizable fortune shipping square timber from Quebec to Liverpool in the 1840s. Their business practices were apparently above reproach until Usborne began overloading their oceangoing schooners with huge slabs of lumber weighing more than a ton each. When he had filled the schooners' holds, he stowed these gigantic beams on the vessels' open decks where, despite their weight, they would frequently slide about in the open ocean, causing vessels to capsize, especially in rough seas. Of course, some of the schooners made it safely to Liverpool, and the firm made a healthy profit.

With this income, Usborne built a great stone house on the heights above Quebec City where he and his wife, Mary, threw lavish parties for the colony's upper crust. One year, on May 1, they filled their mansion's ballroom with a crowd of well-to-do Quebecers to celebrate the departure of another overladen fleet for Liverpool. A sudden loud knocking at the exterior ballroom door disturbed the merry-making. The music stopped and the laughter ceased. When George Usborne threw open the door, he faced a gaunt sailor draped in seaweed, seawater dripping to the ground. While the guests recoiled in horror, the sailor raised his arm, pointed a long, thin finger at Usborne, and appeared to be screaming imprecations at him. But not a word was heard as the apparition vanished, leaving only a puddle of saltwater and sea wrack on the floor. Later, Usborne learned that his ships had sunk on the night of May 1, at the very hour the cursing sailor had interrupted his party.

The phantom at the door did not bode well for Atkinson and Usborne. Their company was soon bankrupted. In addition, Usborne's wife refused to stay in the house on the heights, as the dripping sailor appeared with ghastly regularity every May Day to disrupt their evening. As a result, Usborne moved his family to Portage-du-Fort, north of Ottawa, where the timber industry was just getting started. As far as is known, the dripping sailor did not follow him into the woods. Possibly in a spirit of thankful relief, in 1856 Usborne donated the land where Saint George's Anglican Church still stands in Portage-du-Fort. This once-haunted man with a checkered past died on March 1, 1886, in Belleville, Ontario (mercifully not on May 1, his doleful day of reckoning).

John Kelly and the *Arethusa* departed Quebec on November 11, 1846, one of the last vessels to leave before the winter freeze closed the port for six months. They arrived back in Liverpool on a frosty, fog-shrouded New Year's Eve, accompanied by two other timber-laden ships that had preceded them out of Quebec, the *Helen* (Captain Hicks), which had sailed on November 7, and the *Queen* (Captain Leary), which had left on November 9.

Salt was an essential ingredient for seasoning, curing, and preserving food up and down the Eastern Seaboard of North America in the 1840s. For example, salt cod produced by US and Canadian fisheries became a staple food supply for the continent's growing population. The

*Arethusa*'s next two trips under John Kelly were part of this commercial dynamic. In the winter and spring of 1847, the *Arethusa* transported a cargo of salt and probably passengers to Gardiner, Sager & Company in New Orleans, returning to Liverpool with 371 bales of cotton, corn, lard, hams, and staves. In the summer and fall, she carried another load of salt to D. Burnet at Quebec, returning to Bowden and Quinn in Belfast on November 16, 1847, with the usual shipment of timber.

John Kelly's last two trips with the *Arethusa* took many passengers from Belfast to New York City in 1848. The first spring trip was a forty-two-day passage from Belfast with 250 travelers. Cabin passenger James Frenchy[55] published a letter of commendation in the *Belfast News-Letter* praising John Kelly and chief mate Davey[56] for the "considerate attention" they showed to all the passengers and their skill in bringing them safely to America.

TO THE EDITOR OF THE BELFAST NEWSLETTER.

SIR.—The following resolution of thanks, from the passengers of the Arethusa, Belfast to New York, was unanimously agreed to, as a tribute to the excellent commander of that ship.

JAMES FRENCHY, cabin passenger

New York, April, 1848

Resolution of thanks to John Kelly, Commander of the "Arethusa"

That, at the close of a prosperous and pleasant voyage, in which his professional knowledge had been frequently and fully tested, the undersigned desire to express their approbation of his services, while under his care.

The considerate attention constantly shown to the comforts of each passenger, and the urbanity of manners which have, at all times, characterized Captain Kelly, merit from us, severally, a distinct acknowledgement, and shall be sufficient, at all times, to give us a sincere interest in his welfare.

To Mr. Davey, the chief mate, the warmest expression of our regard is due, for the gentlemanly conduct which has distinguished him throughout the voyage.

Desiring to Captain Kelly our best wishes for his further prosperity, we are respectfully,

[Here follow the signatures of the passengers, 219 in number.]

New York, April, 1848.[57]

John Kelly and the *Arethusa* departed New York on June 12, 1848—the same day that William Kelly and the *Belinda* arrived at New York en route to their date with destiny at Scatarie Island. Two weeks after the loss of the *Belinda* on June 22, the *Arethusa* docked at Liverpool with a cargo of cotton, flour, Indian corn, breadstuffs, sappan wood, and tar consigned to Cook & Smith. It was likely here that John Kelly first heard of his brother's misadventure off Cape Breton, just three years after his own ship *Clio* had come to grief at Hunting Island, South Carolina. Both Kelly brothers had now weathered the master mariner's ultimate test and lived to sail another day.

The *Arethusa*'s next trip was a fifty-six-day passage that departed Belfast on September 15, 1848, and arrived at New York on November 13 with 267 immigrants, including five cabin passengers: Francis and Lady Mary Morin, Adeline Morin, and Robert Dixon and lady.[58] Kelly and the *Arethusa* subsequently departed New York two days before Christmas 1848 and arrived back in the Mersey one month later on Tuesday, January 23, 1849, carrying cotton, flour, wheat, ashes, cornmeal, and turpentine—a fast passage home on what appears to have been John Kelly's last voyage as captain of the *Arethusa*.[59]

Here we leave John Kelly for a time. He had other things on his mind as he brought the *Arethusa* back to Liverpool, and he was not alone in this. El Dorado was beckoning, and the *Liverpool Mercury* fanned popular interest in the gilded news from Northern California with a long article exclaiming, "More gold has been discovered and the supply is literally inexhaustible. About 100,000 dollars' worth is gathered daily; but there is much sickness and suffering at the diggings, from want of all the necessities of life. Two barrels of brandy were lately sold at the mines for 14,000 dollars in gold dust!"

Sometime around 1848 or 1849, John appears to have relocated to California, and there his trail disappears, perhaps at the diggings, perhaps somewhere along San Francisco's waterfront where so many people went missing for a time or forever, with little to lose and everything to gain.[60] It was a time of revolution in Europe, and there was a rush for gold in the California territory. It was a period when individuals were swept into movements. With the 1840s winding down, John Kelly's career blurs into conjecture, as does his brother's.

## William Kelly and the *Dalriada*

Following the loss of the *Belinda* at Scatarie, there is a yearlong transition period in William Kelly's career, time enough for him to have gone somewhere and done something. But his activities from June 1848 to June 1849 are lost in the obscuring fog of indeterminacy that typically settled upon him as he moved from one ship to another. He next appears at Quebec, preparing to take a truly behemoth vessel on her maiden voyage to Liverpool. Losing the *Belinda* had been just a blip in his career.

> THE "DALRIADA,"—This immense ship, of larger tonnage than any vessel belonging to any port in Ireland (or England, with a few exceptions), cleared at Quebec for Liverpool, on the 26th May. Exclusive of some of the magnificent merchantmen which belong to our own port, the Anne, Jeffry, of Dublin, stands next in size. The Dalriada is the property of Mr. Grainger, of this town; one of our most enterprising and extensive ship owners; and she is commanded by Captain W. Kelly, an able and experienced seaman. She brings with her the following immense cargo: — 104 tons oak; 1,652 tons white pine; 4,863 standard pine deals; 5,000 pipe staves; 14,000 white oak staves; and 760 barrels flour.[61]

The *Dalriada* (Official Number 23185) was a gigantic square-rigger with three masts and two decks. Launched from the shipyard of Pierre Brunelle at Quebec for George H. Parke on April 27, 1849, her vital statistics were 206 feet long × 40 feet beam × 25 feet depth of hold, making her 70 feet longer and 20 feet broader abeam than the *Belinda*. She was approximately 1,500 tons registered weight (versus 750 tons for the *Belinda*) and had a whopping 2,500 tons carrying capacity. Constructed of oak, hackmatack, and pine sheathed with yellow copper, her prow was gilded with an impressive male figurehead. Dalriada was the name of a Gaelic kingdom of the late sixth and early seventh centuries that had encompassed the western coast of Scotland and County Antrim in Northern Ireland. David Grainger must have been confident with Kelly's skill and expertise to have entrusted this impressive ship's maiden voyage to him. The *Dalriada* cleared out of Quebec on May 26, 1849, and arrived safely at Liverpool on July 3, a trip of thirty-nine days, slower than Kelly's usual hustle, possibly because of weather or the weight of the ship's massive cargo.

In 1845 the British Board of Trade had instituted a system of voluntary examinations for masters and mates serving on foreign trade vessels. After arriving in Liverpool, Kelly, although he was already a seasoned master mariner, took this examination and obtained his registration ticket.

The *Dalriada*'s first round trip was Liverpool to New Orleans, a route well known to Kelly, who was himself becoming well known to the paying public. For the first time, the advertisement announcing the *Dalriada*'s November departure to New Orleans stated, "Captain Kelly's experience and kindness to emigrants is so well known that comment is unnecessary." This promotional catchphrase would follow Kelly for the rest of his career, reassuring travelers that they were in good hands with him.

The *Dalriada* got away early from Liverpool on November 9, 1849, with over 400 passengers and a cargo of general merchandise including 4,450 sacks of salt and 50 hampers of potatoes. She arrived at New Orleans forty-five days later on Christmas Eve. Two passengers died during the crossing—a four-year-old boy named James O'Brien and a twenty-five-year-old married woman named Mary Hempl.[62]

Kelly had plenty of time to renew old acquaintances in New Orleans. It took three and a half months to fill the *Dalriada*'s immense hold with 4,253 bales of cotton weighing 1,958,078 pounds and valued at $220,419 (equivalent in purchasing power to approximately $8.4 million in 2022). She also carried 100 tierces of beef, 50 barrels of pork, 1,500 staves, and a large quantity of passenger stores—all in all, the largest single cargo ever shipped from New Orleans up to that time.

While loading cargo, Kelly also had to replace a good part of his crew. His carpenter, steward, one apprentice, and eighteen seamen deserted in New Orleans, likely lured away by the exotic attractions of the city. In addition, crewman John Long (age 29) of Liverpool died in the hospital of pneumonia. Fortunately there was no shortage of men interested in leaving the city for any number of reasons; twenty fresh sailors signed on for the return trip to Liverpool on April 15, 1850. The *Dalriada* departed on the same day, with the *New Orleans Picayune* newspaper of April 16 effusively describing her as "a splendid new ship...nearly large enough for a man-of-war...a beautiful model, and as fast as she is spacious and handsome." Interestingly, the crew agreement for this trip lists William Kelly's salary as £10 a month (equivalent in purchasing power to approximately £1,412 in 2022).[63]

Following a forty-seven-day crossing, the *Dalriada* sailed into Liverpool on May 30, one ship among a remarkable flotilla of vessels including the *Jessica* (Captain Hayes), *Transit* (Captain Russell), *St. Clair* (Captain Johnson), *Petona* (Captain Hughes), *Milicate* (Captain Hunter), *Alice Wilson* (Captain Lockhart), and *Viceroy* (Captain McMahon)—all wafting in together from the Crescent City.

The fresh breeze that blew these eight ships into Liverpool on a fine spring day in 1850 was also a wind of change for William Kelly. On the family front, he learned that he had lost a sibling while returning from New Orleans. His youngest sister, Fanny, the erstwhile "Queen of Antrim Town" who had been celebrated in verse in 1826, had died too young in Belfast at age twenty-six on March 15, 1850, cause unknown. On a happier note, as if in compensation, Martha Kelly had given birth to a daughter, and they named this child Fanny after William's deceased sister. Of course, she was also named after their previous daughter Fanny, who had died five years earlier when William was transitioning from the *Dumfriesshire* to the *Belinda*.

As for William's career, the *Dalriada* was loading for Callao and San Francisco with Kelly still listed as her master on June 20, 1850, but when she sailed on June 26, she was under the command of a man named Smith. William Kelly was in play again, moving to a different ship and, this time, a different owner.

The *Dalriada* was Kelly's last Grainger ship. Although she was registered to the port of Belfast, Kelly had always sailed her into and out of Liverpool, and he must have been feeling the tug of that booming mercantile city on the Irish Sea. He was also developing a professional relationship with James Beazley, one of Liverpool's most successful merchant ship owners. An astute businessman, Beazley was building a fleet of speedy, state-of-the-art clipper ships for the China and Australia trade, and he needed experienced master mariners to take charge of his foreign-going ships. William Kelly would soon be looking eastward to the Antipodes and beyond.

## William Kelly and the *Mary Carson*

The ship *Mary Carson* (Official Number 13592; 692 registered tons) was built in Sackville, New Brunswick, in 1849 at the shipyard of Christopher Boultenhouse[64] and subsequently transferred to James Beazley at Liverpool. A Captain Morrison took her on her first run from Liverpool to New Orleans and Quebec early in 1850. Then, on October 12, 1850, she sailed from Liverpool to New Orleans again, this time with William Kelly in command. She arrived at the Crescent City on Thursday, November 28, after a fast thirty-seven-day crossing with 268 passengers and 5,455 sacks of salt.

In the nineteenth-century British mercantile marine, no news was usually good news. If a ship made an uneventful passage, arriving more or less on time with generally healthy passengers and a largely intact cargo, the ship's owners and agents were delighted. This "no news" scenario appears to have been Kelly's standard operating procedure for all three of his voyages commanding the *Mary Carson*. The newspapers had little to note beyond the ship's departures and arrivals. James Beazley was likely gratified with the absence of reportage. On the other hand, there are unfortunately no stories to recount—except for one interesting family circumstance arising from the ship's first trip to New Orleans.

Kelly's arrival in New Orleans on November 28 was just two days after the wedding of his wife's brother Sam Rainey to Maria Louise Hawes on November 26, possibly at the Presbyterian church on the corner of Canal and Franklin Streets. This begs the question: Was Kelly trying to make it to New Orleans for the wedding? If so, he made good time but just missed the date. I wonder if Martha traveled with him to see her brothers and attend Sam's wedding.

After spending Christmas and New Year's in New Orleans, Kelly pointed the *Mary Carson* back to Liverpool sometime between February 11 and 15, 1851. Although there is no departure listed in the *New Orleans Bee*, the *Bee* does note her arrival at Liverpool on March 10 with Kelly in command.

Twenty days later, busy census takers swarmed the streets of Liverpool, recording who was where and with whom in British households on the night of Sunday, March 30. The 1851 census lists William and Martha Kelly with son John visiting Michael Warde, an Irish commercial traveler residing at 39 Quebec Street, close to the Clarence and Stanley Docks. Indeed, it was an Irish gathering of the Kellys and the Wardes with the Warde's Irish maid, Rose Grogan, and a visiting Irish merchant, Thomas Hazlett, also in attendance.

A couple of weeks later, the *Mary Carson* departed Liverpool on April 17, 1851, for New York with 276 passengers. They arrived at New York on May 23; then, following the same route as the ill-fated *Belinda* three years earlier, Kelly took the *Mary Carson* back up the East Coast, past his nemesis, Scatarie Island, to the Saint Lawrence River and on to Quebec, arriving there without incident on July 21. After quickly loading timber and other merchandise, they departed Quebec in good order and arrived safely back in the Mersey on August 29, 1851.

## William Kelly's Paperwork

Upon his return to Liverpool, Kelly had to once again navigate the bureaucratic corridors of the British mercantile marine. Following the voluntary examinations for masters and mates instituted in 1845, the Mercantile Marine Act of 1850 instituted compulsory examinations, requiring seamen who had obtained their voluntary accreditations between 1845 and 1850 to replace their old tickets with new Certificates of Service issued by the Board of Trade. Kelly accomplished this during his month ashore preparing for the *Mary Carson*'s third voyage. Coincidentally, his certificate number is 1,851, the year that he received the certificate.

By September 1851, William's base of operations had moved from Belfast to Liverpool, a perfectly reasonable development given his new employment with the Beazley Line. Indeed, at some point in the early 1850s, William took possession of a house at 52 Upper Stanhope Street in the Toxteth Park section of Liverpool. This neighborhood consisted of a mix of grand merchant houses around Sefton Park and Princes Park, with more modest Victorian terraces bordering on the docks to the west. William and Martha now had a family of three: Agnes (age 10), John (age 4), and Fanny (age 1). It is unclear whether Martha and the children joined William in Liverpool at this time. The family might have remained in Northern Ireland until 1855, when Kelly finally sold his house in the Townhead section of Antrim Town.

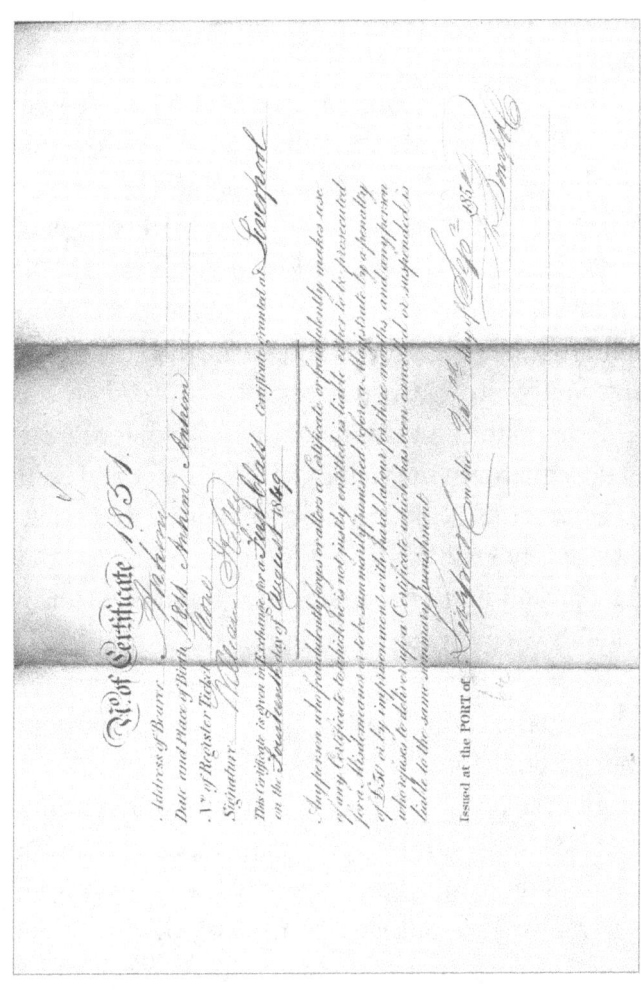

Figure 5: William Kelly's master's certificate no. 1,851, issued at Liverpool, September 23, 1851. Image credit: UK and Ireland, Masters and Mates Certificates, 1850–1927 database (Ancestry.com).

Just a week after renewing his master's certificate, Kelly boarded the *Mary Carson* for his first trip to India as captain of a British merchant ship. With no known surviving records of his service prior to 1836, however, I cannot say definitively that he had not been there before as a seaman.

The *Mary Carson* departed Liverpool on September 28, 1851, with a moderate wind from the northwest that blew her through the chops of Saint George's Channel to the southern tip of Ireland. Here she turned westward, keeping well clear of the Bay of Biscay, with its troublesome inward-flowing currents, and Cape Finisterre, where the Atlantic current set right on shore. She then continued dropping southward, pushed by strong and steady winds west of Madeira, the Canary Islands, and Cape Verde. She crossed the equator in the vicinity of Saint Peter and Saint Paul Rocks, where Kelly kept a close lookout for these islets, which were only visible within ten miles on a clear day. Here they picked up the southeast trade winds. Steering through with yards braced in and topmost studdingsails set, they outran the trades, crossed the Tropic of Capricorn, and picked up the variable winds that drove them around the Cape of Good Hope.

Assuming a November 1851 to March 1852 timeframe, they then headed south from the Cape and east to Saint Paul Island in the South Indian Ocean. Then they pushed north, driven by the southeast trades and the northwest monsoon. Crossing the equator again, they passed about 150 miles west of Banda Aceh, Sumatra, and entered the Bay of Bengal. Keeping west of the Nicobar and Andaman Islands, they eventually reached the Hooghly River and proceeded inland to Calcutta (now Kolkata). They finally arrived at Calcutta on March 23, 1852—an astonishing 177 days at sea for a trip that should have taken somewhere around 85 days.

Why the *Mary Carson*'s passage to India took so long is a good question. There are only two references to her in transit. On October 3, she was hailed near Bardsey, an island off the Llŷn Peninsula in the Welsh county of Gwynedd, north of Land's End. Then, on October 13, she was hailed again standing west at 47°N, 14°W (in the Atlantic, south of Ireland, roughly on a line with Saint-Nazaire, France). Apart from these brief sightings, which occurred early in her trip, there is no word of the *Mary Carson* until she finally arrived at Calcutta. Something significant must have interfered with Kelly's first outbound passage to India—something as yet unknown.

The *Mary Carson* departed Bengal on June 20, 1852, and her log notes two additional crew deaths during the trip home: Alexander Clyde, apprentice, on September 28, and Henry Lewis, seaman, on October 31.[65] The ship arrived home at Liverpool on November 11 after fourteen months at sea. Here William Kelly learned about the latest addition to his growing family. On May 18, 1852, while the *Mary Carson* was loading in Calcutta, Martha had given birth to a boy. She had named him William after his faraway father.

Having completed a satisfactory eighty-four-day return trip, Kelly found his protracted passage out had not jeopardized his standing with James Beazley. Continuing to see promise in his forty-one-year-old captain, Beazley had assigned Kelly to a new vessel that was built for speed in even the lightest of winds—a spanking-new Canadian clipper ship that had just arrived in Liverpool from New Brunswick.

CHAPTER TWO

# WILLIAM KELLY AND THE *MILES BARTON*

## (1853–1856)

Launched in 1853 from the shipyard of William and Richard Wright[66] at Marsh Creek, Courtenay Bay, near Saint John, New Brunswick, the *Miles Barton* (Official Number 1117) was built expressly for voyages to Australia. Here the gold rush in the state of Victoria, four years after the California gold rush began, was attracting a flood of immigrants to Melbourne, in southeastern Australia. The *Miles Barton* was a large clipper ship (175 feet long × 35 feet beam × 22 feet depth of hold) with two decks and a carrying capacity of 995 registered tons. Figure 6 shows a wooden model of the *Miles Barton*, which was sold at Bonhams in New York on May 25, 2011, having previously been part of the Seamen's Church Institute Collection of Maritime Paintings and Decorative Arts (also in New York).[67]

Figure 6: A wooden model of the clipper ship *Miles Barton*, American, early twentieth century. Image credit: © Bonhams 1793 Ltd.

James Beazley named his new ship after the Liverpool cotton broker in whose offices he had served his own business apprenticeship. According to Forwood,[68] Miles Barton the man (1789–1869) was "a picturesque figure, with his genial smile, and his hat drawn over his eyes." A reminiscence of Thomas Ellison helps clarify the allusion,[69] "He usually wore his hat canted to one side of his head, and often low down on his forehead, the brim coming close to the eyes; but the extent of the inclination downwards depended a good deal upon the state of the market: if business was active, the brim was tilted slightly upwards; but if the market was depressed, so was the hat."

So Miles Barton's hat was a business bellwether at the Liverpool Exchange. I wonder if he adjusted his brim in any particularly revealing manner on the days when his ship came in.

*Miles Barton* the ship arrived in Liverpool from New Brunswick on January 26, 1853, whereupon Beazley's shipping agents, Millers and Thompson, immediately assigned her to their Liverpool Golden Line of Packets to Australia. William Kelly would be clipper master on the ship's maiden voyage, departing from Liverpool for Melbourne at the end of April 1853.

An advertisement announcing the *Miles Barton*'s imminent departure[70] declared:

> She is expected to prove the fastest vessel afloat. Her cabins are fitted up in a most superior manner. The between-decks are extremely lofty, and ventilated on the most improved principles. [The ship] has an unusually clear upper deck for the passengers to take exercise on, and which has been proved to be absolutely essential to health on so long a voyage. The fittings will be found to be of a novel and superior description, and baths are provided on deck for the passengers. The dietary is extremely liberal and great care will be used in the selection of the provisions. She will carry an experienced Surgeon.

These carefully chosen words were intended to fill the *Miles Barton*'s passenger accommodations to ensure a profitable venture for the ship's owner, shareholders, and agents.

There are two first-person accounts of the *Miles Barton*'s departure and maiden voyage. First, we have preacher James Buck's vivid description of the religious service he conducted on board prior to the ship's departure. Then there is passenger David Stavely's diary, which he meticulously titled "The Story of the Voyage of David Stavely, Born Rureagh, County Down, Ireland, from Liverpool to Melbourne Aboard the Miles Barton Commanded by Wm. Kelly in 1853."[71]

These two accounts provide fascinating glimpses into this milestone outbound passage, as William Kelly's seafaring career entered a new and larger arena with much greater prospects.

On Sunday, April 24, 1853, the Rev. James Buck of the Liverpool Seamen's Friend Society and Bethel Union visited the ships *Miles Barton* and *Asia*, which were both at anchor in the Mersey. His purpose was to conduct religious services for the ships' passengers and crews prior to their departure. Buck recorded his observations in an article that was subsequently published in the *Liverpool Mercury* of Friday, April 29. The clergyman's vivid words describe the liveliness, noise, color, and drama of a ship on the brink of departure. They also capture the unique character of the writer who rendered all of his observations in a single unbroken—and quintessentially Victorian—paragraph.

RELIGIOUS SERVICES
ON BOARD THE AUSTRALIAN EMIGRANT SHIPS
THE MILES BARTON AND THE ASIA
These two ships, the Miles Barton and the Asia, being in the river, were both visited on Sabbath, the 24th instant, by the Rev. James Buck, of the Liverpool Seamen's Friend Society and Bethel Union, whose own account is as follows:—I left the landing stage at ten o'clock, and after some difficulty, owing to the unusual rapidity of the tide, which rendered

approach to the ship in a small boat not altogether free from danger, got on board the Miles Barton. The chief officer[72] immediately gave orders for the deck to be cleared, preparatory to service. A pious Scotchman and several others rendered their aid in bringing forms from below for the accommodation of the female passengers, and at eleven o'clock the people were all congregated on the mid-deck. The arrangement of this part of the ship, with its various poop-houses, threw the assembly into an unusual form: a large number ranging along the ship's larboard side, in several rows, which at a distance terminated in a crowd; another crossing the ship, between the mainmast and the poop, extending round and filling up the whole space of the starboard deck; a third part thronging, at different elevations, round the mainmast, wherever they could maintain foothold, holding on by the tackling near; and the remainder almost upon me, above on the boat bottoms and planks, which formed a canopy over the heads of the other people. No awkwardness of position, however, could prevent them from being as near me as possible, or from giving that earnest and lively attention throughout the whole service which I have, without exception, found characteristic of my emigrant auditors. The mate of the ship, a very interesting, intelligent, and educated young man, was by my side, one of my best hearers, and the crew, it was pleasing to see, were all interspersed, being known by their blue or red flannel costume.[73] It was a full service as usually celebrated in the non-conforming congregations, and lasted an hour and a half. There was no difficulty with the singing; many good voices, the owners of which manifested anything but a disposition to spare them, were around me, which had evidently been accustomed to unite in congregational psalmody. The prayer was offered amid the most impressive silence. The effect of the whole may partly be judged of from the eagerness many of the people showed to have an account of the service sent to their friends at home. After the benediction had been pronounced, I intimated my intention to have such an account inserted in one of the local papers, and that if any of them wished to have a copy sent to their friends I would gladly charge myself with the trouble of carrying their wishes into effect. Forty-five addresses were sent in during the half hour which followed, each one, of course, bringing also the price of the paper. Some of these addresses were of parents, others of brothers and sisters, and not a few of young women in favour of whom the correspondents cherished the hope of a still closer relationship than any of these. The homes to which they pointed embraced as many points as the compass itself. Long distances in Ireland, Wales, Scotland, and England were to be traveled by those tokens of remembrance, indicating very significantly the wide range of those sympathies which, in such lively exercise, were radiating from the deck of that one emigrant ship, and also from what far-off and varied scenes unseen eyes and bosoms were looking and throbbing towards that promiscuous community who were, pro tempore, the dwellers within the wooden walls of that city afloat. It was a beautiful testimony to the sweetness of home and the value of friends from those who were in the best position to give such testimony, having so recently taken farewell of both. How becoming did the many anxious charges which were given me seem! "Be sure, sir, not to lose my address!" "Be sure, sir, not to forget to send my paper." I could only assure them their wishes should be faithfully fulfilled. This work finished, I shook hands with many, among whom was a Captain Grove, who, with his wife, were passengers on board. He had been wrecked some time ago in a brig which bore his name, and of which he was owner, and his wife, who was with him at the time, was in the main-top twelve hours before her rescue could be accomplished. A painting of the ship hung up in the cabin, representing her with the sea beating over her and carrying away all her boats, as a memorial of their merciful deliverance. Having hailed a passing boat, I reached the landing stage about half-past two o'clock, and in half an hour took another boat for the Asia, which was lying far up in the Sloyne. [There follows a description of the service held on the ship *Asia*.]

David Stavely's diary sheds light on the days immediately preceding the *Miles Barton*'s departure, although his entries here are fragmentary and difficult to decipher. Two days after Buck's religious service, the loading of passengers was thrown into confusion when the ship's agents, Millers and Thompson, brought carpenters on board to build additional berths in the steerage sections. The agents obviously wanted to squeeze in as many paying passengers (and wring out as much profit) as possible.

Those who were already on board the *Miles Barton* saw the tiny space allotted to them dwindling even more as the new berths were snugged in. Human nature being what it is, one group of passengers, those believing in direct action, began tearing out the extra beds as fast as the carpenters put them in. Another group, leaning more toward due process, formed a committee, wrote a petition, and elected three representatives to present their case to Beazley and his agents. They even took up a collection in case they needed to file a lawsuit. It might have been this gambit that finally brought Beazley himself to the ship, along with a somber delegation from Millers and Thompson. In the end, Beazley blinked. He ordered the extra berths removed, and the additional passengers were sent ashore. A spokesperson for the original group of passengers returned thanks to Beazley for his kindness, and the insurrection ended with tremendous cheers for him, Kelly, and the crew of the *Miles Barton*, probably punctuated with jeers for the shipping agents and their henchmen.

## Voyage 1: Liverpool to Melbourne, Calcutta, and Bombay

The *Miles Barton* sailed from Liverpool's Salthouse Dock at 4:00 p.m. on Thursday, April 28, 1853, with a crew of thirty-five. She carried 382 passengers (including 30 children)[74] and a cargo of general merchandise bound for Melbourne. David Stavely's diary provides a fascinating day-by-day account of the *Miles Barton*'s outbound passage with, every now and then, a brief appearance by Captain Kelly. For example, just two days after departing, the ship had a close call just south of Ireland when Kelly narrowly averted colliding with another vessel, "but by good management and the assistance of God there was no harm done with the exception of a Seaman who fell from the yard arm but [was] not dangerously hurt."

On Wednesday, May 4, Kelly assembled the passengers and read them the rules so everyone would know what was expected of them. On Friday, May 13, a baby girl was born. At Kelly's suggestion, her parents named her (in a manner of speaking) after their ship, Emilia Barton Filles, which reveals something of the influence wielded by a ship's master at sea.[75] On the same day, Kelly convened a court of inquiry to investigate a fight between two passengers and attempt to resolve their differences.

On a Saturday evening toward the end of May, while beating southward with generally fine weather and a stiff breeze, the *Miles Barton* crossed the equator with much merriment. Here, traditional ceremonies initiated those who were "crossing the line" for the first time. First, the crew stealthily tipped a tub of burning tar overboard to deceive the passengers into thinking there really were "lights on the line." Then a congenial "Nepkin" (Neptune, God of the Sea) and his wife visited the ship. They were, of course, sailors dressed in sheepskins. After being dragged fore and aft on a sled, the couple joined Captain Kelly on the quarterdeck where Nepkin informed him that "he had come on board to pay him a visit and shave all his children, as he considered it his right and duty to do so on all ships that came his way." Playing along, Kelly said he was very happy to see Nepkin and hoped he would treat his children decently, "as they were all of a superior breed and brought up at boarding schools... that they were nearly all of them English but a good many were Scotch and the greater part of them Irish." Kelly invited Nepkin to pay him another visit in two days and bring with him "a silver razor and some of Her Majesty's double-refined, scented soap that would raise Her Majesty's softest leather." After shaking hands with each of them and wishing them both good night, Kelly received an extravagantly low bow from Nepkin and a curtsy from his wife. When the sheep-skinned sailors returned two days later, razors in hand, Kelly astutely vetoed the shaving, "lest there should be anyone hurt."

One day early in June, Kelly hauled out his hailing trumpet to speak with the captain of a passing vessel, the *Elizabeth George,* which was running between Callao and New York. As the two ships hove to in the open ocean, the captains arranged a last opportunity for Kelly's passengers to send letters home via a hastily convened mid-Atlantic exchange. "It was then like a writing school for a few minutes," noted Stavely. "We only got then about 10 minutes to write when I wrote a few lines to my Brother and a great many put a wrong address on their letters as the small boat was going down."

On Wednesday, June 22, they passed the Cape of Good Hope and commenced their eastward run across the southern Indian Ocean in a line with Saint Paul and Amsterdam Islands. Stavely noted strong winds and heavy rains rounding the Cape punctuated by another passenger fight between decks.

They were now racing directly toward Australia, propelled by the circumpolar storm track nicknamed the

Roaring Forties (south of the fortieth parallel). Here, winds forced ships on their sides through mountainous seas often for days on end. Stavely began jotting down their daily longitudinal gains in excited anticipation of arriving at their destination.[76]

Through the first half of July, as the *Miles Barton* sailed as far from land as any time during the trip, conditions were generally boisterous and stormy with sudden changes of wind and wild wet weather. During the worst of it, Stavely describes enormous seas "so large that some of the passengers [were] swept from one side of the deck to the other." On the night of July 12, as the rough weather continued, four of the "committee" (apparently four of the passengers' elected leaders) drank too much and fought among themselves; one of them even tried to jump overboard—twice! Kelly prudently stopped all liquor sales.

On July 18, there was another birth on board at 3:35 in the morning. As the day progressed, Kelly took advantage of a fresh breeze to overtake and hail the ship *John George*, ninety-eight days out of London, also bound for Melbourne. The *Miles Barton* scudded ahead so rapidly that they lost sight of the *John George* by dark.

Finally, early in the morning of Thursday, July 21, 1853, Stavely caught his first glimpse of the famous Cape Otway lighthouse west of the entrance to Port Phillip. Word began rapidly spreading through the ship that their journey's end was near. Kelly brought the *Miles Barton* carefully into Bass Strait, where the winds and currents, especially around King Island, required careful attention. A deep-water pilot was required to negotiate the narrow channel at Port Phillip Heads, where a powerful ebb tide created high, confused, and tumbling seas. That evening a strong gale forced Kelly to tack about and drop anchor in the strait off the entrance.

They finally picked up a light breeze around three o'clock Friday morning, but they had drifted so far back with the wind and tide that it took until ten o'clock that morning to come up as close to the channel as where they had been the night before. When the pilot came on board to take them through the Heads, they were again becalmed until one o'clock Saturday morning, when a dilatory breeze finally blew them into Port Phillip Bay where new lives would begin for 382 weary but exhilarated travelers.

After another day of excruciatingly slow progress under tow by a tug steamer across the large, shallow bay, they were still ten miles from Melbourne. Standing on deck, David Stavely saw several little huts and tents with his naked eye and a great many more in the distance with his eyeglass. He also saw cattle "as fine as ever I saw a sight in summer at home and the moon arose so beautiful on the unfurled water, it was most delightful."

On Sunday morning, July 24, Kelly went ashore and engaged a schooner and a steamer to take his passengers and their luggage to Melbourne's piers. That night there was another final, probably liquor-fueled fight on board, just yards from the bed where a sick female passenger lay at death's door.

Stavely finally left the *Miles Barton* at three o'clock on Tuesday afternoon, July 26, and arrived at Melbourne Town around five p.m. There he treated himself to a cup of hot tea and a celebratory beefsteak at a local inn. The sick woman on board had died just fifteen minutes before he disembarked. She was the only fatality during the *Miles*

*Barton*'s impressive eighty-four-day run from Liverpool to Melbourne.

Incongruously, the English poet John Dryden captures the very different immigrant experiences of David Stavely and the anonymous woman who never made it ashore: "Like pilgrims to th' appointed place we tend; the world's an inn and death the journey's end."[77]

David Stavely's diary is replete with interesting observations of wind and wave, "insufficient Sunday services," and gladdening seabird sightings interspersed with stand-up fights among unruly men confined too long in steerage. The Irishman also noted a couple of instances when Kelly recruited passengers to supplement his crew under certain conditions.[78] On June 24, for example, "about 6 o'clock in the morning the Capt came and called for the North Country gold diggers to get up and help them to house sail for the gale." Then, on July 7, with the *Miles Barton* laboring in an Indian Ocean storm more than two thousand miles from Melbourne, Stavely notes that "the storm increased so during last night that the Captain was obliged to call upon some of the passengers about midnight to help him to lower sail. The storm eased in the morning but still a tremendous heavy sea and the ship continuing to roll...very heavy running under double reefed top main mizzen and fore sails. At 7 pm took a lee lurch and shipped very heavy seas all night. Long. 99 degrees E; Lat. 44 degrees South."

Stavely, who was a North Country digger himself, also knew a thing or two about ships. He gamely assisted with the pulley-haul on ropes to vary the trim of the sails on that tempestuous night as the *Miles Barton* fought her way eastward through swelling seas.

Stavely's diary contains many references to the *Miles Barton* overtaking and passing other vessels on the way to Melbourne—corroborating William Kelly's reputation for hustle. Indeed, his eighty-four-day outward passage tied with the Black Ball Line's *Indian Queen* (Captain Mills) for the third-fastest trip from Liverpool to Melbourne in 1853. The *Miles Barton* and the *Indian Queen* were outpaced only by the famous Black Ball clipper *Marco Polo* (Captain "Bully" Forbes, seventy-six days) and Beazley's new *Star of the East* (Captain Robertson, seventy-eight days). On June 18, four days off the Cape of Good Hope, Stavely records "a good wind continuing, ran 14 miles from 5 o'clock am to 6 o'clock am." He also notes a friendly wager in which Kelly won two pounds off "Captain Williams, who was convinced no ship could do it. Distance made from 12 o'clock yesterday to 12 o'clock today, 310 miles. Course ESE."

Kelly made an excellent showing on his maiden passage to Melbourne, exploiting the Roaring Forties and the Antarctic Circumpolar Current to sail her through in excellent time. Depending on the season, clipper masters would sometimes drop down into the Furious Fifties to make even better time, although these latitudes required a sharp lookout for storms and ice packs. Sea captains were wholly dependent on sailing know-how and the science of voyage-making. As Villiers points out, "The study of ocean sailing conditions is as old as the story of discovery by sea itself, for the two went hand in hand. A sailing ship on an ocean voyage was not at all concerned with making the shortest passage between two points, measured in miles.

What she sought was the best and shortest usable passage, measured in terms of winds and weather."[79]

The desired outcome was always, of course, the safe arrival of the ship with healthy passengers and cargo intact. The *Miles Barton*'s passengers, as listed in the *Melbourne Argus* of Tuesday, July 26, 1853, were, in the cabins, Miss Williams; two Misses Jackson; Miss Marsden; Mr. and Mrs. Peel; Mrs. Johnson and family; Mr. and Mrs. Anson; Messrs. Williams, Glasser, Bartlett, Trumble, Edwards, Lowey, and Stanton; Dr. Maise, surgeon; and 367 in the intermediate and steerage compartments. Her cargo included 5 hogsheads for S. Kinder; 7 cases and 1 cask for T. Broadbent; 8 crates, 13 packages, 16 cases, and 1 bale for Parker and Kinder; 1 case for C. Swan; 5 chests and 5 cases for M. Glaser; 1 case for J. W. Richardson; 1 case for R. Fleming; 1 case and 6 packages for D. Wood; 1 case and 1 cask for Berry and Guest; 8 packages for G. Glue; and 8 cases for H. J. Eshelby.

Upon arrival, the *Miles Barton*'s grateful passengers presented Kelly with a complimentary letter and a valuable gold watch and chain, as detailed in the following account that was subsequently published in the *Belfast Northern Whig*:

> THE CLIPPER SHIP "Miles Barton," of Liverpool, Captain Wm. Kelly.—At the time this vessel was fitting out for Australia, we gave a description of her, and we are very much gratified to find that we have not been disappointed in our expectations, as this vessel has performed the voyage from Liverpool to Melbourne in eighty-four days, and delivered her passengers in good health and spirits, and

well pleased with both vessel and captain.—We have been favoured, through a friend, with a copy of the resolution at a meeting on board, held on the 21st of June, which we have great pleasure in publishing, as it is a confirmation of the opinions we expressed of Captain Kelly at the time he joined this ship; and should the Miles Barton again take the berth for Australia, we are certain she will get a decided preference. It will be very gratifying to the friends of those who sailed in this vessel to know they have been so comfortably situated on their voyage; and it speaks well for their generosity to find they have appreciated Captain Kelly's services, and marked their approval of his conduct in a suitable manner:—Ship, Miles Barton, June 29th, 1853.

At a meeting held this day, Dr. Johnson in the Chair, the following resolution was unanimously passed: —Resolved, that the passengers on board the ship Miles Barton, now fast approaching the termination of their voyage from Liverpool to Melbourne, Australia, duly appreciating the uniform kindness evinced by Captain William Kelly, and his anxiety to promote on all occasions the health, comfort, and harmony of all on board, are anxious to express their grateful feelings towards him; at the same time, they wish to bear testimony to the unceasing attention, and the ability displayed by him in the discharge of his arduous professional duties, and their admiration of the very superior sailing qualities of the noble vessel under his command. As a lasting memento of their feelings, as above mentioned, and with best wishes for his prosperity and happiness, they beg his acceptance of the accompanying gold watch and chain: Committee – Messrs. Finlay, Beckett, Dowling, Coleman, Ryan, Flatow, Fox, Trumble. Richard Johnson, M.R.C.S., Chairman; Joseph Wilson Richardson, Treasurer; Robert R. Morgan, Arch., and C.E., Hon. Secretary.[80]

The forty-two-year-old Kelly would treasure this gold watch for the rest of his life. It is likely the same watch and chain that appear in our family photographs of him, which were taken many years later. This prized memento would ultimately pass to Kelly's oldest son, John, by the terms of his wife's will when she passed away in 1884.

The *Miles Barton* remained in Melbourne only a little over a week, departing on August 2 for Calcutta (now Kolkata) and Bombay (now Mumbai).[81] I know nothing of the ship's freight on this trip to India beyond a newspaper reference to her carrying part of her original cargo from Liverpool on to the subcontinent. At this time of year, they probably took the northern route out of Melbourne, sailing into the Tasman Sea and up the east coast of Australia through the Torres Strait and Arafura Sea to the Indian Ocean, skirting the Sunda Islands, and entering the Bay of Bengal. This route, leveraging the seasonal monsoon connecting the Pacific and Indian Ocean trade winds, was the quickest route to the mouth of the Hooghly River at this time of year.

Entering the Hooghly at its funnel-shaped estuary called the Sandheads, the *Miles Barton* cautiously worked her way under pilotage 120 miles upriver to the bustling port of Calcutta. This city was Bengal's major administrative and mercantile center and the capital of British India until 1912. The Hooghly presented a challenging obstacle course with continuously shifting sandbanks and other navigational hazards, including seven-foot tidal bores during the monsoon season.

I do not know when the *Miles Barton* arrived at Calcutta or when she departed. I can only surmise that she left sometime in the fall, sailing southward around the British crown colony of Ceylon and perhaps calling in at Colombo before working her way up the west coast of India to Bombay, where she arrived on October 7, 1853. Here she remained for a little over a month and a half to discharge her remaining cargo and load new consignments and provisions for her return to Liverpool.

The *Miles Barton* departed Bombay on November 25 in company with another Liverpool-bound ship, the *Genghis Khan* (Captain Bond). They sailed directly across the Indian Ocean, through the Mozambique Channel, and down the east coast of Africa in the Mozambique and Agulhas currents. While rounding the Cape of Good Hope, probably with a strong westerly wind, they kept no more than fifty miles from shore in the shallow Agulhas Bank. In this way, they avoided the treacherous seas farther out, where the warm Indian Ocean and the cold Atlantic mingle as the seafloor falls away to the abyssal plain. Then, continuing northwestward into the deep ocean, the white-winged ships shaped a course for Saint Helena and the Ascension Islands. Here they crossed the equator and set a northerly course, picking up the northeast trades and westerlies that blew them by the Azores and home to the Irish Sea.

The *Miles Barton* arrived back at Liverpool on Wednesday, March 8, 1854 (one day after the *Genghis Khan*), completing her maiden voyage of approximately thirty thousand nautical miles in ten and a half months. Kelly's homecoming was sweetened by the arrival of yet another child in the house at 52 Upper Stanhope Street. Mary McConnel Kelly had been born on September 20, 1853, while her father was sailing from Calcutta to Bombay.

In commemoration of the *Miles Barton*'s successful maiden voyage, William Kelly received an engraved silver snuffbox from Mr. Thomas Haigh of Elm Hall, Wavertree, near Liverpool. Haigh was a well-known Liverpool cotton broker described by Forwood as "the courtly and stately chief of Haigh and Co."[82] He was a businessman with close ties to both Miles Barton (the man) and James Beazley. In 1851 Barton had served as president of the Liverpool Cotton Brokers Association; in 1857 Thomas Haigh served in the same capacity. Between 1863 and 1867, Haigh and Beazley sat together on the Liverpool board of directors of the Union Maritime Insurance Company. These business associations point to this Thomas Haigh as the man who presented Kelly with the silver snuffbox mentioned in the following letter, written in January 1928 to the editor of *Sea Breezes* magazine by Kelly's grandson William Gourley Moore, the son of Kelly's daughter Fanny and her husband, John Moore.

> Relic of Miles Barton
>
> In your excellent little magazine for September I notice the ship Miles Barton mentioned, and the death of an old sailor in New Zealand who was an apprentice in this famous ship which my grandfather, Captain Wm. Kelly, sen., at one time commanded. I have lying before me a very finely-worked silver snuff box bearing the following inscription:

—"Presented to Captain Wm. Kelly, of the ship Miles Barton, on the successful completion of his first voyage in that vessel, by Thomas Haigh, Liverpool, 8th March, 1854."

My grandfather was a famous old skipper in days of sail, and he commanded, built and owned the Merrie England. He was in the Express, Mary Carson, and other fine ships.

I wonder if there is anyone alive today who remembers him or anyone who can tell me what the end of the Miles Barton was.

Captain Kelly's two sons, Captains John and William Kelly, junr., were in sail and later in steam. They were all fine seamen, and the three of them have sailed on the last long voyage.

We used to have oil paintings of several fine ships in my old home in Ireland, but where they are now I cannot say. One of the Miles Barton in a heavy sea I remember well.

W. G. Moore, Johannesburg, S.A.[83]

## Voyage 2: Liverpool to Melbourne and Calcutta

There was little time wasted in preparing for the *Miles Barton*'s next voyage. On March 14, just six days after her return to Liverpool, she entered for loading and was ready to depart again for Melbourne by early May—but she would not get away without another visit from that "most happy man," the preacher James Buck. Kelly invited Buck to conduct another of his farewell religious services—an engagement that the clergyman enthusiastically accepted and wrote up, as before, for the *Liverpool Mercury* in his own inimitable fashion.

## RELIGIOUS SERVICES ON BOARD OF AUSTRALIAN EMIGRANT SHIPS

The tide of emigration for the season appears to have set in with real earnestness. The multitudes who are daily thronging the pier-heads, eager for their departure, are truly wonderful. Cart-loads and wagon-loads of boxes arrive in quick succession, accompanied by men, women and children—Irish, Scotch, English, and German—all mingling together in a strange and confused medley, bringing into requisition every kind of carriage vehicle, and the labor of carters and porters, and making the humble fortunes of a host of shoeblacks and orangegirls to an extent really astonishing. Steam tug companies reap a large harvest also, and the boatmen of the river come in for no inconsiderable portion of the spoil, while, higher up in the social state, our shipowners and brokers must feel little temptation to go to the diggings in search of gold, through the extreme facility with which they can conjure the precious commodity into their credit account by the ordinary routine of brisk and prosperous business.

My own labours are, from the same cause, in increasing demand. The number of ships ready about the same time renders the economising of time and judicious foresight indispensable to enable me to meet the multiplied calls, so as, if possible, to disappoint none of what is now felt to be, if not an essential element, at least a beautiful propriety of the preparation of an Australian emigrant ship for the proper commencement of her long voyage. In connection with my other work among the sailors of the port, I find myself continually and delightfully busy. If enjoyment of this life consists in activity in the best of causes, then I am a most happy man. My opportunities of fulfilling my vocation are certainly most abundant. Since my communication in last Tuesday's paper I have visited the Miles Barton and the Red Jacket.

THE MILES BARTON
This ship, sailing under the firm of Millers and Thompson, went into the river on Saturday last, the 29th ult. Her commander had requested, through the passenger-agent, that his ship should have divine service on board on the day following; but, unfortunately, the note did not reach me until Sabbath evening, just as I was about commencing my service at the North Bethel. On Tuesday, however, the 2nd Inst., I was on board of her by a little after one o'clock, and on alighting on her deck was most kindly received both by Captain Kelly and his chief officer, Mr. Tate, both of whom I immediately recognized as the same men from whom I had received so much attention on my last visit to her in April, 1853, for a similar purpose. Dinner being quite ready, our first attention was duly rendered thereto. Immediately after, my notices announced half-past three o'clock as the time of commencing divine service. During the interval, I went about

among the people, and found all of them apparently well content with the arrangements made for their comfort, and overheard many expressions of sympathy and favor of the proposed service. When the time came round, all the crew were relieved from work, that they might have a fair chance of attending. I went among them before beginning, and found they purposed to be present; but they said, "We suppose we must come in last of all." I said, "What for?" "For fear there may not be room for all," they replied. I, however, assured them their presence would be as acceptable to me, and was as much contemplated in my design, as the presence of any other parties, and they were at liberty to go down at once and take the best place! Poor fellows! It seemed to put the matter in a new light before them, as they said, "We'll come; we'll come, Sir." They were nearly all present, as was also the chief officer (the captain had meanwhile gone ashore). The service was held down in the intermediate cabin, a fine roomy place, and 200 were carefully counted as composing the congregation. As usual with me, it was a full service, consisting of praises, prayers, and preaching and occupied an hour and a half. It was evidently greatly prized by the people, who, in every suitable manner, afterwards gave expression to their thankful appreciation of my visit and labors. Many of them were very sorry that no like-minded man was going out with them, and wished they could take me. But they agreed with me that my work seemed cut out before me on this side of the sea, and they hoped that as I could go out with none, I might not fail to visit all. Every service I hold on board of these vessels serves to deepen the impression of the importance of the work, and to augment my thankfulness that physical and mental strength is vouchsafed, so as to enable me to perform it efficiently. Half an hour was spent after all was over in taking the addresses of their friends at home, of which I received eighty, to whom strictest charge was given me not to fail duly to forward this printed statement of my visit. Many were much affected, and wept, on my bidding them farewell and taking my departure. Leave-taking being over, and a small boat alongside, I was soon conveyed ashore. She is expected to sail to-day.

James Buck<br>Liverpool Seamen's Friend Society and Bethel Union<br>May 4, 1854 ~ Liverpool paper[84]

True to Buck's prediction, the *Miles Barton* left Liverpool on May 4, 1854, with 264 passengers and a cargo of general merchandize. She passed Land's End on May 8 and two days later exchanged signals with the General Screw Company steamship *Indiana* (Captain Lambert) approximately 300 miles west of Tenerife. Then she was hailed again on June 8, thirty-five days out, approximately 650 miles northeast of Rio de Janeiro. Thereafter, with no passenger diary to enlighten us as to the details of her trip, there is no further word until her arrival in Melbourne on July 22. According to an Australian newspaper, "Not a single disturbance had occurred on board during the whole passage."[85] Compared with her previous eighty-four day outbound trip, this speedy, seventy-four-day passage out had apparently been totally brawl-free. Either people had behaved better on this trip, or William Kelly had learned something about crowd control during his first trip out and he put this valuable know-how to good use the second time around.

Kelly's passengers presented him with a purse of sovereigns, a piece of silver plate, and the following complimentary letter, which was also published in the *Argus* of July 24, 1854.

> To Captain William Kelly
> Dear Sir,—At the termination of our passage from Liverpool to Melbourne, we, the undersigned passengers in your vessel, beg respectfully to tender our most hearty thanks for the uniform kindness and attention we have experienced at your hands, and to assure you of our highest opinion, both as a gentleman and a mariner.
>
> Our passage, accomplished as it has been, although the vessel was heavily laden, in the short space of 74 days, is of itself a testimonial of your ability as a navigator.
>
> To your chief officer, Mr. Tait, and the officers and crew generally, is due the highest encomiums that can be passed.
>
> Wishing you every prosperity,
> We remain, dear Sir, yours respectfully,
> Signed on behalf of the Passengers,
> FRANK CHALMER & ROBERT BIRNEY[86]
> On board the Ship Miles Barton,
> Hobson's Bay, July 22nd, 1854

Kelly replied punctually with the following response dated the same day.

> Ship Miles Barton,
> Hobson's Bay, July 22nd, 1854
> Gentlemen,—I have received your handsome testimonial and beg respectfully to thank you for the very high and flattering manner in which you have expressed yourselves towards myself, officers, and crew, and to assure you that no exertion shall ever be wanting on my part, to forward the interests of those whom I may have under my charge.
>
> I remain, Gentlemen, your faithful servant,
> (Signed) Wm. Kelly

There is little to say about Kelly's return trip to Liverpool via Calcutta. On Saturday, August 12, the *Miles Barton* moved into Hobson's Bay near the mouth of the Yarra River to commence her tug-assisted crawl across Port Phillip Bay to the Heads and the open sea beyond.

Eleven days later, on Saturday, August 23, she departed Port Phillip, one of six ships that left the bay that day, including the *Carpentaria* for Hong Kong, the *Balaret* for London, the *Janet* for Newcastle (New South Wales), the *Childe Harold* for Guam, and the *Juliet* for Baltimore.

The *Miles Barton* arrived at Calcutta on October 18, 1854, and departed from Saugor Island (where the Hooghly River flows into the Bay of Bengal, now Sagar) on November 19. She arrived back in Liverpool on February 28, 1855. A large fleet of ships entered the Mersey with her. Contrary winds had held many vessels in the channel for weeks, and a deep frost had closed the port for days. Now, with the winds improving and the city thawing, workers returned to the docks, eager to offload weary ships wafting in from all directions.

The *Miles Barton* had accomplished her second run out and home, via Melbourne and Calcutta, a voyage of approximately 28,700 nautical miles, in nine months and twenty-four days—an achievement the *Liverpool Mercury* saw fit to highlight in its Shipping Intelligence column. The *Courier* (Hobart, Tasmania) applauded her ninety-nine-day passage from Calcutta in which she outperformed many ships that had left the Hooghly a month to six weeks before her.

Back in the United Kingdom, William Kelly, now one of the premier clipper masters of his day, appears to have finally completed his family's migration from Antrim to Liverpool. The following announcement provides an inkling of the spacious family home the Kelly family left behind in Antrim.

> TENEMENT IN THE TOWN OF ANTRIM.
> TO BE SOLD, BY PRIVATE CONTRACT, that very commodious DWELLING HOUSE and Premises, situate in the Townhead of the Town of Antrim, at present in the occupation of Mrs. Captain Kelly. The premises measure in front 28 feet 3 inches, in rear 32 feet 6 inches, and in depth 146 feet, be the same more or less. The Dwelling-house contains Parlour and Drawing-room, three Bed-rooms, Larder, Kitchen and Scullery, all in the best possible state of repair. There is a good enclosed Yard, with Offices and Garden in the rear, entered by a gateway from the front street. The Railway Station is within ten minutes' walk of the house. The above

is held by Lease under Lord Viscount Massereene, bearing date November, 1839, for 21 years and a young life, at the yearly rent of 2£.

Proposals will be received on the Premises up till the last day of February next; or, at Belfast, by JAMES PHILLIPS, 12, Queen's-quay.

Antrim, 1st January, 1855.[87]

## Voyage 3: Liverpool to Melbourne, Manila, Anjer, and Rotterdam

On her third voyage, the *Miles Barton* changed her affiliation but not her destination. Beazley moved his ship from Millers and Thompson's Golden Line of Packets to Henry Fox's up-and-coming Fox Line, which the postmaster general had authorized to carry the Australian mails. In this new capacity, the *Miles Barton* was scheduled to depart Liverpool in May 1855 following in the wake of Fox's celebrated Boston-built clipper the *Blue Jacket* (Captain Underwood), which had left for Melbourne in March. William Kelly, now suitably styled in the announcements as "well known in the trade," remained in command of the *Miles Barton*.

A puzzling human tragedy preceded the *Miles Barton*'s departure on this voyage. Around nine p.m. on Monday, May 14, 1855, a Welsh clergyman who had booked a single passage to Melbourne was boarding the ship at Salthouse Dock on the River Mersey when he lost his footing on the gangway and fell into the river, striking his head severely against the side of the wharf and the ship as he plunged into the water.[88] A nearby police officer hurried to the spot and succeeded in keeping the clergyman's head above water until assistance arrived. Other helping hands carried him up from the dock, unconscious, to a nearby house, where he was declared dead. His forehead and chin were severely bruised, almost black. His pockets contained seven one-pound Australian notes, six pounds in gold and silver, and a watch with a guard chain. When the authorities removed his luggage from the ship, they found a valuable set of inscribed silver plate that had been presented to him by his parishioners as a token of their appreciation for the time he had served as their vicar.

*Lloyd's Weekly Newspaper* speculated that the "reverend gentleman" might have stepped into questionable company, "no doubt being allured by what are termed in Liverpool 'Man-catchers,' with which the port abounds. It would seem that these harpies succeeded in inducing the deceased to partake pretty freely of intoxicating beverages, it is supposed with the view of ultimately robbing him, but whether they were successful in the disgraceful plot, so far as money is concerned, has not been satisfactorily ascertained."[89]

The paper money, coins, and watch found in the vicar's pockets would seem to argue against this supposition. Whatever its cause, a single miscue dashed the vicar's high hopes of starting over in a new place. Instead, his bright prospects disappeared in the murky waters of Salthouse Dock, and his ship sailed without him just four days later on Friday, May 18, 1855. Surgeon superintendent James Hester was comfortably installed in the *Miles Barton*'s passenger cabin, while 155 other travelers occupied the ship's intermediate accommodations. The Welsh clergyman would surely have been with them there, but for his tragic misstep on the gangplank.

On May 22 a passing ship hailed the *Miles Barton* off the southern tip of Ireland, and on May 28 she was signaled again off Cape Finisterre. From there she fought headwinds to the equator, which she crossed around June 16, thereafter experiencing lighter winds and calms. She passed the Cape of Good Hope around July 16 (William Kelly's forty-fourth birthday) and from there completed the run to Port Phillip Heads in twenty-five days, arriving there on Sunday, August 12. Coming through the Heads between two and three o'clock on Sunday afternoon, the *Miles Barton* ran into a spot of trouble at the entrance to the south channel. Here she ran aground at six o'clock and was stuck until eleven o'clock Sunday night, when the flood tide floated her off, fortunately with no damage.

The *Melbourne Argus* of Tuesday, August 14, reported the grounding incident in a curiously oblique manner that placed no blame for the incident, stating, "Of course the occurrence will be officially reported to the Pilot Board by the pilot who was in charge of the ship, and the Miles Barton having been aground is merely recorded here as a fact, and without attributing blame or censure to anyone. This investigation is left entirely in the hands of the board, under whose special jurisdiction these matters more particularly fall; and we feel assured the decision the gentlemen constituting it will acquit themselves of their responsibilities in a satisfactory and proper manner."

After this minor inconvenience, the *Black Eagle* tug paddle steamer brought the *Miles Barton* up to Hobson's Bay, where they dropped anchor off Melbourne at 2:15 a.m. on August 14, 1855. Later that day, the passengers presented Kelly and his officers with flattering testimonials for their kindness, attention, and gentlemanly conduct during the passage out.[90] The *Argus* opined that "Capt. Kelly, who is long known and deservedly respected in the Australian trade, has made a tolerably good run, the time occupied in the passage being 86 days." In addition to mentioning one birth and one death among the passengers during the trip, the paper printed a detailed listing of the *Miles Barton*'s cargo, which consisted of 70 tons of coal along with cast-iron water pipes, nails, anvils, axles, bellows, cordage, glass, books, clothing, silk, pork, bacon, hams, oats, rice, cheese, sauces, beer, and more.[91] It was a load of mixed merchandise that Melbourne's settler and business communities would have enthusiastically welcomed.

On September 17, 1855, a little over a month after her arrival in Melbourne, the *Miles Barton* set sail again with sixty tons of coal bound for Manila on the northern Philippine island of Luzon. This might have been William Kelly's first excursion to the Philippines as a ship's master.

Based on the *Miles Barton*'s mid-September departure from Melbourne, an educated guess at the route she sailed is the Eastern Passage (Figure 7): from Bass Strait into the Tasman Sea and up the eastern coast of Australia; into the Coral Sea west of New Caledonia and through the Solomon Islands, crossing the equator at roughly 160°E longitude; then turning northwest and sailing between the Caroline Islands and Palau for Luzon. This was not the most direct route, but it avoided the obstacle course of the Indonesian islands, with their many confusing reefs, straits, and passages. This course also positioned the *Miles Barton* where she could race with the wind. The open monsoonal ocean offered few obstructions to the fastest passage, especially for a ship's master who might have been sailing these waters for the first time.

Alternatively, Kelly might have taken his chances with the Torres Strait Passage—a much shorter route but one typically recommended for use only in July and the beginning of August (Figure 8). After passing through Bligh's entrance to the Torres Strait, this route would have taken him between the Tenimber and Arrou Islands to the passage between Ceram and Bouro into the Molucca Channel, then round the northeast end of Celebes Island into the Celebes Sea, through the Basilian Channel into the Sulu Sea, through the Mindoro Strait to the China Sea, and then direct to Manila via the Palawan Channel. The azure waters of this route were riddled with reefs and other obstacles. The route was also plagued by contrary currents and tides that could easily have taken the *Miles Barton* off course. If the channels had been properly surveyed by the mid-1850s, Kelly might have taken this more direct route to shave a few hundred miles off his trip. However, to avoid losing his sixty tons of coal on a wayward shoal, he probably opted for the longer but relatively safer Eastern Passage.

I have no dates for the *Miles Barton*'s arrival at or departure from Manila. All I can say is that she discharged her sixty tons of coal there and loaded 33,603 bags of sugar, a major export commodity of the Philippines. The *Liverpool Mercury* lists her as "at Manila and cleared for Queenstown on January 31." The next *Mercury* listing has her "at Anjer, from Manila, for Queenstown" on March 3. Anjer was a town in West Java (now Banten), not far from Jakarta. A major transit point for ships passing from and to the United Kingdom, Anjer would be totally destroyed in 1883 by a one-hundred-foot tsunami caused by the volcanic eruption of Krakatoa.

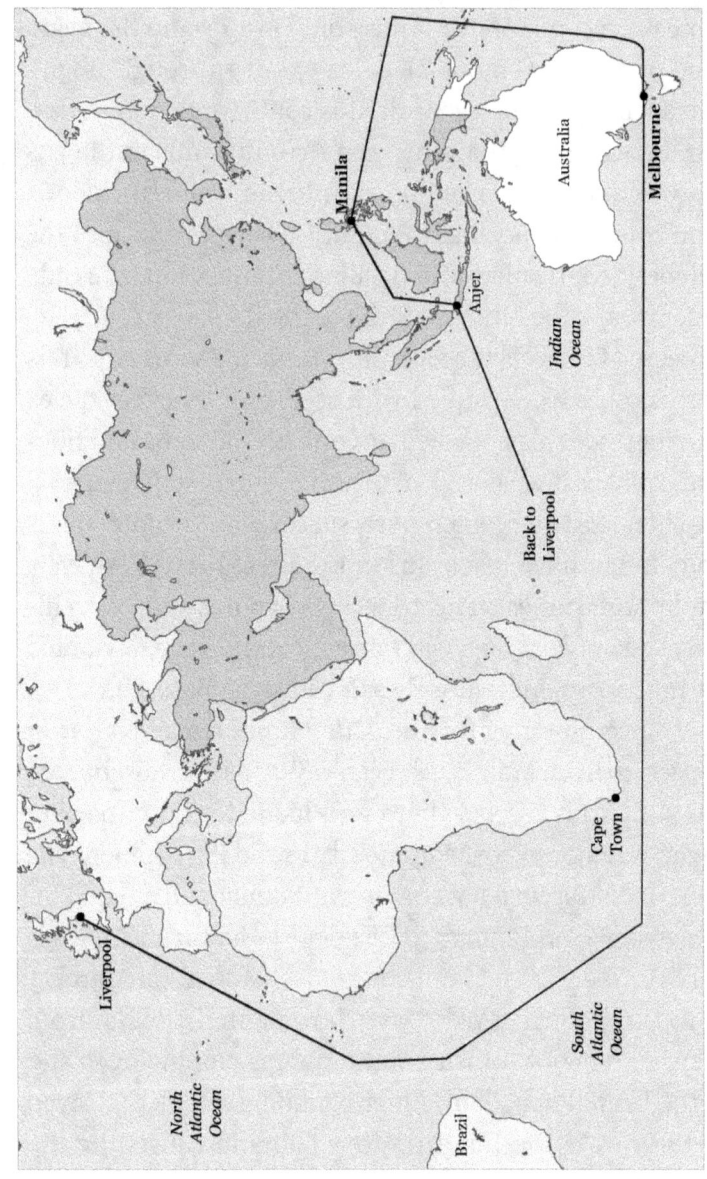

Figure 7: *Miles Barton*, voyage 3, option A—Eastern Passage, Melbourne to Manila.

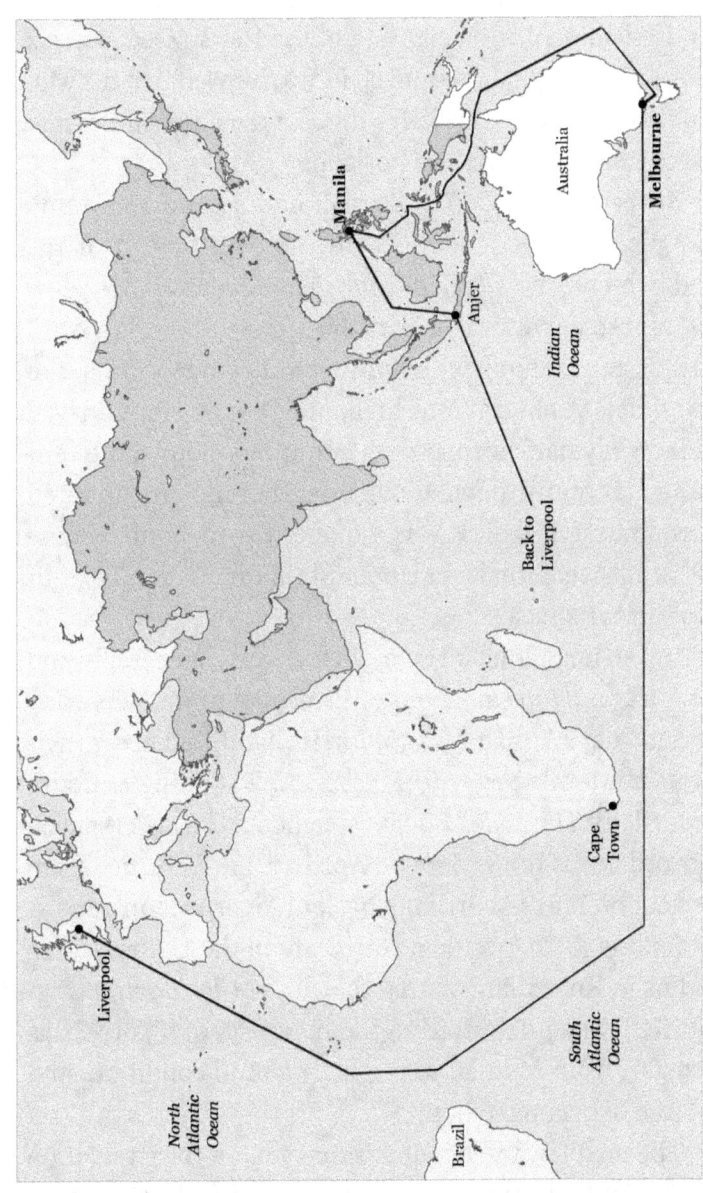

Figure 8: *Miles Barton*, voyage 3, option B—Torres Strait Passage, Melbourne to Manila.

Here in the island-dotted Sunda Strait between Java and Sumatra in the vicinity of a then-slumbering Krakatoa, Kelly had his first sighting of the Indian Ocean in six months and might have mused idly to himself that his wife and children were still twelve thousand nautical miles and two oceans away over the horizon.

From here the *Miles Barton* had a good run home via Queenstown, a seaport on the south coast of Ireland, which is now called Cobh. The *Liverpool Mercury* announced her arrival back in the Mersey on Friday, April 4, 1856, in company with another ship from Manila, the *Alchymist* (Captain Winteringham). The two ships arrived under a sky half-heaped with cumulous clouds, the remnants of a rain-drenched morning that had precipitated a brief burst of hail. It was a fine day for a homecoming and family reunion at 52 Upper Stanhope Street, Toxteth, after a year at sea.

It was not a long layover. Just a week later, Kelly and the *Miles Barton* sailed out of Liverpool again, departing on Saturday, April 12, 1856, for Holland to convey their cargo of Manila sugar to Messrs. A. T. Solling & Co. of Rotterdam. The *Miles Barton* touched at Brouwershaven on April 26, at Rotterdam on April 29, and returned from Helvoet on May 25, arriving back in Liverpool on June 4.

Solling & Co. posted a certificate in the Underwriters' Rooms in Rotterdam stating that "the *Miles Barton* (Captain Kelly) had delivered to them a cargo of 33,603 bags of sugar, from Manila, in perfectly sound condition, and not one bag damaged!"[92]

The next few weeks constituted yet another transition in William Kelly's career. However, now that he was one of Liverpool's best-known clipper ship masters, his next move is easier to discern. On June 25, the papers announced that the ship *Miles Barton* would join the *Mermaid*, the *Tiptree,* and the *White Star* in Pilkington and Wilson's White Star Line of Packets to carry the Australian mails. The *Miles Barton* was scheduled to leave for Melbourne on July 20, not under Kelly's command but under Captain John Darlington. This time the clouds obscuring Kelly's next assignment would clear without delay.

On July 12, the following announcement appeared in the *Liverpool Mercury* confirming that James Beazley had selected William Kelly to take yet another brand-new vessel on her first extended voyage. Once again, he would be tasked with putting ship and crew through their paces to assess their collective capability to make a quick and smart voyage at sea.

> SHIP LAUNCH.—A large ship of 1,700 tons burthen [carrying capacity] was launched on Friday week from the building yard of Mr. Albert White, Ferry-bank, Waterford. She was named the Merrie England, and is to form one of a fleet of vessels belonging to Mr. James Beazley, of this town. She is intended for the India and China trade, with a view to which she has been adapted for great speed, and is expected to rival in sailing qualities any of the noted fast ships now afloat...She will be commanded by Captain William Kelly, late of the Miles Barton, also one of Mr. Beazley's ships.[93]

Before turning to the *Merrie England*, I will close out the *Miles Barton* years with a sidelong glance at three artifacts related to this period: William Kelly's revolver, Joseph

Heard's painting of the *Miles Barton* in a heavy sea, and John Kelly's paperwork.

## William Kelly's Revolver

A little over one hundred years after William Kelly commanded the *Miles Barton*, sometime in the mid-1960s, a man brought a package to the National Maritime Museum at Greenwich. The package contained a five-chambered percussion revolver stowed in a wooden box, along with a screwdriver, a nipple wrench, a ramrod, a nipple primer, a steel patch cutter, a ball and bullet mold, and a wooden tompion (or stopper) for the gun's muzzle. The gun had a checkered walnut grip with a steel butt plate incorporating a hinged trap. The solid steel frame and steel trigger guard were lightly decorated with engraved scrolls. Manufactured between 1851 and 1855, the revolver was inscribed "DEANE ADAMS & DEANE, 30 King William Street, London Bridge." The brass plate on the wooden box was inscribed "Captn Wm. Kelly Miles Barton."

The man who donated the revolver to the Maritime Museum was Kelly's grandson William Kelly Wallace who had retired as chief civil engineer of the London, Midland and Scottish Railway (1933–1948).[94] Wallace died in 1969, and the gun is still part of the Maritime Museum's Firearms Collection. Coffee mugs emblazoned with an image of the revolver and its components have been sold in the museum gift shop and were available for purchase online in 2012. As a result, William Kelly's percussion revolver has continued to serve commercial interests into the twenty-first century—over 150 years after it helped him keep the peace during three sea voyages from Liverpool to Melbourne and beyond.

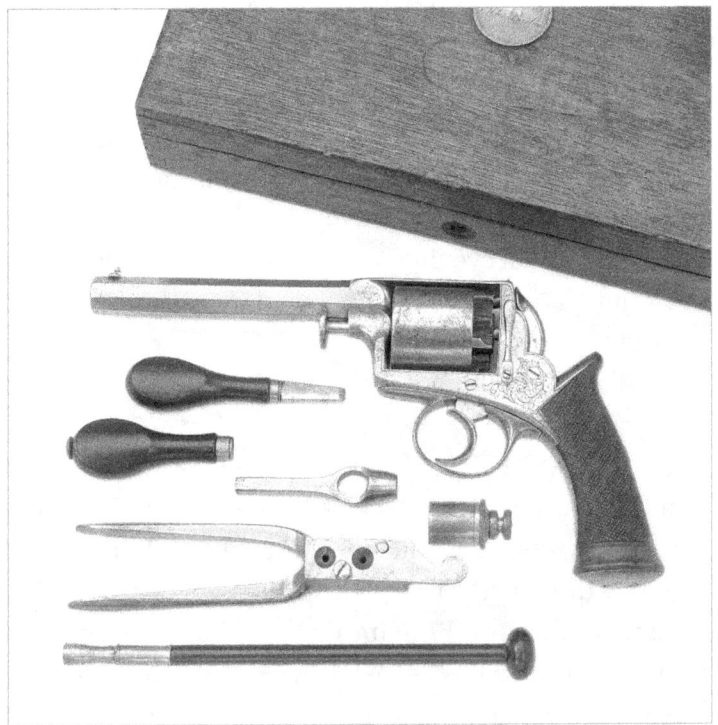

Figure 9: William Kelly's percussion revolver dating from his *Miles Barton* days. Image credit: National Maritime Museum, Greenwich, accession number E8665-2.

## *The Miles Barton in a Heavy Sea*

In a letter written to *Sea Breezes* magazine in January 1928—referenced above in "Voyage 1: Liverpool to Melbourne, Calcutta, and Bombay"—William Kelly's grandson W. G. Moore writes, "We used to have oil paintings of several fine ships in my old home in Ireland, but where they are now I cannot say. One of the Miles Barton in a heavy sea I remember well."

Moore's implied question "Where is the painting of the *Miles Barton* now?" would be answered sixty-four years after he wrote this letter. On January 5, 1992, the *Miles Barton* painting appeared in an episode of the BBC's *Antiques Roadshow* filmed at the Deeside Leisure Centre in Queensferry, North Wales, just fifteen miles south of Liverpool. Dr. Bob Foy, who had been independently researching Kelly in the early 1990s, happened to be watching the show that evening. He was utterly astounded when the painting and its owner appeared unexpectedly on his televison screen.

While researching Kelly's will, Foy had learned that Kelly's daughter Fanny had inherited her father's painting of the *Miles Barton*. Consequently, Foy thought it highly likely that the man who brought the painting to the *Roadshow* was a descendant of Fanny and John Moore. Working through the BBC, Foy wrote to the owner, asking if he was related to William Kelly. Foy also requested a photograph of the painting and inquired if the owner knew the whereabouts of any other paintings of Kelly's ships. Unfortunately, the man declined to identify himself and did not provide any information about the painting's provenance.

In 2021, twenty-nine years after Foy's TV encounter with the *Miles Barton* painting and ninety-three years after W. G. Moore's initial query to *Sea Breezes*, I stumbled on a video recording of the 1992 Queensferry episode on the internet. There, standing next to an intriguing painting of a ship in a heavy sea, I saw a tall, grey-haired man in a grey tweed jacket and grey striped tie—a man with unmistakably hooded "Kelly" eyes. He explained to the *Roadshow*'s art expert that the painting of the *Miles Barton* had been in his family since the 1850s. He had inherited it from his mother when she passed away in 1959.

Since the 1920s, advertisers have said a picture is worth a thousand words. Accordingly, I spent many months trying to license a screenshot of the painting so that I could include it in this book where it belongs. Regrettably, I was unable to obtain a license with acceptable terms, so I have not included the painting here. Turning the old adage upside down, I must now rely on something approaching a thousand words to capture the essence of one painting.

The *Antiques Roadshow* painting surprised me in more ways than one: first, in its unexpected appearance online; then, in its depiction of the ship. Instead of the plain, unpainted hull of the wooden model of the *Miles Barton* (Figure 6), I saw a striking, pitch-black hull with thick, white dashes (or checkering) running from bow to stern. The painting depicts the ship in a conventional port view, her prow slicing downward into a churning sea.

Above the vessel, towering cumulous clouds (or possibly cumulonimbus thunderheads) mixed with feathery patches of blue sky suggest unsettled weather. There is a rugged landmass in the distance, a faraway paddle steamer off the ship's starboard bow, and a spectacular iceberg looming beyond her starboard aft quarter. Based on these clues, the painting's owner and the *Roadshow* expert immediately agreed on one thing: the ship must be somewhere in the South Seas. Indeed, the distant coastline might be one of the most remote places on Earth, the Kerguelen Archipelago, also known as the Desolation Islands. The *Miles Barton* would have passed these windswept volcanic outcrops on the way to and from Australia. The islands are approximately equidistant between Africa,

Antarctica, and Australia—over two thousand miles from the nearest populated places.[95]

The *Miles Barton* is depicted running before the wind with reduced sails to avoid capsizing. Only four sails are fully deployed: the jib at her bow, two sails at the foremast, and one at the mainmast. The wind-filled jib and foresails function as airfoils helping to lift the ship through the turbulent sea. Halfway up the mizzenmast at the vessel's stern, a fifth, loosely reefed sail billows in the wind. Five signal pennants fly from the top of the mizzenmast. The Red Ensign at the ship's stern blows stiffly toward the prow, in the direction the wind is gusting.

The *Miles Barton*'s precarious situation is accentuated by a deep well of darkness undulating across the bottom of the painting. Almost as black as the ship's hull, this menacing undercurrent rises into a maelstrom of turbulent, greyish-green waves capped by curling, wind-driven arcs of spray that encircle and buffet the ship. The massive iceberg they have just passed points a frozen finger toward the top-right corner of the painting. The vessel's plunging prow slants to the bottom left. These opposing dynamics draw the observer into the scene. With confusion, speed, fragility, and uncertainty struggling for dominance, the painting elicits a visceral, vertiginous response. There is little wonder that Kelly's grandson remembered the painting well from his old home in Ireland.

The *Roadshow* expert attributed the painting to the well-known maritime artist Joseph Heard (1799–1859). The nautical painter and author Roger Finch states that "[Heard] was ranked with Samuel Walters as one of the two finest ship portraitists of [Liverpool], sought after by shipping companies and the commanders of crack vessels, sail and steam."[96]

In his book on Liverpool's former maritime painters, A. S. Davidson lists a few distinguishing traits of Heard's paintings, asserting, "He is very fond of depicting the vessel with the appropriate flag hoist giving her number according to Marryat's Code....When depicting moderate to very rough seas, he employs a very characteristic comma-shaped plume of spray blown off the curving wave top....Under the same conditions, the vessel has a...forward curving, downward tumbling bow wave....Very frequently a distant paddle steamer aids perspective and adds to the interest."[97]

All of these elements are present in the *Miles Barton* painting that surprisingly appeared at Queensferry in 1992. There the *Roadshow* art expert declared the painting to be "a very nice picture" and valued it at somewhere between £8,000 and £12,000. The painting's owner agreed with this assessment, and the show moved on to consider two delightful pieces of Scandinavian furniture.

Today I have no idea where the *Miles Barton* painting is or even if it still exists. I can only hope that it is hanging on someone's wall somewhere. Ideally, it is with a new generation of Kelly descendants who might want to know more about the master mariner who commanded the *Miles Barton* on her maiden voyage—and who subsequently commissioned Joseph Heard to immortalize his ship in oils.

## *John Kelly's Paperwork*

In June 1856, John Kelly jumped through the same bureaucratic hoops his older brother had successfully navigated in 1851. John replaced his old seaman's ticket (certificate no. 72,262) with the new Certificate of Service required by the UK Board of Trade. The particulars of service listed in his application are invaluable in piecing together John's career, beginning with the time he first went to sea, from the brig *Jessie* through the *Margaret Johnson*, the *William Herdman*, the *Lord Seaton*, the *Clio*, and the *Arethusa*. Most interestingly, the paperwork notes that he had been "residing in California since 1848." The certificate also indicates that John was using his brother William's Liverpool address as his home base. Most significantly, William Kelly witnessed John's claim, and John requested that his new certificate be sent to the shipping office at the Port of Waterford, where William's new ship, the *Merrie England*, was about to be launched. What did the Kelly brothers have up their sleeves in the summer of 1856?

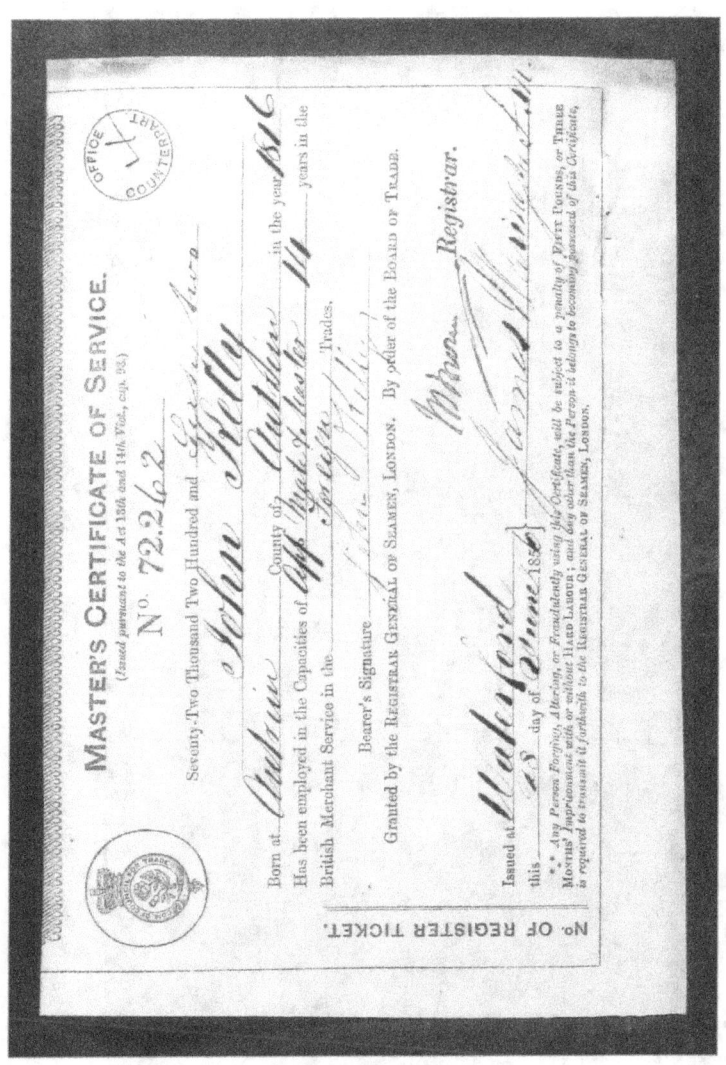

Figure 10: John Kelly's master's certificate no. 72,262, June 1856. Image credit: UK and Ireland, Masters and Mates Certificates, 1850–1927 database (Ancestry.com).

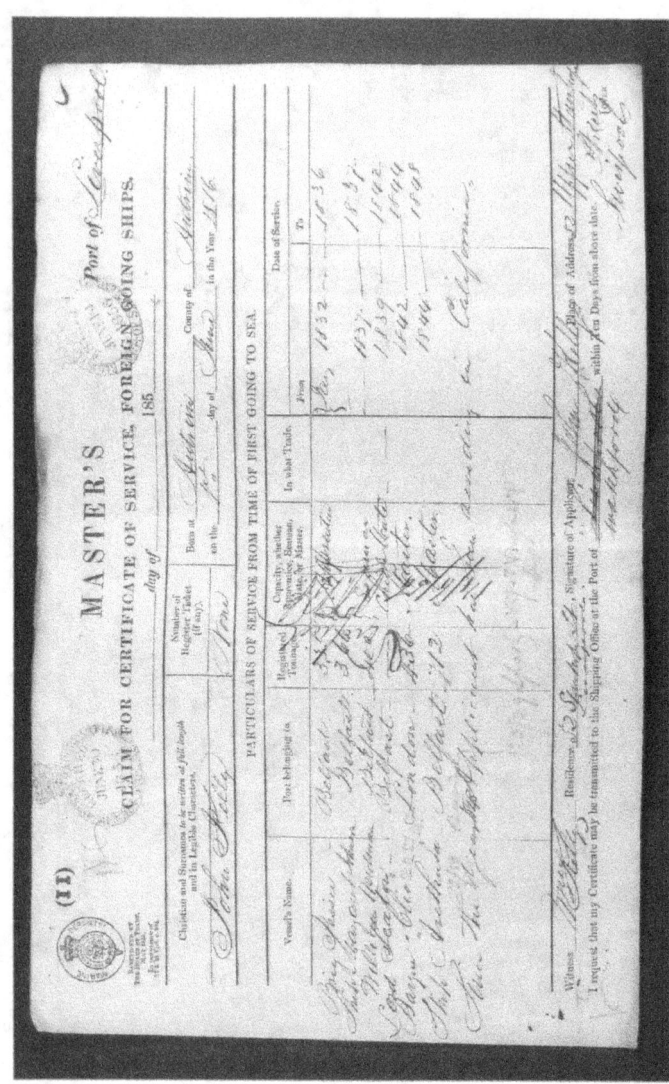

Figure 11: John Kelly's Claim for Certificate of Service, June 1856. Image credit: UK and Ireland, Masters and Mates Certificates, 1850–1927 database (Ancestry.com).

CHAPTER THREE

# WILLIAM KELLY AND THE *MERRIE ENGLAND*

(1856–1862)

The *Merrie England* (Official Number 16847) was an exceptionally handsome ship and much admired in Liverpool in her day—as she was in Waterford, Ireland, where she was launched from Albert White & Company's shipyard at ten minutes before seven o'clock on the morning of Friday, July 4, 1856. The *Waterford News* described her launch as "a splendid one...one of the most graceful and beautiful that ever took place in this city" and went on to say, "Her owner is James Beazley, Esq. of Liverpool, and she is to be commanded by an able seaman, Captain Kelly, an Irishman, as his name indicates....She is intended for the India and China trades, and is expected to rival in speed any of the clippers now afloat."[98] The *Liverpool Albion* further detailed the ship's impressive launch as follows: "[With] a tastefully-decorated bottle dashed against her bow by the lady of Captain Kelly, she began to move, and went off in splendid style. Her great weight and length gave her enormous impetus; she appeared to be beautifully checked, however, by her two large bower anchors, which were let go at once, and she swung gracefully round in mid-stream....She is painted of a neat dark green, and elegantly finished. Her bow is adorned with a representation of the British Lion, which has an exceedingly striking, yet graceful effect."[99]

At 225 feet long × 36 feet beam × 22 feet depth of hold and 2,500 tons carrying capacity, the *Merrie England* was the largest and finest ship ever built at Waterford and arguably the largest built in Ireland to that date. She was the last full-rigged sailing ship constructed by White's shipyard. She cost £21,735 to build, and Beazley paid £20,000 for her. When purchased, she was the second-largest ship in Beazley's fleet, just twelve feet shorter than his *Star of the East*. In seven voyages trading to East India and Australia, she would accumulate profits of £14,692 for Beazley before he sold her to Kelly in 1867.[100]

Reprinting an article picked up from the *Cornwall Chronicle*, the *Sydney Morning Herald* of January 5, 1857 described the *Merrie England* as "a ship of great carrying capacity and admirable mould. Her lines are remarkably fine in the cut-water and bow and sweep gracefully aft to a limber and handsome stern. She is deep and is well rounded in the waist, with a very flat floor, and is evidently designed to carry a large amount of cargo and a wide spread of canvas.... She is classed A1 at Lloyd's for ten years."[101]

The same article states that her Irish oak framing beams and ribs were strengthened by iron knees and straps, and she was completely copper-fastened throughout. A small house forward on her large, red pine deck contained berths for the ship's officers and cooking galleys. Aft she had a full poop deck, fifty-five feet in length. This provided an exercise area for the first- and second-class passengers whose sleeping berths were beneath the poop along with the main saloon and two staterooms accommodating up to eight first-class passengers. Up to eighteen second-class passengers occupied the forward portion of the poop. The ship's saloon was described as "a most complete and comfortable snuggery of moderate size and tastefully furnished." There were baths and other sanitary arrangements close to the saloon. The intermediate and steerage passengers were all accommodated in the main between-decks area, which offered suitable ventilation and lighting along with spacious nine-foot ceilings.

On Tuesday, September 9, 1856, after two months of fitting-out and sea trials, the *Merrie England* departed Waterford for Liverpool under tow by the steam tug *Blazer*, the most powerful of the Liverpool tugs, which Beazley had sent to fetch her.

She arrived at Liverpool on Friday, September 26, the first vessel to be received into the new dry dock of Messrs. Clover & Royle at Woodside, Birkenhead. Here she underwent her final preparations for delivery to Pilkington and Wilson's White Star Line of Royal Mail clipper ships.

A newspaper correspondent at Liverpool reported glowingly of the *Merrie England*:

> This beautifully-constructed and well-found ship has been entrusted to the command of Captain William Kelly, late of the Miles Barton, belonging to the White Star line. In the last-named vessel, Captain Kelly secured for himself the reputation of being one of the most successful of our Australian navigators. He has made numerous voyages to Melbourne, and in no instance was he more

than 78 days out; but when the fine model and beautiful proportions of the Merrie England are taken into consideration, that is no unreasonable expectation which points at seventy days, or less, as the average duration of his future voyages.[102]

Indeed, there were great expectations for the *Merrie England* and her master William Kelly, who would be ably assisted on the vessel's maiden voyage by another experienced master mariner—William's first mate and brother, John Kelly.

Even William Kelly's old friend James Buck weighed in on the merits of the *Merrie England* after conducting a religious service on board for passengers and crew (as he had done twice previously on the *Miles Barton*). Buck wrote, "The Merrie England is considered to be exceedingly well-built, and to have capacity for sailing fast; while her accommodation for passengers is exceedingly satisfactory. The saloon cabin is a very chastely ornamented one, taking in it eight best cabin passengers, which is the extent of its accommodation. Her second cabin, under the same poop deck, is a very comfortable place, and eighteen make it their lodging. Between decks is lofty and well ventilated where the rest of the people live, to the number of 224; her complement altogether being 250."[103]

As first mate and chief officer of the *Merrie England*, John Kelly would be his older brother's right-hand man, his second-in-command and sounding board. In many respects, John would be the joint-commander of the ship with responsibility for her day-to-day running, crew discipline, and cargo management. At sea, he would supervise the crew and manage the watches along with the ship's second and third mates; he would relay his brother's orders to the crew, inspect the ship each day, and ensure that all fixtures, supplies, and tools were in order; and he would keep the ship's logbook, recording wind and weather conditions, distance traveled, and daily positional readings. In port, he would maintain the ship's records, supervise the loading and unloading of cargo, and manage the procurement and stocking of supplies. John would be like the *Merrie England*'s chief operating officer. As the ship's master, William would be more like the chairman of the board, still very much the ultimate decider pertaining to all things aboard the ship.

Together, the Kelly brothers constituted a remarkably experienced and proficient executive tag team for Ireland's grandest clipper ship on her extended maiden voyage to Australia and China.

## Voyage 1: Liverpool to Melbourne, Ceylon, India, Hong Kong, and Shanghai

As advertised, on the afternoon of Monday, October 20, 1856, the *Merrie England* stood out to sea for Melbourne with planned onward passages to Point de Galle (Ceylon), Bombay, Calcutta, Hong Kong, and Shanghai. Her passengers included the two Misses Rose; Mrs. Young and family; Mr. and Mrs. Wright; and Messrs. J. Ross, Meyer, Thomas, Sylvester, Chalmers, McConn, and Taylor in the stern; plus another 250 in steerage. As for cargo, she carried approximately 900 tons of mixed merchandise.[104]

Her sister White Star ship, the *Star of the East* under Captain Gaggs, departed for Melbourne the next day with approximately three hundred passengers and one thousand tons of cargo. The *Morning Chronicle* (London) hinted at a bracing competition between the two ships, reporting that "much interest is attached to the respective passages,"[105] especially as no vessel that had yet sailed with the *Star of the East* had beaten her to Melbourne.

The *Merrie England*'s trip was not reported in the papers, but her crew agreement and official log provide a few details of her passage to Australia.[106] On November 1, while sailing south between the Azores and Portugal, William Kelly ordered the crew to come aft every day at twelve-thirty for their required dietary allowance of lime juice and sugar, a half ounce of each per day, which was required by law to prevent scurvy. This practice generally commenced about fourteen days into a voyage, but sailors rarely took the requirement seriously in temperate waters outside the tropics. The *Merrie England*'s crew neglected to come aft on November the first and again on the second, whereupon Kelly noted he "gave them Sugar for their Pudding," apparently conceding this round to the crew.

In December two male children were born, one on December 17 to John and Mary Darnley while the *Merrie England* was in the middle of the South Atlantic, and another born on December 29 to parents whose names are illegible in the log, with no locational coordinates recorded.

After rounding the Cape of Good Hope, the *Merrie England* proceeded eastward across the broad and notoriously hazardous Southern Indian Ocean toward Australia. While traversing between the Roaring Forties and the Furious Fifties, the Kelly brothers had to deal with a difficult personnel issue—a pair of unruly seamen, verging on mutinous, who sorely tested the authority and patience of the ship's officers in these remote, dangerous, and highly unpredictable waters.

The incident began in the early morning of New Year's Day 1857, when first mate John Kelly told his older brother that two seamen, James Knox and John Collins, were refusing to come on deck. Captain Kelly went forward, where he found Collins fighting with a passenger and Knox cheering him on. Kelly ordered Knox aft, but the twenty-six-year-old Scot refused to comply, twice stating that his shipmates were "a parcel of muffs," and if they were of his mind, they would soon let everyone know who was master of the ship. When Kelly threatened to clap him in irons, Knox declared "he would follow Kelly and his brother all his life, but he would have his revenge." Kelly put Knox in irons and locked him in the cabin storeroom with bread and water. He also confined John Collins in the sail room for disturbing the peace of the ship. A log entry made the same evening indicates the charges against Knox were read to him, whereupon he acknowledged having threatened the master and mate but denied the mutinous language.

The resolution of this difficulty played out in a classic application of authority and forbearance on the part of the Kelly brothers. They isolated the troublemakers, defused the volatile situation, and ultimately brought the offenders back into line. On January 2, as the *Merrie England* passed south of the Kerguelen Islands, William Kelly visited John Collins and asked him if he would behave like an adult. Collins refused to answer. On January 3, the captain visited Collins again, this time accompanied by the boatswain and carpenter as representatives of the crew. Again he asked the sailor to conduct himself properly with officers and passengers. Stubbornly, Collins replied that "he would not promise anything this side of Melbourne." On January 4, with Kerguelen now well behind them, James Knox promised to conduct himself properly in the future. John Collins would hold out until January 9, when he made the same undertaking, and John Kelly finally set him free.

One week later on January 16, 1857, the *Merrie England* arrived at Melbourne, where the Kelly brothers discovered that the *Star of the East* had arrived a week before them. Captain Gaggs had reported slow progress with light, baffling winds crossing the equator, but they had then swept from the Cape of Good Hope to Australia in a fast twenty-three days, hustling into Melbourne on January 10. Perhaps the *Merrie England* had also been slowed by the equatorial doldrums but had not been able to make up time after rounding the Cape, running eastward with southern winds that failed to live up to their breakneck reputation.

The *Melbourne Argus* printed a detailed inventory of the *Merrie England*'s impressive cargo. Indeed, the manifest reads like a wish list of basic staples and necessities for a remote outpost of the British Empire—candles, butter, cheese, raisins, nails, hams, boots and shoes, hardware, clothing, iron bars, books, plate glass, and innumerable cases, barrels, bales, parcels, and packages including a small box addressed to a gentleman whose name stands out from the rest: Le Comte de Chabrillan. What was this French nobleman doing in Australia in 1857? As it turns out, the story is worthy of a television costume drama, even if Gabriel-Paul-Josselin-Lionel de Guigues de Morton de Chabrillan (1818–1858) might be better known today for his wife than for his life.

## The French Consul's Wife

Lionel de Chabrillan was a French aristocrat and diplomat who lost a fortune gambling in Paris in the early 1850s. While there, he also took as his mistress a woman with a shady past, which further alienated him from his noble family. Elizabeth-Céleste Vénard had grown up rough on the streets of Paris, even living in a brothel for a few months at age sixteen, but she rose out of squalor with flamboyant flair. Taking the stage name Céleste Mogador, she became a dancer, a bareback horse rider at the Paris Hippodrome, an actress, a courtesan, and a writer of some note. In 1854 she published her *Mémoires*,[107] which caused something of a scandal in Paris.

Having emptied his family's coffers at the card tables, de Chabrillan added insult to injury by marrying Céleste in January 1854. He then left with her for Australia to take up an appointment as French consul-general in Melbourne—a remote posting obtained for him by his exasperated family who apparently expected to see no more of him.

Ultimately, de Chabrillan served honorably as consul, but it was Céleste who found her true calling in Australia. Initially ostracized by most of Melbourne society, as word of her notorious *Mémoires* preceded her, Céleste took up her pen again with a vengeance. She became an early chronicler of the immigrant experience in Melbourne and the nearby Ballarat gold fields in novels like *The Gold Robbers* (1857) and *Miss Powel* (1859). French authors Alexandre Dumas Sr. and Alexandre Dumas Jr. were both great supporters of the countess, with Dumas the elder writing: "During the years she spent away from France she re-educated herself completely; not only did she learn

English but re-learned French....During two nights I sat up until dawn reading 'Les Voleurs d'Or.'"[108]

After two years in Melbourne, Céleste returned to France, apparently to collect money owed to her and her husband. During the Franco-Prussian War, she established a nursing organization, Les Soeurs de France, to care for wounded soldiers; she also opened her Australian-style country villa at Le Vésinet (appropriately named le Châlet Lionel) as a home for orphans of the war. A woman of letters with a remarkable life story, Céleste de Chabrillan would complete twelve novels, twenty-six plays, seven operettas, and numerous songs and poems before she died at a retirement home run by the Sisters of Charity on February 18, 1909, at age eighty-five. This much is known.

Regrettably, I do not know the contents of the small box carried in the *Merrie England*'s enormous hold for delivery to Céleste's forty-year-old husband, Lionel, just a year before he died of dysentery in Melbourne in December 1858.

The *Merrie England* departed Melbourne in early February 1857 bound for Bombay via Point de Galle, Ceylon (see Figure 12). It appears she left just a few days before the *Star of the East* followed her on the same route. At this time of year, December through April, the Kelly brothers likely used the southern route out of Australian waters to take advantage of the prevailing easterly winds along the south coast of the continent. This meant a direct run from Bass Strait across the Great Australian Bight to Cape Leeuwin, rounding the Cape, standing to the northwest, and laying a direct course for Ceylon. Blown by the northwest monsoon,

Kelly's crew would have kept a weather eye open for Indian Ocean hurricanes at this time of year.

The *Merrie England* arrived at Point de Galle between March 10 and 16, 1857, and from there might have made a run up to Bombay. The newspapers state she was bound for that port without noting her arrival or departure.

From Bombay, she would have worked her way back down the west coast of India, around Cape Comorin, and north into the Bay of Bengal. She arrived at Calcutta on April 2 with no passengers. Here, on April 15, seaman John Collins, possibly still chafing from his run-in with the ship's commanding officers on the trip out, "absented himself from the ship," a sardonic way of saying he deserted. William Magee of Antrim, the ship's twenty-year-old steward who had previously served with Kelly on the *Miles Barton*, died of unknown cause on April 24 at Calcutta. Two days later seamen Thomas Manning and Moses Durant also deserted.[109]

What was the Kelly brothers' cargo for the next leg of their voyage? The *London Sun* of June 1, 1857, reported that the *Merrie England* was to carry "18,000 bags of rice at 1 dol. 20c. to China."[110] Thus, they must have departed Calcutta sometime around May 10 bound for Hong Kong and Shanghai with rice in the hold.

On this passage, they sailed across the Indian Ocean, past the Andaman and Nicobar Islands, and into the Strait of Malacca between Sumatra and the Malay Peninsula to Singapore. Between May and September, the southwest monsoon dominated the Strait of Malacca, bringing with it squalls from the southwest called Sumatras. Moderate to strong gales could descend suddenly, especially at night, with accompanying thunder, lightning, and rain. Nor'westers were also common in the Malacca Strait during the monsoon season. They were typically preceded by a black cloud arch that rose rapidly from the horizon, providing little time to reduce sail before the full force of the storm struck.

After passing through the Singapore Strait, the *Merrie England* sailed northeast into the South China Sea, probably taking the inner, or Cochin China, route. She followed the Malay coast from Pulo Aor to Redang Island, subsequently crossing the Gulf of Siam (now the Gulf of Thailand) and following the coast of Cochin China to Touron Bay (now Da Nang Bay, Vietnam). From there, she sailed across the Gulf of Tonkin and along the east coast of Hainan Island, direct to Hong Kong.

I do not know when the *Merrie England* arrived at Hong Kong. According to the *North China Herald* of July 11, 1857, she departed there on June 26 and arrived at Shanghai on July 7 carrying sundries consigned to Turner & Co. Here she appears to have remained for up to a month. I know they were there between July 20 and August 3 because the log states, "Monday, 20 July, Shanghai: For refusal to obey orders, Robert Jones was sent to Jail for one month by HB [Her Britannic] Majesty's Consul."[111]

The *North China Herald* of August 15, 1857, subsequently notes the *Merrie England*'s departure on August 9 from Woo Sung (a port town fourteen miles downriver from Shanghai) for Point de Galle in ballast. Her next reported location—on December 7, 1857—was Akyab in Burma (now Myanmar). Akyab (now Sittwe) was located on an estuarial island at the confluence of the Kaladan, My, and Lemyo Rivers where they empty into the Bay of Bengal. Along with Rangoon, Bassein, and Moulemein, Akyab was one of Burma's four main rice-exporting centers. Here the *Merrie England*'s log documents yet another incident with a crew member, seaman John Parry, who abandoned work for the relative comfort of his hammock and, when reproached by the second mate, responded with "abusive epithets not fit to be repeated." William Kelly wrote Parry up for this but did not record the final resolution.

Kelly topped up his cargo with rice prior to departing Akyab on December 7, 1857. On the passage home, the *Merrie England* experienced light winds and fine weather, except for two days off the Cape of Good Hope at the end of January when she encountered heavy gales.

The *Merrie England* arrived back at Liverpool on Sunday, March 21, 1858. William and John Kelly had successfully completed the ship's inaugural voyage: Liverpool to Australia (Melbourne), Ceylon (Galle), India (Bombay, Calcutta), China (Hong Kong, Shanghai), Burma (Akyab), and back to the United Kingdom in 518 days—the better part of a year and a half at sea.

## Voyage 2: London to Calcutta and Back

The *Merrie England*'s second voyage under William Kelly, this time without his brother as first mate, was a ninety-seven-day passage from Liverpool to Calcutta (departing June 18, 1858; arriving September 23, 1858) and a 103-day return from Calcutta (departing December 17, 1858; arriving at the Custom House in London on March 30, 1859). The London dailies reported the ship's arrivals and departures but offered no details regarding her cargoes and passengers.

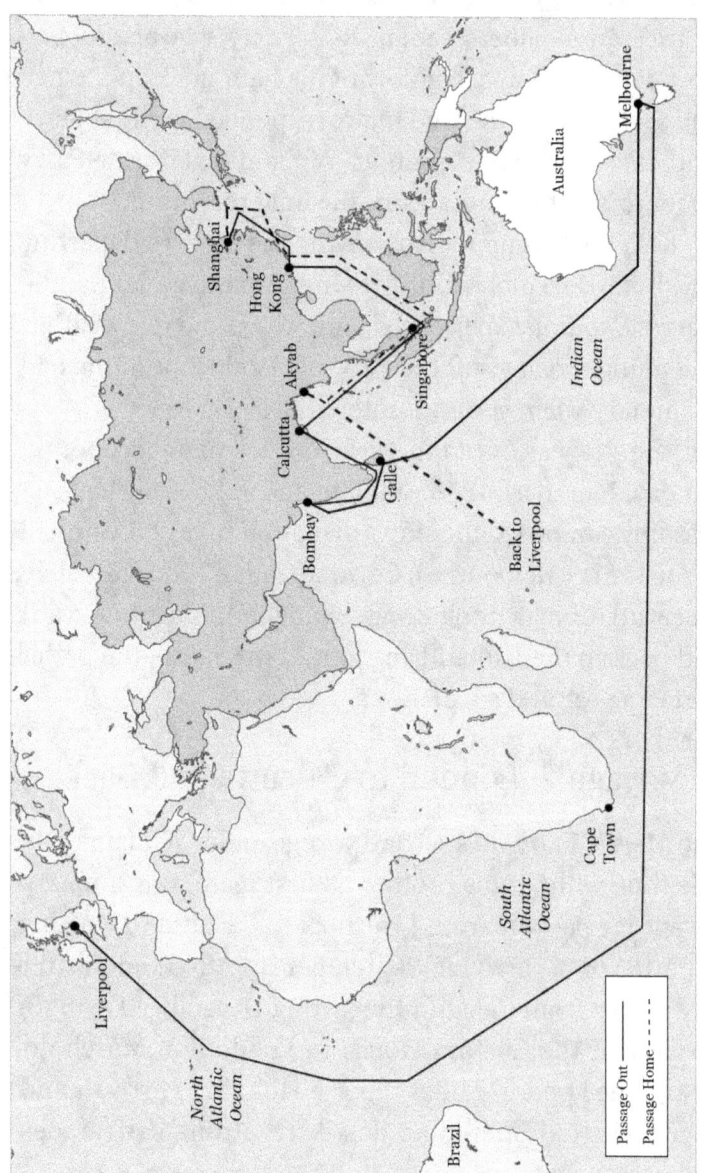

Figure 12: *Merrie England*, voyage 1—Liverpool to Australia, Ceylon, India, China, and Burma.

## The Burning of the Dalriada

On March 1, 1859, four weeks before the *Merrie England* arrived back in London from her second voyage, the great ship *Dalriada*, which Kelly had commanded ten years earlier, met her end in an epic conflagration at sea. The *Belfast News-Letter* of Monday, May 23, 1859, covered this disaster extensively.

The *Dalriada* had sailed from Bombay on February 3, 1859, with a cargo of seed, cotton, and oil and a crew of thirty-six under Captain Ewing, who was accompanied by his wife and child. They had a pleasant passage with light winds until five p.m. on March 1, when they were in the middle of the Indian Ocean, southwest of Diego Garcia in the Chagos Archipelago. Here the crew noticed smoke pouring from under the covers of the forward chain pipes. Subsequently they found the ship was burning on the port side. All hands set to work cutting holes in the deck and pouring water into the hold, but by midnight the stubborn fire had spread to the starboard side and aft, and the foremast began to burn.

About one a.m., they heard a crackling sound close to the water's edge behind the fore-rigging. There they found pitch boiling out of the seams, smoke seeping through, and the planks scorching hot. Captain Ewing ordered the longboat and lifeboats out in preparation for abandoning ship. By three a.m., there was three and a half feet of water in the hold, likely due to the water they had poured in to extinguish the fire. Flames were now burning forward as high as the topmast stays, and sails were alight. At four a.m., a heavy squall struck the ship, fanning the flames and filling the poop and cabin with smoke. Ewing put the ship before the wind to clear the smoke, and the crew began provisioning the boats.

At six a.m., there was nine feet of water in the hold, and the fire had burned through the ship's side to the water's edge. With all hope of saving the *Dalriada* now lost, the boats were brought alongside, and at seven a.m., with the foremast beginning to fall apart, all hands disembarked and pushed away from the ship. The *Belfast News-Letter* reported, "In about fifteen minutes the flames burst up fore and aft; at eight a.m. the foremast fell over the side; and at 9 o'clock the main and mizzen masts fell with a tremendous crash, and the ship was enveloped in one mass of flame."

Now distributed among three boats, the crew made sail to the northeast, hoping to meet with a ship or reach an island in the Chagos Archipelago. The next day, finding that the smallest boat was not sailing as well as the others, they consolidated the entire party to two boats: the captain, his wife and child, and twenty-one men in the longboat and the first mate with thirteen men in the lifeboat. In the afternoon of the sixth day after leaving the burning wreck, they reached the island of Diego Garcia, where the ship *Futteh Salaam* (Captain Croad) picked them up and took them back to Calcutta.

The *Belfast News-Letter* concluded, "And so, fortunately, is recorded a happy escape from the dangers and horrors of fire at sea from spontaneous combustion; a terrible accident which often leaves no survivor to relate it."

## Voyage 3: London to Calcutta and Back

The *Merrie England*'s third voyage was a repeat of trip two. The ship departed London in mid-May 1859 and arrived at Calcutta in August 1859, then departed Calcutta in November 1859 and arrived back at London in March 1860. This time the daily press provided a good accounting of the exotic cargo Kelly's ship carried from the subcontinent back to the United Kingdom. The *Merrie England*'s hold was packed with 47,777 pounds of Assam tea, 7,659 cow and buffalo hides, 636 corahs (plain, unbleached, and undyed silk cloth or undressed cotton cloth), and 871 bags of sugar, along with boxes of castor oil, jute, lac dye (the crimson or yellow resinous secretions of lac insects used in the pigment and cloth dyeing industries), linseed, mustard seed, safflower, saltpetre, shellac, and more.[112]

## Voyage 4: Liverpool to Calcutta, Demerara, and New Orleans

As shown in Figure 13, the *Merrie England*'s fourth voyage was a return to Calcutta with a lengthy round trip back to Liverpool via Demerara in British Guiana (Guyana today) along with a brief stop in New Orleans. Departing the Mersey on Wednesday, May 9, 1860—a beautiful spring day interspersed with light showers—the ship retraced her now well-worn route down the Irish Channel, past Land's End and southward in the Atlantic, around the Cape of Good Hope, into the Indian Ocean, and northeastward to the Bay of Bengal, probably arriving at Calcutta sometime in September 1860. There Kelly took on board a contingent of 350 indentured laborers bound for the sugar plantations of Demerara. The *Merrie England* was about to play a facilitating role in one small episode of a controversial nineteenth-century migration.

## Crossing the Kala Pani

The importation of indentured laborers into the British West Indies had begun in 1838, five years after the British Parliament passed the Slavery Abolition Act. When the African slaves who had worked the sugar plantations of Demerara for over 150 years were freed, the planters needed a dependable replacement workforce to support the colony's sugar industry. India, with its booming population, fractured economy, and high unemployment, emerged as a major source of both willing and unwilling indentured laborers for this and other colonies of the British Empire.

In the early 1860s, the majority of Indian immigrants came from Calcutta and Chota Nagpur, a group of plateaus two to three hundred miles west of Calcutta. The immigrant laborers were indentured for five years but had to work for ten years before they were eligible for free return passage to India. Once sucked into the plantation system, their lives were not unlike those of the slaves they had replaced. Strict labor laws included contractual obligations to complete specific weekly tasks for which they were typically paid five shillings. Failing to complete tasks, refusing to work, being absent without leave, misbehaving, and so on were all considered breaches of contract, which could result in prosecution and loss of wages. As early as 1840, Colonial Secretary William Russell called indenture "a new system of slavery,"[113] and Joseph Beaumont, the chief justice of British Guiana, referred to it as "a monstrous, rotten system, rooted upon slavery, grown in its stale soil, emulating its worst abuses."[114] The indenture system would continue for over three-quarters of a century until it was finally abolished in 1917.

The *Merrie England* sailed from Calcutta on October 5, 1860, in company with the ship *Camperdown* (Captain Denny), which carried another 350 Indian laborers for the plantations. As Basdeo Mangru suggests, the long and tedious passage to the West Indies was emotionally and physically challenging for the immigrants. Most importantly, crossing the kala pani (Hindi for "black water") meant the unravelling of family connections, loss of reputation, and even caste defilement. Other concerns included long periods of detention, threats to their religion, dietary anxieties, and the many challenges of a lengthy journey at sea, especially when those overseeing them did not care about them or their customs.[115] Thus burdened, many of the indentured laborers isolated themselves belowdecks, and mortality on the ships from Calcutta was often high. The *Merrie England*'s maximum passenger count was supposed to be 250 people. Three hundred and fifty immigrants far exceeded her capacity. Fox Smith observed:

> All the ships leaving Calcutta this season had a rather large percentage of deaths. The *Camperdown* lost 36, the *Loodiana* 20, the *Merrie England* 31, the *Ulysses* 65, and the *Alnwick Castle* 32. A good many of those who died were children, and most of the casualties occurred shortly after leaving Calcutta. All authorities agree that the first three weeks were the worst part of the voyage, owing to the fact that, in spite of all precautions, epidemics such as measles sometimes made their appearance after the ships had sailed. Another point worth noting in this connection is that another large number of deaths took place immediately before

reaching Demerara—bearing out the old sailor superstition that however ill a man may be he will not die before he smells the land.[116]

The *Merrie England* and the *Camperdown* arrived together at Demerara, probably sometime in early January 1861. There they offloaded their Indian laborers, subjecting them to the whims of the planters who would monopolize and exploit them for as long as they remained in the colony.

In all, approximately 240,000 Indian immigrants would arrive in British Guiana between 1838 and 1917. Of these, approximately 76,000 found their way back to India after serving their indenture.[117] Those who chose to remain in the colony became the pioneer generation of a vibrant Indo-Guyanese community that is still active within Guyana. Today the descendants of indentured workers constitute the largest population segment in the country—and they continue to play an essential role in the economic, political, and cultural life of the region.

As for Kelly, he did not linger in the West Indies. The *Merrie England* put to sea again, sailing across the Gulf of Mexico to a place Kelly had once known well, a seething, rambunctious city on the threshold of rebellion.

## *Secession in New Orleans*

Upon arriving in the Mississippi delta, the *Merrie England* was brought up to New Orleans from the Passes by the towboat *Anglo Saxon* and deposited at her berth along the quay on Monday, January 28, 1861. Kelly had arrived at a time of breakaway excitement in the Crescent City.

Just two days before the *Merrie England* arrived, the Louisiana state government in Baton Rouge had adopted the Ordinance of Secession, declaring the state an independent republic and transferring the seat of government from Baton Rouge to New Orleans. Louisiana would subsequently join Alabama, Florida, Georgia, Mississippi, South Carolina, and Texas as the first Confederate States of America. They would soon be bolstered by Arkansas, North Carolina, Tennessee, and Virginia in the southern alliance against the northern states. The American Civil War was stirring to life with the free flag of Louisiana floating over New Orleans.

However, the North's naval blockade of southern ports would not begin until April 1861. The *Merrie England*'s arrival could not have been better timed, and a bustling wharf greeted Kelly despite the political turmoil gripping the city. The *Bee* declared on the day after his arrival, "The quay continues blocked up with cotton bales, piled up in some places five tiers deep, and the largest quantity of sugar, molasses and produce we have ever seen on the wharf at any one time. Steamboats find great difficulty in discharging and receiving from the scarcity of gangways."[118]

A curious Captain Kelly was likely eager to go ashore and ascertain the state of affairs by looking up Martha's family. His wife's brothers—James and Sam—would certainly have firsthand knowledge of what was happening in the city.

Martha's older brother James Rainey, now a wealthy fifty-one-year-old cotton broker, had been in New Orleans twenty years earlier when William and Martha had lived there. James and his wife, Catherine, had passed the intervening years very much in the family way. Ten children now made the Rainey residence at the corner of Prytania and Thalia Streets a lively place indeed.

Her brother Sam had arrived in New Orleans from Antrim in 1844 at age sixteen, just a couple of years after William and Martha had returned to the United Kingdom. Sam was now an enterprising thirty-three-year-old bookkeeper with his wife, Maria; a four-year-old daughter named Emma; and a one-year-old son named William Kelly Rainey after his seafaring uncle. Sam and his young family were snugly housed in their own more modest residence at 385 Saint Charles Street with two Irish domestics, Margaret Mullen and Mary Mahan, rounding out the household.

For Captain Kelly, there were plenty of Rainey in-laws and other Irish folk with whom to while away some shore leave. The next three weeks were likely monopolized by kin, while intervals of loud secessionist fervor probably intruded from time to time into the family reunion.

On the morning of Tuesday, February 12, for instance, William, James, and Sam might have found their way to Lafayette Square to watch the newly adopted flag of the Louisiana Republic hoisted for the first time. The politicians were there along with the Washington Artillery, the First Company of Louisiana Riflemen, the Louisiana Guards, the Montgomery Guards, and the Sarsfield Rifles in all their spit and polish. Precisely at 11:00 a.m., the flag was raised atop the Municipal Building. The troops presented arms, the crowd cheered, an artillery gun thundered, and the telegraph bells pealed. After a twenty-one-gun salute, the presiding officer invited the politicians to review the troops after which the soldiers paraded and were duly dismissed. If Kelly was not in the crowd, he might have heard the commotion.

With a ship to return to Liverpool, Kelly filled the *Merrie England*'s hold with over three thousand bales of cotton and a quantity of oil cake[119] and got away on Monday, February 25, 1861—a sparkling, almost spring-like day in New Orleans, according to the papers. On March 8 they passed the steamship *De Soto* (Captain Johnston) in the Florida Strait between Key West and Cuba. Then, when clear of the Gulf of Mexico, they stood north through the northeast trades and passed Bermuda, shaping a course direct for England. The *Merrie England* arrived back at Liverpool on Saturday, April 20, 1861, with another year at sea encrusted on her hull.

This time Kelly went home to a different residence. He had moved his family from 52 Upper Stanhope Street to 18 Upper Parliament Street, still in Toxteth Park. The new house was just a short walk from the previous one, between Blair Street and Brook Street in a cluster of five houses called Cemetery View because they overlooked the burial ground of Saint James's Cathedral.

The 1861 UK census, which was enumerated two weeks before Kelly's return from New Orleans, listed his family as shown in Table 2, with Martha's mother, Agnes Rainey, either living or visiting them at the time.

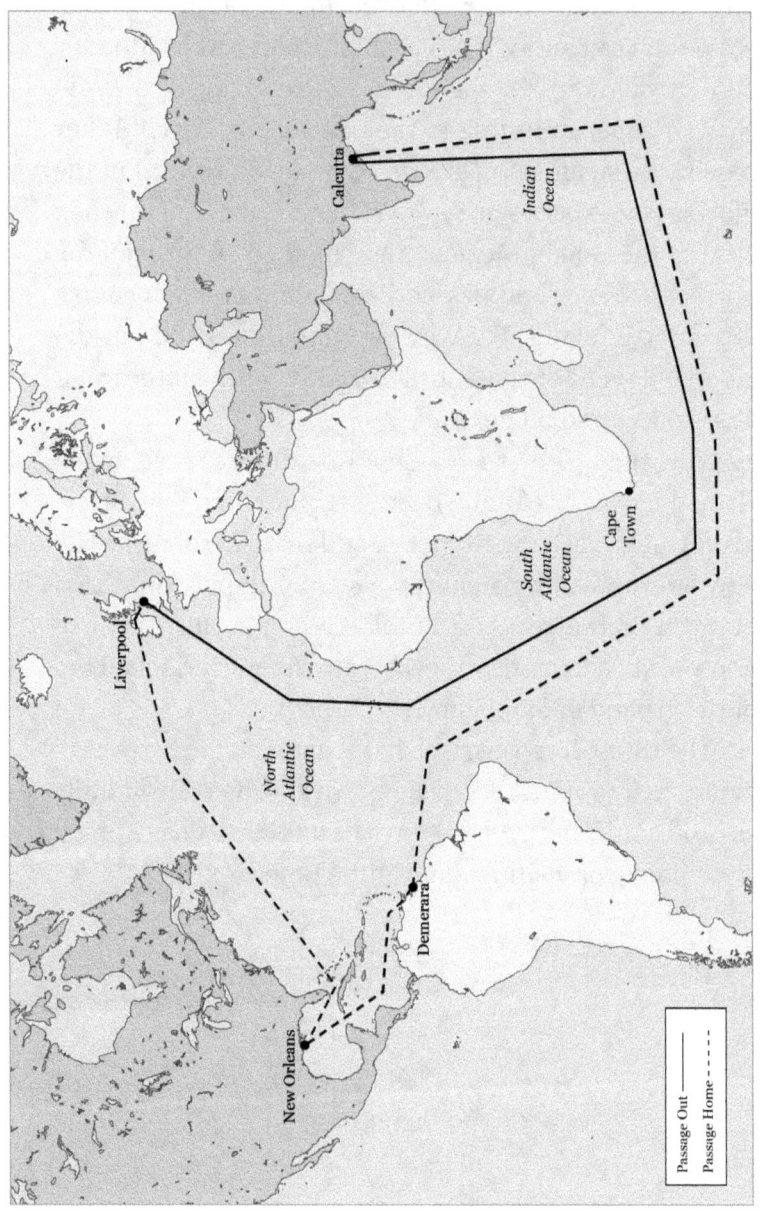

Figure 13: *Merrie England*, voyage 4—Liverpool to Calcutta, Demerara, and New Orleans.

## Table 2: 1861 UK Census, 18 Upper Parliament Street

| | | | | | |
|---|---|---|---|---|---|
| Martha Kelly | wife | mar | 43 | Wife of master mariner | Born Ireland |
| Agnes Kelly | daughter | un | 20 | | New Orleans |
| John Kelly | son | un | 13 | Scholar | Ireland |
| Fanny Kelly | daughter | un | 11 | " | Ireland |
| William Kelly | son | un | 9 | " | Ireland |
| Mary Kelly | daughter | un | 7 | " | Ireland |
| Agnes Rainey | mother-in-law | wid | 74 | | Ireland |
| Mary Ann Riley | servant | un | 21 | Domestic servant | Ireland |

Date: Sunday, April 7, 1861, Parish of Toxteth Park, Municipal Borough of Liverpool, Municipal Ward of North Toxteth, Ecclesiastical District of St. James

Comfortably installed in his new residence, Kelly probably began thumbing through newspapers to catch up with world events. The nineteenth-century news cycle was slow and sporadic compared with the continuous and instantaneous news flashes of the internet age. Having just returned from New Orleans, he would have been especially interested in bulletins from the United States—where the union was rapidly unraveling.

By the arrival of the ship *Africa*, the *Liverpool Mercury* of Tuesday, April 23, 1861, had received the following intelligence from New York (up to April 10):

> However difficult it may be at the present moment to form anything like an accurate estimate of the terrible convulsion which is shaking the constitution of the United States to its very foundation, it is quite clear that the turning point is now reached, and that within a few days we shall witness either the inauguration of a civil war or the quiet acquiescence of the Southern Government to policy apparently, though only apparently, opposed to the interests of the Confederacy. This latter view is not regarded in the States as at all probable, and, therefore, dismissing it from further consideration, they seem to prepare for the greater evil—a struggle between fellow-countrymen.

As Kelly perused his pile of newspapers, he learned that South Carolina had demanded the surrender of the federal garrison at Fort Sumter on April 11. Major Robert Anderson had refused to concede defeat with the stipulation that he would soon be forced to do so if not relieved. The Civil War officially began on April 12, 1861, at 4:30 a.m. when Confederate shore batteries under Louisiana-born General P. G. T. Beauregard opened fire on Fort Sumter, forcing the garrison to surrender on April 13 and evacuate the next day. On April 19, the Union blockade of southern ports was declared, shutting down 3,500 miles of Confederate coastline and twelve ports, including New Orleans and Mobile. Devouring the news, Kelly must have wondered how his wife's family were coping with the rapidly unraveling situation in the American South. Would he ever again sail to New Orleans?

## Voyage 5: Liverpool to Calcutta

The *Merrie England*'s last voyage under William Kelly was a magical mystery tour with only arrivals listed in the papers. She departed Liverpool on an unknown date (although probably toward the end of February 1861), and the papers noted her arrival at Calcutta on August 18. She departed Calcutta sometime in the fall and arrived at Capetown on January 27, 1862, then left Capetown on another unknown date and arrived back at Liverpool on February 16, 1862, after a year at sea. The general merchandise she carried from Calcutta consisted of standard items from the subcontinent, including 10,928 boxes of rice, 2,861 bales of jute, 1,301 boxes of linseed, 1,353 boxes of saltpetre, 200 boxes of castor oil, and 186 boxes of shellac.[120]

This scantily documented voyage portends yet another transition in William Kelly's career. The next time the *Merrie England* departed from Liverpool for Melbourne and Calcutta on March 15, 1862 (with no captain listed), she arrived at Calcutta in June under the command of a Captain Lowry.

In the early years of this new decade, William Kelly was again moving on—this time from master mariner to master and managing owner of yet another ship. He also would have to grapple with a looming family tragedy—the mysterious disappearance of the man who had sailed by his side during the *Merrie England*'s successful maiden voyage. The fate of his brother, John, would take many months to unravel, ascertain, and fully comprehend.

CHAPTER FOUR

# John Kelly's Last Voyages

(1858–1860)

Two months after accompanying his brother on the *Merrie England*'s impressive first trip, John Kelly assumed full command of another Beazley vessel when he replaced Captain Findley of the *Flora* (Official Number 10589). This ship of 728 tons built in 1851 in New Brunswick was preparing to leave England for Bombay. With Findley ill, John Kelly took over for him at the Welsh port of Milford Haven on Wednesday, May 19, 1858, and the *Flora* departed for India two days later. The voyage out and back appears to have passed without incident. They arrived at Bombay in the fall, departed in mid-November, and returned to Liverpool on April 4, 1859.

In June 1859, John signed on as first mate of the ship *Epaminondas* (Official Number 15388) under Captain Heasley. Built in 1850 at Quebec by George H. Parke and owned by David Grainger of Belfast (as were John's earlier ship *Arethusa* and William's *Belinda*), the *Epaminondas* was a lovely three-master with a single deck, a square stern, and an imposing figurehead of the fourth-century BCE Theban military commander and statesman after whom the ship was named. Her dimensions were 161 feet long × 34 feet beam × 23 feet depth of hold. Her capacity was 1,171 tons, and she carried up to 220 passengers. The title page of this book includes a charcoal tracing of the *Epaminondas*. The original drawing purportedly once hung in David Grainger & Son's office at Prince's Dock in Belfast.

Kelly served as mate on the *Epaminondas* for three voyages: Liverpool–Quebec (June–September 1859, carrying salt), Liverpool–New Orleans (December 1859–May 1860, cargo unknown), and Liverpool–Quebec again (May–September 1860, cargo unknown).[121]

## The Catastrophe of the *Hilton*

In October 1860, John Kelly transferred (again as first mate) to the ship *Hilton* (Official Number 23158) for a routine voyage from Liverpool to Calcutta. Owned by Halhead, Fletcher & Co. of Liverpool, the *Hilton* had earlier seen duty in the Australian immigrant trade. Now sailing on lower profile cargo runs under the command of Captain McLeary, she departed Liverpool for India on Friday, November 2, 1860, with a cargo of salt. An old sailing superstition once held that it was unlucky to commence a sea voyage on Friday. The *Hilton* corroborated this notion because she never arrived in India. Months went by with no word from her or of her, and her owners, agents, and the families of her crew and passengers began to despair, growing more discouraged as time went by with no word of her fate.

On Friday, June 7, 1861, eight months after the *Hilton*'s departure from Liverpool, the *London Evening Standard* noted the high premiums being quoted by

Lloyd's underwriters for two homeward-bound New York ships that were overdue (the *Nantucket* at 50 guineas; the *Equal Rights* at 30 guineas). The same article reported that "60 guineas premium [had] been offered on the ship Hilton, outward bound from Liverpool for Bombay...but the rate was refused."[122] It seems that vague concern was hardening into grim acceptance of the inevitable. The general consensus was that the *Hilton* would not be heard from again.

In July the *Birmingham Daily Post* commented, "Much anxiety continues to be felt in Liverpool in consequence of the supposed loss of...the ship Hilton, Captain McLeary, sailed from Liverpool for Calcutta with a cargo of salt, since which she has never been heard of. It is believed that the vessel must have commenced leaking, and the salt dissolving, capsized. All hopes are given up as to the safety of the Hilton."[123]

William Kelly, on board the *Merrie England* transporting indentured Indian laborers to Demerara, had no idea that John was in peril two oceans away; indeed, it took him many months to piece together what happened to his brother.

Eventually William believed he had figured it out, and he added a memorial inscription to the large flat stone set in the ground next to the Kelly monument at Muckamore burial ground: "Captain John Kelly...lost in a hurricane off Mauritius, January 1860, Aged 45 years." In fact, the *Hilton* was actively engaged from January 1860 through almost the end of that year. John Kelly transferred to her in October, and she subsequently departed for India on November 2. Then, as noted in Lloyd's Captains Register, the *Hilton* sank on November 28, 1860, with all hands lost.

The Muckamore gravestone with the problematic month probably reflects the best information that William Kelly had at the time he added the inscription to the gravestone.

Two books shed some light on the fate of the *Hilton* and her crew. They are Allister Macmillan's *Mauritius Illustrated* (1914) and Robert Jackson's *Ocean Passages for the World* (1895). Macmillan states that the hurricane season around the island of Mauritius runs from December through April. A late November hurricane would have been early but still within this timeframe. Macmillan also suggests that hurricanes in this vicinity "form as a rule to the north or north-east of Mauritius, between latitudes 8° and 12° south in the belt which exists between the S.E. trade current and the N.W. monsoon. These two currents, rising by convection, give birth to a vortex motion in the superheated areas of the tropical calms."[124] Jackson's *Ocean Passages* recommends that "sailing vessels should pass to the eastward and round the north end of Mauritius to avoid the calms near the S.W. part of the island."[125] Based on these authorities, the *Hilton* most likely sank in the South Indian Ocean somewhere north or northeast of Mauritius.

According to Macmillan, the winds around Mauritius normally blow from east to east-southeast. As the hurricane approached the *Hilton*, Captain McLeary and First Mate Kelly would have observed increasing winds veering steadily to the southeast. They also would have noticed an ominously falling barometer and a thickening skein of wispy, cirrostratus clouds filling the sky. The officers' apprehension would have increased as the wind picked up, blowing in irregular, fitful gusts that shredded the watery stratus above. As the squalls strengthened in force and frequency and the sea rose around them, McLeary would have ordered all hands on deck to haul in sails, while a smaller group of exhausted, anxious seamen worked the pumps in the hold. Sheets of heavy, pounding rain washed over the ship, sweeping her deck and inundating her cargo spaces. Finally, the salt-choked pumps of the eight-year-old vessel could no longer keep the in-rushing ocean at bay. The *Hilton*'s heavy cargo of salt shifted catastrophically, causing her to keel over with a loud groan of splintering timbers and muffled cries. An all-enveloping scud of ocean foam and stabbing spray obliterated the sky, and the *Hilton* vanished into a swirling vortex of debris, taking the drowned and the drowning with her.

The UK Register of Deaths at Sea lists John Kelly as one of thirty-three seamen lost with the *Hilton*. The register lists his total wages as £25 (in debt), which was paid at the Liverpool Shipping Office on January 22, 1862. This scant information made its way to the Board of Trade on January 30, 1862. It took this long—some fourteen months—for the authorities to close the book on the *Hilton*. The incorrect month carved into John's memorial inscription on the Kelly family granite at Muckamore burial ground was by then long forgotten, and so it remains to this day.

# John Kelly's Last Voyages                 141

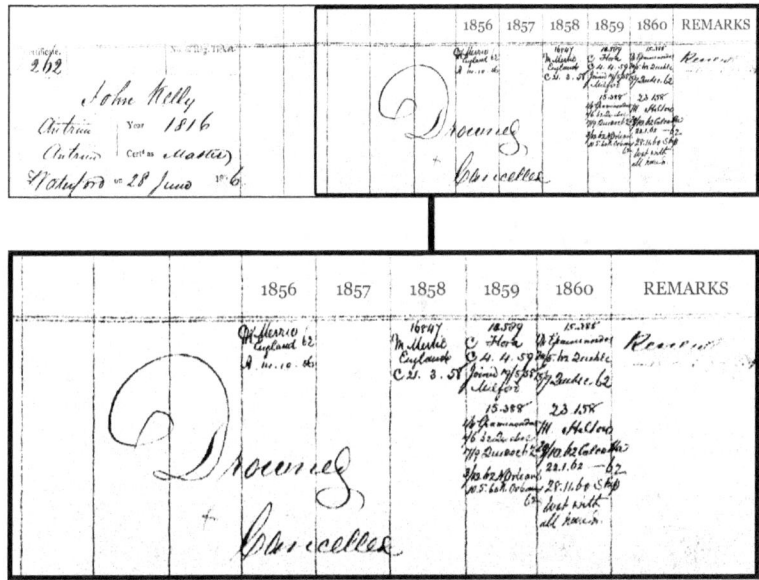

Figure 14: Report of John Kelly's death by drowning in the sinking of the *Hilton*; "23158 Hilton, 28.11.60, ship lost with all hands." Source: Lloyd's Captains Registers BT 124/14; recorded service 1851–1860; certificate numbers 70,000–74,027; National Archives (UK).

Figure 15: John Kelly's gravestone inscription, Muckamore burial ground. Image credit: Dr. Bob Foy, 2013.

CHAPTER FIVE

# Conflagration and Destruction

(1861)

Having lost John in the foundering of the *Hilton*, William Kelly might well have wondered if his brother's death marked the beginning of a cascade of similar circumstances for him. Were ships he had sailed likewise poised on the brink of obliteration? Indeed, two ships from William's past would soon follow the *Hilton*. Instead of appearing dockside at Liverpool where they were expected, they would show up in the daily news cycle, where curious readers eagerly devoured the high drama of their final hours.

## The Conflagration of the *Mary Carson*

On January 16, 1861, the American ship *Henry Brigham* commanded by Captain John R. Potter of Savannah was sailing before a stiff gale in the middle of the North Atlantic. Suddenly the ship's mast-top lookout observed a light on the horizon. Suspecting a ship in distress, Potter spread every available inch of canvas and raced to the southeast, sailing approximately thirty miles out of his way until he encountered a large vessel burning furiously from stem to stern.[126]

The hulk's masts were floating against her leeward flank, her topsides and decks were burned through, and flames were raging in her center. As the *Henry Brigham* sailed past the bow of the unfortunate vessel, the stern of the hulk broke off and crashed hissing into the sea. Expecting that her crew had abandoned her, Potter ordered a strict lookout for survivors in the water. One hour later they came upon a longboat containing the ship's first officer, her carpenter, and several seamen; then standing to the northeast, they found another boat with the ship's master, Captain Daniel Jones, and thirteen others. The *Henry Brigham* rescued the entire crew.

Captain Jones identified his burning vessel as the British ship the *Mary Carson* bound from Charleston to Liverpool with 2,500 bales of cotton and 500 barrels of pine resin. The crew was at a loss to explain how the fire began, but they recounted how rapidly it had spread and how impossible it had been to contain with such a highly combustible cargo. They had abandoned ship about 300 miles east of the Grand Banks and had spent many freezing hours contemplating the worst in heavy seas.

Their struggles were not over after their rescue. For the next three days, the *Henry Brigham* rode out a series of revolving gales and a furious hurricane before finally making it to Liverpool. Of the *Henry Brigham*'s multitasking master, the *Liverpool Daily Post* reported:

> Captain Potter deserves great credit for the accurate manner in which he has recorded the incidents of the extraordinary storm which his ship

encountered. His observations, recorded while the ship was in the most imminent danger, will—for none know better than seamen that "knowledge is power"—enable those who may be called upon to contend with similar dangers to bring increased resources to aid them in the conflict. If the same system of recording the events of voyages were generally followed by our merchant captains, the gain to science would be immense.[127]

While noting regretfully the spectacular demise of his old ship, William Kelly would likely have applauded the humane conduct and daring seamanship that saved her crew. Indeed, Captain Potter's fame spread internationally. For his efforts, he received a beautiful four-and-a-half-foot telescope in a tube case of fine white Russian leather packaged in a solid mahogany box inscribed: "Presented by the British government to John R. Potter, Master of the American vessel Henry Brigham, of Savannah, for humanity in picking up at sea, on the 16th of January, 1861, the crew of the Mary Carson, of Liverpool."[128]

## The Destruction of the *Miles Barton*

Less than a month after the *Mary Carson* inferno, one of the most prestigious and highly regarded of Kelly's ships—the *Miles Barton*—was lost under similarly newsworthy circumstances off the coast of South Africa. She had been chartered as a troop ship to carry officers and 320 men of the 1st Battalion, Third (Royal East Kent) Regiment of Foot (also known as the 3rd Buffs) under Major King from Hong Kong home to England after the Second Opium War.[129]

The ship, with a crew of thirty-two under the command of Captain James Shelford, was under full sail proceeding westward around the Cape of Good Hope when, around midnight on February 8, 1861, she struck a reef about thirty miles east of Cape Agulhas, the southernmost point of Africa and the dividing line between the Indian and Atlantic Oceans.[130]

The officers and men of the Buffs, startled from sleep by the suddenness of the ship lurching and grinding into something unknown, emerged bleary-eyed from their quarters to find the crew attempting to free the vessel from a reef by jibing (shifting her sails from one side of the ship to the other); but they abandoned this maneuver for fear that the ship was so damaged that she would sink if taken into deep water. To add to the confusion, about half an hour after the ship struck the reef, a fire broke out in the galley, which the crew quickly extinguished. Because the sea was running high and they had no sense of how far they were from the coast, Captain Shelford wisely advised against attempting to land the troops that night. Instead, the soldiers passed the long night assembled on deck in good Birkenhead order, only stepping forward to take their turn at the pumps when commanded.[131]

At daybreak they ascertained that they were about two miles from a long, sandy, and desolate shoreline pounded by high waves. As the morning sun rose higher, the difficult and dangerous process of removing the men from the ship began. They launched the ship's longboats and brought them up to the vessel's side, but high waves washed away the wooden ladders that they had dropped over the side, and the men had to clamber down ropes to reach the boats. A few men fell into the ocean, but their mates rescued them.

A powerful wave hurled one of the longboats high up on the beach, shattering it. After many hazardous trips back and forth from the disintegrating ship to the treacherous shore, the last of the soldiers finally arrived safely on the beach around four o'clock in the afternoon. Only then did Captain Shelford, his officers, and crew follow the troops to the beach.

Figure 16: Approximate location of the *Miles Barton* wreck site (east of Cape Agulhas and Arniston, South Africa). Image credit: Bill Bradley, 2019.

There were no casualties during the disembarkation, but sadly, one soldier drowned the next day when he accompanied several of the crew back to the ship to retrieve needed materials. Their longboat capsized, and Private Macnamara, described as "one of the finest, cleanest and smartest men in his regiment," did not survive his plunge into the sea.[132]

On February 12, the steamer *Cyclops* picked up the soldiers and crew and brought them around to Table Bay near

Cape Town. When the *Cyclops* left the scene of the wreck, her rescued passengers observed the *Miles Barton* broken in two but still clinging stubbornly to the reef, which to this day is known as Miles Barton Reef.[133] A lot of valuable property went down with the *Miles Barton*, including many rare articles taken by the troops from the Summer Palace of the Chinese emperor in Peking (now Beijing)—items variously classified as "curiosities" or "loot," depending on the sensitivities of the newspapers reporting the incident. Subsequently, the local Lloyd's agent conducted a public sale of the ship's hull, masts, rigging, stores, and other salvaged items, which recouped £180 (approximately £23,814 in 2022 currency).[134]

The most intriguing possibility surrounding the wreck of the *Miles Barton* is the strong likelihood that William Kelly's oldest son, John, was on board when she went down. John Kelly's "Statement of Service from First Going to Sea," which he submitted with his 1869 application for an ordinary master's certificate, lists him as "boy" serving on the *Miles Barton* from May 1860 to February 1862 (this is erroneous, as the ship sank in 1861). If John Kelly was indeed on the *Miles Barton* when she sank, the adventuresome fourteen-year-old had an early initiation into the inscrutabilities of surviving a catastrophe at sea. Captain William Kelly took the *Miles Barton* seaward on her maiden voyage to Australia and India in 1853; his son saw the same ship broken on a South African reef eight years later. The *Miles Barton* was a family affair for this father-and-son pair.

It is also worth noting that James Beazley's *Star of the East*, the clipper ship that the *Merrie England* had raced to Melbourne during her maiden voyage in 1856–1857, was herself lost on April 10, 1861, while returning to Liverpool from Bombay. She sank just two months after the *Miles Barton*—in approximately the same location off the coast of South Africa, fortunately with all hands saved.

The English hymnist William Whiting wrote "Eternal Father, Strong to Save" in 1860, just a year before the *Mary Carson* and the *Miles Barton* sank (and in the same year the *Hilton* went down). This well-known hymn is generally thought to have been inspired by the dangers of the sea as described in Psalm 107 (the same Psalm carved into the Kelly family monument at Muckamore burial ground).

> Eternal Father, strong to save,
> Whose arm doth bind the restless wave,
> Who biddest the mighty ocean deep
> Its own appointed limits keep,
> O, hear us when we cry to thee
> For those in peril on the sea!

Beginning with the *Dalriada* and moving through the *Hilton*, the *Mary Carson*, the *Miles Barton*, and the *Star of the East*, the loss of these former, familiar ships that brothers William and John Kelly had sailed on, or competed against, during the height of their careers foreshadows a momentous change ahead for William Kelly. He was moving closer to a time when he would manage ships from the shore instead of sailing them in the moment, with the white canvas aloft and the lifting deck beneath his feet. But he was not quite there yet. There would be one last extended deep-sea voyage before Kelly would "swallow the anchor."

CHAPTER SIX

# Swallowing the Anchor

## (1862–1872)

SWALLOW THE ANCHOR: A maritime term to indicate giving up, or retiring from, a life at sea and settling down to live ashore.

*The Oxford Companion to Ships and the Sea*

## William Kelly's Acquisition of the Ship *Express*

William Kelly's next ship was an enigmatic vessel with a perplexing and catastrophic fate. Why an enigma? The ship *Express* (Official Number 44633) does not appear in the UK Lloyd's Register of Shipping or the UK Mercantile Navy List, even though she was registered in Liverpool. However, she is listed in the US Lloyd's Register of Shipping as a 1,118-ton ship with two decks, dimensions 215 feet long × 36 feet beam × 22 feet depth of hold, built in 1854 at Saint John, New Brunswick. Surviving crew agreements list her date of registration as March 1862. This was probably the month she was overhauled, metaled, and surveyed in Liverpool. The *Express* was heavier than the *Miles Barton* by about 120 tons and lighter than the *Merrie England* by about the same amount. I know more about this ship's dreadful end than I know about the four years she sailed under Kelly's ownership.

The *Express* was the first ship William Kelly commanded as both master and managing owner. This did not necessarily mean that he was the sole owner. Sailing vessels were expensive propositions and prone to disappearing in the many situations of doubt, difficulty, and danger encountered by ships at sea. Because of this, it made sense to spread the risk of ownership across multiple shareholders, distributing the financial exposure among family, friends, and other interested parties who typically held multiples of a sixty-fourth part of the vessel.

Of course, Kelly was the top man who not only hired and commanded the ship's crew but also managed her affairs—soliciting cargoes; booking passengers; maintaining contacts in ports-of-call; arranging for insurance, maintenance, and repairs; filling out paperwork; and reporting to shareholders on the state of the ship at regular intervals.

## *Liverpool to Aden, Singapore, and London: A Gift of Ostrich Eggs*

According to the crew agreement for the first voyage of the *Express* under William Kelly's ownership, twenty-eight men and boys signed on at Liverpool between April 14 and April 16, 1862.[135] Kelly's own listing in the agreement indicates that his previous ship was the *Merrie England* (February 1862), and a glance at the crew list shows that he brought three men with him from that ship—John Peterson of Dover (age 36), boatswain; Henry Green of

Belfast (age 24), steward; and Thomas Dodd of Whitstable (Kent) (age 35), cook. Kelly's first mate on the *Express* was Hugh Wisnom of Antrim (certificate no. 13,956), a thirty-two-year-old sailor who will appear again in this narrative. The rest of the crew was an international mix hailing from Dumbarton (Scotland); Ballymena, Belfast, and Cork (Ireland); Norway; Sweden; Denmark; Poland; Shetland; and Jamaica. The crew also included a fourteen-year-old boy named William Patterson who was on his first voyage as ship's boy and a sixteen-year-old apprentice seaman named John Kelly. This was William Kelly's oldest son, who was already a seasoned sailor, having survived the wreck of the *Miles Barton* just two years earlier. John was on board to continue learning the ropes under his father's watchful eye.

The *Express* left Liverpool for Aden on April 24, 1862, with no mention of her departure in the *Liverpool Mercury*. This uncanny ability to come and go unnoticed was typical of many of Kelly's arrivals and departures. The only incident that interfered with their departure this day was the requirement to put a thirty-three-year-old sick seaman named Charles Williams ashore while they were still in the Mersey shortly after departing.[136]

With this accomplished, Kelly took the *Express* out again on the route he knew by now like the back of his hand, dropping southward off Ireland; clearing the Bay of Biscay and Cape Finisterre; leaving in his wake Madeira, the Canary Islands, and Cape Verde; traversing the equator; and dropping to the southern tip of Africa, where they arrived off the Cape of Good Hope sometime around the end of June. After rounding the Cape, they headed northward, beating through the Mozambique Channel between the African mainland and the island of Madagascar in the full force of the southwest monsoon. They then skirted the Comoros and Seychelles Islands, recrossed the equator, and proceeded along the Somali Coast to Ras Asir (Cape Guardafui today). Here, at the easternmost point of Africa, they swung to the west into the Gulf of Aden, hugging the African coast as far as Burnt Island, a barren, guano-encrusted rock five miles off the north Somali coast. Here Kelly finally shaped a northeast course across the gulf direct for Aden Harbor.

The iridescent waters of the Arabian Sea might have been new to Kelly. Their variable tides, currents, and winds could be difficult to navigate, and peculiar wonders of the deep sometimes startled and amazed the unwary. As noted in *The Gulf of Aden Pilot*, "The sea of these coasts is remarkable for its occasional peculiar brilliancy at night; without any warning it will become suddenly illuminated, as if on fire, causing alarm to the stranger who may be unacquainted with the phenomenon, by giving him the idea of his vessel being amongst breakers, but on casting the lead the deception becomes apparent. It occurs in the open sea as well as near the land, and whether calm or with a breeze."[137]

This rare, night-time phenomenon, known as a milky sea, appears to be a vast expanse of luminous water stretching as far as the eye can see. The dark sky above and the bright ocean below create an eerie scene resembling a negative photographic image. On a moonless night, ship passengers have been known to read by the light of a milky sea.

Some investigators believe the spectacle is caused by a bioluminescent marine bacterium that colonizes microscopic plankton floating on the surface of the ocean. When this symbiotic population reaches a critical concentration, a faint but steady glow develops in the presence of high oxygen levels in the water. A high concentration of signaling molecules then causes the colony to glow—an example of "quorum sensing" in which bacteria communicate with chemical signaling.

With no surviving logbook documenting the *Express*'s passage through the Arabian Sea in the summer and fall of 1862, there is no way to confirm (or refute) whether the *Express* experienced a milky sea while transiting these beguiling waters. All I can say is the ship was in the right place at the right time of the year. Her crew might very well have sailed, wide-eyed and wondering, over glowing, milky-blue "snowbanks" beneath a moonless sky in the Gulf of Aden.

Aden was situated in the crater of an extinct volcano attached to the Arabian mainland by a low isthmus. The place had been a British settlement since 1839, when Royal Marines occupied the harbor to counter attacks by local pirates against British ships on the way to India. Then administered by the Government of Bombay, the settlement was a major watering, coaling, and trans-shipment station for vessels traveling back and forth between the United Kingdom, India, and the Far East (with its importance growing after the Suez Canal opened in 1869).

Kelly and the *Express* likely arrived at Aden sometime in August 1862, when hot, sandy winds from the north known as the *shamal* prevailed within the crater. Why Kelly brought the *Express* to Aden at this inauspicious time of year is open to conjecture. The ship might have carried a mixed cargo of coal, cotton goods, liquor, wine, and other sundries—at least, these were among the settlement's major imports at the time.

Another interesting import from closer at hand was ostrich feathers from the Somali and Dankali coasts of Africa.[138] White, brown, grey, and black feathers were brought into Aden, where local inhabitants cleaned and packaged them for onward shipment to England, France, and Egypt. There they became feather dusters or were put to other decorative uses. The small black and brown feathers that had been damaged during cleaning found their way into muffs and boas.

The ostrich feathers are worth mentioning because our Kelly family memorabilia includes a letter written by William Kelly's brother-in-law John McFerran of Kemptville, Ontario, to McFerran's daughter, Mary Elizabeth Grothier, in upstate New York (dated May 8, 1867). The letter states, "Uncle William sent me a great curiosity in this country two Ostrich Eggs. The[y] are the largest you ever see. The[y] are six inches long and the[y] are sixteen and one-half inches in circumference." It might have been during this stop at Aden that Kelly acquired the ostrich eggs that found their way to Canada (or he might have picked them up during the *Merrie England*'s stopover at Cape Town earlier in the year). Exactly where the eggs came from is just a detail. The larger point is: William Kelly collected souvenirs during his travels, and he was quick to share them with his extended family, astonishing and delighting them in the process. I wonder how he packaged these fragile keepsakes so that they survived the trip from Liverpool to the backwoods of the Ottawa Valley in 1867, the year that Canada achieved Confederation.

The *Express* departed Aden sometime in September 1862, possibly with coffee or honey in her hold but most likely in ballast, given that her next destination was the major rice port of Akyab in Burma's western coastal state of Arakan (now Rakhine). They probably passed out of the Gulf of Aden north of Socotra Island, and then sailed across the Arabian Sea and around the southern coast of Ceylon. They might have stopped at Point de Galle before heading north in the Bay of Bengal and sailing west of the Nicobar and Andaman Islands direct to Akyab.

According to the crew agreement, they were at Akyab on October 17, 1862. William Kelly had last been there five years earlier in December 1857, with his brother, John, at his side, during the *Merrie England*'s maiden voyage to Australia and China. This time, his son, John, was at his side, but Kelly might have been burdened with the knowledge of his brother's disappearance, or even his death, assuming the *Hilton*'s fate was then known. In either case, William was likely eager to complete his business in Burma and move on. After taking on a cargo of rice, the *Express* sailed southward through the Strait of Malacca to her next port of call—Singapore at the tip of the Malay Peninsula. The *Singapore Straits Times* reports her arrival there from Akyab on November 22, 1862, and there she discharged and loaded cargo into early December.

According to the *Liverpool Mercury*, "the *Express*, Kelly, from Singapore" was at Hong Kong on February 4, 1863. She arrived back at London five months later on June 7, 1863, after a little more than a year at sea.

## Sunderland to Calcutta and London: The Captain Steps Down

Two months after returning to London, the *Express* next appears at the Port of Sunderland, one of the chief shipbuilding towns in the northeast of England, where the River Wear flows into the North Sea. There I found Kelly's ship in August 1863, possibly undergoing repairs or a refit before returning to sea. The crew agreement for her next voyage indicated an indeterminate trip from "Sunderland to Calcutta, thence as may be required to any port, ports, place or places, in the Indian Ocean or Bay of Bengal, China Seas, Australia, north or south Atlantic Ocean or Pacific, West Indies, Mediterranean, trading to and fro as required and back to a port of discharge of Cargo in the United Kingdom or the continent of Europe...calling for orders where required; voyage not to exceed three years."[139] In other words, the ship's twenty-three-man crew would go wherever Kelly took them, pretty much anywhere in the world, during their three-year-maximum tour of duty.

Two crewmen from the *Express*'s previous voyage accompanied Kelly to Sunderland: carpenter James Annandale and loyal follower Henry Green, both of whom had served with him on the *Merrie England*. Green moved from steward on the *Express*'s first trip to third mate on her second. Most interestingly, it appears that Kelly was initiating his youngest son into the seafaring life at a very early age. The crew agreement lists a William Kelly of Liverpool (with no age listed) in the block reserved for "apprentices on board." This was probably eleven-year-old William Kelly Jr.'s first voyage as part of a ship's crew. Amazingly, his father logged him in, not as a ship's boy, but as an apprentice. William Jr. was on the fast track to becoming a ship's officer.

The *Express* got away from Sunderland on Monday, August 17, 1863, without a first mate. Sanderson Brown, the forty-one-year-old sailor from Hull who had signed on at this position, was discharged by mutual consent before they left port, possibly for health reasons.[140] An even greater upheaval was about to occur. One week later, when the *Express* put into Portsmouth, the ship lost her captain too, as recorded on the certificates page of the crew agreement:

Custom House Portsmouth, 22 August, 1863
I hereby certify that Wm. Kelly the master has been obliged to leave the ship owing to illness and Geo. H. Sunderland engaged as mate.

(Signed) W. Harward

This unspecified illness might have been simmering for months, or it might have emerged suddenly between Sunderland and Portsmouth. Whatever its cause, it marked the end of William Kelly's seafaring career in the merchant marine. It was perhaps the first sign of heart disease. The fifty-two-year-old seaman would continue to own ships and play an active role in the shipping communities of Liverpool and Belfast for another fourteen years, but he appears not to have sailed again as ship's master on a deep-sea voyage—and William Kelly Jr. also left the ship in Portsmouth.

As managing owner of the *Express*, Kelly replaced himself with a twenty-nine-year-old master mariner from Sunderland named Samuel Riggall (certificate no. 12,979), who took the ship on to Calcutta, arriving in January 1864. There they lost one man who drowned in the Hooghly River—a twenty-three-year-old seaman named William Brown who appears to have been the only other casualty of the voyage.

By the time Riggall and the *Express* arrived safely back in London on July 29, 1864, a still recuperating William Kelly was already closely scrutinizing a new ship that had recently arrived in UK waters from the East Coast of the United States.

Table 3: William Kelly's career as a ship's master at sea (1836–1863)

| VESSELS | PORTS OF CALL | DAYS | NM* |
|---|---|---|---|
| *MARGARET JOHNSON* | | | |
| Voyage 1 | 1836–37: Liverpool–New Orleans–Liverpool | 110 | 9,714 |

| *AMBASSADOR* | | | |
|---|---|---|---|
| Voyage 1 | 1840: New Orleans–Liverpool | 49 | 4,857 |
| Voyage 2 | 1840–41: Liverpool–New Orleans–Liverpool | 95 | 9,714 |
| Voyage 3 | 1841: Liverpool–New Orleans–London | 96 | 9,547 |
| Voyage 4 | 1841–42: London–New Orleans | 38 | 4,690 |

| *DUMFRIESSHIRE* | | | |
|---|---|---|---|
| Voyage 1 | 1843: Liverpool–Quebec–Belfast | 94 | 4,980 |
| Voyage 2 | 1843–44: Belfast–Mobile–Liverpool–Belfast | 160 | 9,485 |
| Voyage 3 | 1844: Belfast–Quebec | 39 | 2,430 |

| *BELINDA* | | | |
|---|---|---|---|
| Voyage 1 | 1845: Belfast–Quebec–Belfast | 58 | 4,860 |
| Voyage 2 | 1845–46: Belfast–New Orleans–Liverpool | 94 | 9,669 |

| VESSELS | PORTS OF CALL | DAYS | NM* |
|---|---|---|---|
| Voyage 3 | 1846: Belfast–Quebec–Liverpool | 77 | 4,980 |
| Voyage 4 | 1846–47: Liverpool–New Orleans–Liverpool | 150 | 9,714 |
| Voyage 5 | 1847–48: Liverpool–Callao–Liverpool | 290 | 19,785 |
| Voyage 6 | 1848: London–Bremen–New York–Scatarie† | 79 | 4,212 |

| DALRIADA | | | |
|---|---|---|---|
| Voyage 1 | 1849: Quebec–Liverpool | 39 | 2,550 |
| Voyage 2 | 1849–50: Liverpool–New Orleans–Liverpool | 92 | 9,714 |

| MARY CARSON | | | |
|---|---|---|---|
| Voyage 1 | 1850–51: Liverpool–New Orleans–Liverpool | 149 | 9,714 |
| Voyage 2 | 1851: Liverpool–New York–Quebec–Liverpool | 134 | 6,303 |
| Voyage 3 | 1851–52: Liverpool–Calcutta–Liverpool | 261 | 21,320 |

| MILES BARTON | | | |
|---|---|---|---|
| Voyage 1 | 1853–54: Liverpool–Melbourne–Calcutta–Bombay–Liverpool | 313 | 29,259 |
| Voyage 2 | 1854–55: Liverpool–Melbourne–Calcutta–Liverpool | 300 | 28,763 |
| Voyage 3 | 1855–56: Liverpool–Melbourne–Manila–Anjer–Queenstown–Liverpool | 321 | 29,053 |
| Voyage 4 | 1856: Liverpool–Rotterdam–Liverpool | 53 | 1,060 |

| MERRIE ENGLAND | | | |
|---|---|---|---|
| Voyage 1 | 1856–58: Liverpool–Melbourne–Ceylon–Calcutta/Bombay–Hong Kong–Shanghai–Akyab–Liverpool | 518 | 36,362 |
| Voyage 2 | 1858–59: Liverpool–Calcutta–London | 286 | 23,764 |

| VESSELS | PORTS OF CALL | DAYS | NM* |
|---|---|---|---|
| Voyage 3 | 1859–60: London–Calcutta–London–Liverpool | 323 | 23,920 |
| Voyage 4 | 1860–61: Liverpool–Calcutta–Demerara–New Orleans–Liverpool | 346 | 29,345 |
| Voyage 5 | 1861–62: Liverpool–Calcutta–Cape Town–Liverpool | ? | 22,637 |
| *EXPRESS* | | | |
| Voyage 1 | 1862–63: Liverpool–Aden–Akyab–Singapore–(Hong Kong?)–Calcutta–Liverpool | 409 | 31,737 |
| Voyage 2 | 1863: Sunderland–Portsmouth‡ | 5 | 240 |
| | **TOTAL** | 4,978 | 414,378 |

*Approximate nautical miles †Wrecked on the way to Quebec

‡William Kelly discharged due to illness, end of active career at sea

## William Kelly's Acquisition of the Ship *Sterling*

The ship *Sterling* (Official Number 50493) was launched from the South Boston yard of Briggs Brothers Shipyard at four o'clock in the afternoon on Wednesday, April 27, 1864.[141] She was a twin-decked vessel of 770 tons measuring 156 feet long × 31 feet beam × 21 feet depth of hold, and she came from a shipyard with an exemplary pedigree and reputation.

Edwin and Harrison Briggs were the sons of master carpenter and shipbuilder Cushing Otis Briggs of Scituate, Massachusetts.[142] Their shipyard at South Boston Point, which they had established in about 1848, produced some of the fastest and most renowned American clipper ships of the nineteenth century, including the *Northern Light*

(1,050 tons, built in 1851), which made the quickest passage between San Francisco and Boston via Cape Horn in 1853 (the ship's seventy-six-day record still stands for single-hull vessels). Other Briggs ships included the *Meteor* (1,050 tons), the *Golden Light* (1,050 tons), the *Saracen* (1,300 tons), the *Marmaluke* (1,300 tons), and the *Fair Wind* (1,300 tons). After making enough money to retire comfortably, the brothers shut down their shipyard in 1865. The *Sterling* might have been one of the last ships they built.

About a month and a half after her launch, the *Sterling* sailed from Boston to Liverpool, and sometime in the summer or fall of 1864, William Kelly bought the ship at London for £6,250 (equivalent to approximately £882,000 in 2022).[143] She first appears in the UK Lloyd's Register of Shipping in 1865 with Captain Hall listed as master and "W. Kelly" as owner. For a couple of years, Kelly would be the proud owner of both the *Sterling* and the *Express*, but there was a dark cloud on the horizon for one of these fine ships.

## The Disaster of the *Express*

After her return to London in 1864, the *Express* maintained the characteristically low profile of most Kelly ships, with no arrivals or departures noted in either the UK or North American papers for the next year. I can only assume she was quietly going about her business during this time, possibly still with Captain Riggall at the helm, plying the waters somewhere and, with a bit of luck, proving to be a good investment for William Kelly. When the *Express* eventually did burst back into print, it was with a dramatic narrative that made ship owners flinch and experienced seamen confront their worst fears.[144]

The *Express* had departed the Tyne-side town of South Shields on October 2, 1865, with a crew of twenty under the command of Captain Roland Savage of Belfast (born in Portaferry, certificate no. 47,187), who was accompanied by his wife. The first part of the voyage is not known, but by March 1866 they were close to the home stretch—bound from New Orleans to Saint John, New Brunswick, with a load of sand as ballast. There they were supposed to exchange the ballast for timber and return to the United Kingdom.

Around March 18, the *Express* ran into a succession of northwest gales in the mid–North Atlantic and sprang a leak. It was only by pumping day and night that crew members were able to keep the water in the hold from reaching the ballast. About a week later, they encountered heavy weather again. A hurricane, this time from the south, caused the ship to labor and the leak to worsen. Despite constant pumping, the water eventually inundated the ballast, and the pumps became clogged with sand. With the ship under bare masts, Captain Savage gave orders to set the fore topsail and headsails to get the vessel before the wind. The sails were no sooner loosed than they were blown to ribbons.

Desperate, Savage ordered the crew to cut away the mizzen mast to get the ship before the wind, but this had no effect. As a last resort, they cut down the main mast, but this still failed to bring the vessel's bow downwind (in the direction that the wind was blowing). To make matters worse, the *Express* began rolling over on her beam ends. Eventually she went over so far that they cut away the foremast, leaving her a total wreck.

The next day the weather improved, and some of the crew attempted to abandon ship in the longboat without the captain's consent. They got the boat into the water, but before all the men were able to get on board, Captain Savage cut the line. The few seamen in the boat jumped into the ocean and were hauled on board again.

By the morning of March 27, the water had risen more than three feet above the tween deck.[145] Captain Savage, seeing that the situation was hopeless, finally gave orders to abandon ship and brought his wife on deck so that she could find a place in the remaining longboat. They got the boat into the water with considerable difficulty, but there was not room in it for everyone. The mate and four seamen decided to return to the wreck rather than take their chances with the others. As the longboat pushed away from the vessel, a tremendous wave swamped it, dragging everyone into the water, where all drowned. The seamen who had returned to the wreck were helpless witnesses to seventeen deaths, including the captain and his wife.

At 1:00 p.m., less than an hour after the longboat disappeared, another heavy sea swamped the *Express*, washing off the whole of the poop deck where the five survivors were huddling. Only one seaman, a twenty-two-year-old man from Coventry named Thomas Williams, was able to swim back to the poop. There he saw his four companions clinging to different parts of the wreck. In this vulnerable condition, the ship continued to break up. Eventually there was so little left that the survivors dropped off one by one and sank beneath the waves. Williams, however, held on tight to his piece of the wreck until he was finally rescued on April 4 by a passing schooner, the *Coalition* of Quebec, on her way from

Barbados to Havre de Grace, Maryland. The exhausted but determined sailor had survived seven days exposed in the open ocean.

Meanwhile, William Kelly had been waiting for the *Express* at Saint John, New Brunswick, from March 28 with a cargo of timber for his ship's return to Liverpool. It was not until April 20 that he picked up a copy of the *Portland Evening Star* and read of the disaster that had befallen the *Express* and her sole survivor. To limit his liability, Kelly immediately recorded a protest before a notary at Saint John: "Fearing that the master of the said ship may be lost, and that the seaman so saved may be unable to make a protest." He swore on the "Holy Evangelists of Almighty God," and after recounting his knowledge of the voyage, protested against the "winds, seas, weathers, accidents and occurrences aforesaid, and against all losses or damages suffered or to be suffered."

Some five months later, on September 12, 1866, there was little consolation for William Kelly when he signed off on the 124 pounds, 9 shillings, and 6 pence total wages for the next-of-kin of the nineteen seamen who had disappeared with the *Express*. The man who had saved the *Belinda*'s crew at Scatarie in 1848 declared the final accounting to be true with the prudent, handwritten stipulation, "to the best of my knowledge and belief." He then signed his name where Captain Roland Savage would normally have signed, scratching out "Master" on the form and writing in "Owner." The immediacy of this moment, revealed in a twenty-first century photocopy of a 150-year-old bookkeeping record, caught me off guard. Viewing the handwritten proviso, the strike-out, and the correction made me feel that I was looking over Kelly's shoulder, hearing his pen scrape the paper.

It was as if I had witnessed his signature.

The story of the *Express* does not end here. The ship's nineteen "dripping sailors" would haunt William Kelly for the rest of his life, and they will reappear in this narrative.

## William Kelly's Acquisition of the *Merrie England*

The loss of the *Express* put Kelly in the market for a new ship. His continuing business and personal relationship with James Beazley made this possible. Although retired from the sea now, Kelly was still employed as shore manager for Beazley's Liverpool fleet. This job would have kept him busy overseeing the finances, cargoes, and crews for a large shipping company. Along with his other business ventures, Beazley was also a founder and managing director of the British Ship Owners' Company, an innovative trade group that he and others had formed in 1864 with capital of £2,000,000 to charter ships to other companies, including the Anchor Line; the American Line; the New Zealand Shipping Company; Shaw, Savill & Albion; and Cunard. The company not only chartered ships but built them too, and Kelly was likely in the thick of this venture—an enterprise that might also have motivated him to set about rebuilding his own embryonic fleet by acquiring a companion ship for the *Sterling*.

According to Bill Irish,[146] "Beazley made a sizable profit trading to East India and Australia [with the *Merrie England*] before disposing of her to William Kelly...in 1867"—"disposing" being the operative word here.

When she was built in 1856, the *Merrie England* had

been classed A1 at Lloyd's for ten years. By 1867, she was eleven years old and probably worse for wear. Indeed, on October 5, 1864, she was one of over 150 vessels that were lost or stranded during a devastating cyclone that swept over Calcutta. According to numerous news accounts of the disaster, the storm left the *Merrie England* "wrecked," "much damaged but afloat," or "aground, back-broken." She was repaired after this, but her days as a renowned passenger transport to the colonies were over. She was a tramp trader now, hauling dead-weight bulk cargoes like South Australian grain, North American timber, Chilean copper ore, and Peruvian guano—the kinds of heavy, potentially damaging cargoes that further accelerated her decline. Guano, for instance, was hard on a hold's ironwork and also decayed its wooden ceilings and planking.[147] This was the *Merrie England* that Kelly acquired in 1867.

The *Sterling* and the *Merrie England* were both active in the East Indian and South American trades in the 1860s, even running into each other from time to time as they crisscrossed the oceans. As well as furthering Kelly's mercantile pursuits, the two ships served as oceangoing incubators for his sons, who were swiftly following in his footsteps. Kelly's oldest son, John (whom we last encountered serving as an apprentice with his father on the *Express*), served as second mate on the *Sterling* from September 1864 to May 1867.[148] William Kelly Jr. also sailed on both ships as second and third mate. As teenage sailors, John Kelly and William Kelly Jr. rapidly learned the ropes and worked their way up the nautical chain of command thanks to the extraordinary opportunities offered by their father and his ships.

## Two Voyages of the Ship *Sterling*

The *Sterling* is continuously listed in the UK Lloyd's Register of Shipping with "W. Kelly" as owner from 1865 through 1876, with a string of masters including Hall (1865–1869), Wisnom (1870–1872), and Seabourne (1873–1876). Two surviving crew agreements provide some idea of the *Sterling*'s activities between 1868 and 1871. They also introduce two new master mariners with interesting stories to relate.

### Cardiff to the Seychelles, Bassein, and London: A Birth at Sea

The *Sterling* departed the Welsh port of Cardiff on July 1, 1868, bound for the Seychelles Islands in the Indian Ocean northeast of Madagascar under the command of thirty-nine-year-old Captain Hugh Wisnom of Broadisland, Antrim.[149] Wisnom, who had previously served as Kelly's first mate on the *Express* in 1862 to 1863, was accompanied by his wife, Jane, and a crew of sixteen seamen, including first mate Alexander Wilson and second mate Robert McAlpine.

The *Sterling* arrived at the Seychelles archipelago on October 23, 1868, probably at the colony's main port of Victoria. They spent a little over a month in the islands before departing on December 2 for Bassein (now Pathein), a major rice-milling and export center at the western edge of Burma's Ayeyarwady River delta. After arriving there in February 1869, Wisnom lost two of his crew to cholera. Seaman James Elmer of London (age 17) died on February 20, leaving just a small personal bag for delivery to the superintendent of shipping. The other casualty was the ship's carpenter, Isaac Groundwater (age 25) of Longhope,

Orkney, who died on March 1. He left two sea chests for disposition, which probably contained his tools. A twenty-four-year-old Portuguese seaman deserted on March 7, and sometime after his disappearance the *Sterling* too departed Bassein with three replacement crewmen to begin the long journey home.

Two months before their homecoming, a happy event occurred somewhere at sea. On June 27, 1869, Captain Wisnom's wife, Jane, gave birth to a son and, as required by the 282nd section of the Merchant Shipping Act of 1854, her husband dutifully entered this fact in the section of the crew agreement reserved for "Births, Marriages and Deaths that Have Occurred on Board during the Voyage." He did not enter a name for the child. Captain and Mrs. Wisnom must still have been pondering it. According to the entry, Jane Wisnom's maiden name was McAlpine, which leads me to wonder if she might have been the sister of the *Sterling*'s second mate, Robert McAlpine.[150] Hugh's handwritten record of the birth has a pronounced upward-veering slant, perhaps indicating his delight at the successful delivery of his son at sea.

When the *Sterling* finally sailed into Queenstown on August 30, 1869, she was met by William Kelly, who relieved Wisnom of command and took charge of the ship. The Wisnom family was discharged there, and Kelly took the *Sterling* on to London, depositing her at the recently opened Millwall Dock near the center of the Isle of Dogs on September 7.[151]

There is an epilogue to this event. The apple did not fall far from the tree (or the wave's trough far from its crest). The boy born on the *Sterling* followed in his father's footsteps, becoming a master mariner himself. John McLain

Wisnom received his certificate of competency as master (certificate no. 21,633) on September 12, 1892, at Belfast. In his application, he wrote that he had been born at sea on June 28, 1869. Captain John Wisnom might have mistakenly celebrated his birthday a day late throughout his life. His father clearly noted in the crew agreement that his son was born on June 27, not June 28.

## *Cardiff to Aden, Callao, Barbados, and London: An Attempted Homicide*

The *Sterling*'s next voyage was long, difficult, and confounded—a headache for William Kelly Sr. but a stroke of luck for William Kelly Jr.[152] The *Sterling* departed Cardiff on October 23, 1869, this time under the command of George Edward Teague (certificate no. 88,664), a thirty-six-year-old American from Bangor, Maine, who had replaced Hugh Wisnom as captain. According to the crew agreement, they sailed first to the island of Saint Vincent, Cape Verde, arriving there in late November and then moving on to the island of Brava, Cape Verde, in mid-December. Then there is a four-month gap in the record until May 1870 when the crew agreement shows them at Aden. Here there was a major shake-up in the crew. For some undisclosed reason, two mates and the boatswain were discharged, and Captain Teague was replaced on May 25 by forty-three-year-old Captain Clement Bowen (certificate no. 10,708).

Fortunately, Captain R. H. Davis, a twentieth-century authority on Belfast's merchant marine heritage, reveals the facts underlying the turmoil at Aden. Davis writes that "Captain Teague...on a passage out to Aden had some trouble on board which resulted in him being badly stabbed by a seaman in the face and neck....Captain Bowen, who had sailed with Captain Kelly as mate of the Merrie England, was sent out to Aden to take charge and Captain Teague came home."[153] This incident accounts for the four-month silence between Cape Verde and Aden. Somehow word got back to Kelly that Teague was in trouble and would have to be replaced. Accordingly, Kelly recalled Teague and arranged for Bowen, an experienced seaman with whom he had sailed in the past, to take command of the ship. The following article provides a few additional details.

> ATTEMPTED MURDER ON THE HIGH SEAS.—
> The Mary, steamship, from Algoa Bay, bound to London, put into Dartmouth harbor, on Tuesday, having on board three men—one of whom was handed over to the authorities on a charge of attempted murder, the other two being witnesses in the case. It appears that the barque Sterling of Liverpool left Cardiff for Aden, and shortly after leaving that port one of the crew, named William Boyle, from Ireland, made an attempt on the captain's life, and stabbed him in the neck. The vessel then put into Cape Vincent, one of the Cape de Verde Islands, where the Mary, s.s., arrived for a supply of coal. The British consul handed the men over to the captain of the Mary, requesting him to pass them over to the authorities at the first port he made. At the time of the Mary's leaving St. Vincent the captain of the Sterling was doing well, and hope was entertained of his recovery.[154]

The attack on Teague is not documented in the crew agreement, which simply records that three seamen were discharged at Saint Vincent on November 24, 1869, "by order of the British Consul." These men were William Boyle, a twenty-three-year-old able-bodied seaman from Donegal, along with two witnesses: second mate A. Jones and another seaman named George Wilkinson. "By order of the British Consul" is not a common cause for leaving a ship and indicates official involvement in their discharge; it appears the three seamen had indeed been taken into custody.

A further digression regarding Captain George Teague involves an incident that occurred six years prior to the violent attack upon him at Cape Verde. The Union blockade of Southern ports at the beginning of the American Civil War only intensified when the fledgling Confederate Navy began bringing the war to the Union at sea. In this regard, Captain Teague of the *Sterling* played a minor role in a marginal Civil War skirmish at sea near Cape Charles, Virginia. In June 1863, when Teague was master of the schooner *Kate Stewart*, he happened upon an altercation involving three vessels with one ship in flames. A Confederate privateer, the CSS *Clarence,* under the command of Lt. Charles Read, had seized two Union vessels, the barque *Tacony* and the schooner *M. A. Schindler*. Lt. Read had set the *M. A. Schindler* ablaze and was in process of transferring his own crew to the *Tacony*, which he had assessed to be a better ship than the *Clarence*.

Drawn by the burning *M. A. Schindler*, an unsuspecting Teague sailed the *Kate Stewart* into the melee to offer assistance. The audacious Lt. Read ordered the schooner to surrender, and Teague complied (under the misconception that the Confederate raider was well armed when she was, in fact, equipped only with "Quaker guns," wooden logs painted black, designed to deceive). Read boarded Teague's schooner with a view to setting her alight too, until he discovered that her passengers included twenty women. Finding now that he had more prisoners than crew, Read transferred all of his prisoners to the *Kate Stewart* and allowed Teague to sail on with them. Cunningly, Read also announced within Teague's hearing that a large Confederate fleet was on its way to attack the eastern United States. This statement was just a ruse intended to create panic among Union authorities.

Sure enough, when the *Kate Stewart* arrived in New Jersey, Teague dutifully passed Read's "intelligence" on to the powers that be. Within days, thirty-eight armed Union ships were combing the eastern seaboard looking for the CSS *Clarence*—a ship that no longer existed. Read had burned the *Clarence* after transferring his crew to the *Tacony*. The Confederate raider would go on to capture or sink fourteen Union vessels as the Civil War roiled on.[155]

Six years later, the unfortunate George Teague would command William Kelly's *Sterling* on another troubled voyage when a crewman would attempt to murder him. Teague's somewhat erratic seafaring career appears to have been as unpredictable as the sea itself.

With Clement Bowen still in command, the *Sterling* departed Aden toward the end of May 1870. Her final port of call was 8,500 miles away at Callao, Peru, where she lingered for only a week in mid-October 1870 before sailing north to the Guañape Islands, an island group off the north coast of Peru that attracted seamen for only one reason. Like the Chincha Islands visited by William Kelly in 1847, Guañape was a rich guano-harvesting ground. Here there was a Kelly reunion of sorts as the *Sterling* exchanged signals with the *Merrie England*, which was there on a similar undertaking.

There was also a curious exchange of personnel at Guañape on January 11, 1871. Able-bodied seaman Charles Graeber (age 19) transferred from the *Sterling* to the *Merrie England*, and third mate William Kelly Jr. (also age 19) moved from the *Merrie England* to the *Sterling*. Managing owner William Kelly Sr. was shifting the chess pieces within his tiny fleet, bulking up the problematic *Sterling* with a known quantity—his youngest son—to help bring his ship home safely.

The *Sterling* left Guañape shortly after these personnel transfers. She sailed southward, rounded Cape Horn without incident, headed north to Barbados for a spell (June–July 1871) and then sailed northeast direct to the English Channel, arriving at London on October 7, 1871, after a precarious and protracted voyage of just under two years.

As fate would have it, assigning William Kelly Jr. to the *Sterling* was an auspicious move for the young seaman. The other shoe was about to drop. The *Merrie England* would not make it around Cape Horn, let alone back to the United Kingdom—much to the dismay and consternation of the ship's managing owner in Belfast, William Kelly Sr.

## The Sinking of the *Merrie England*

To backtrack and retrace the *Merrie England*'s movements prior to her arrival at Guañape, the old ship had been well on her way to accomplishing a complete circumnavigation of the globe when she called in at the islands to load guano.[156] She had departed Cardiff for Japan on January 22, 1870, under the command of Captain Robert McMahon of Belfast (age 30, certificate no. 27,517) with John Vines Seabourne (age 28, certificate no. 81,525) as first mate, Archibald Darroch (age 22, certificate no. 83,010) as second mate, William Kelly Jr. (age 18) as third mate, and seventeen additional crewmen. They had sailed east from the Cape of Good Hope, arriving at Yokohama on July 12 and Kanagawa on July 15. Continuing east across the Pacific, they had arrived at Callao, Peru, on November 1 (about two weeks after the *Sterling*) and had then followed her sister ship north to the Guañape Islands, arriving there on January 11, 1871, the same day as the crew exchange that transferred William Kelly Jr. from the *Merrie England* to the *Sterling*. Thomas Webb (age 35), a seaman already aboard the *Merrie England*, replaced Kelly as third mate on the older ship.

The *Merrie England* got away from Guañape about January 24, sailing south to the Chincha Islands to top up her hold with more nitrates. Then she headed south for Cape Horn and home. Unfortunately, while off the coast of Chile before they had even reached the Horn, John Seabourne's log entries reveal that the *Merrie England* was laboring with water in the hold.

On Sunday March 5, 1871, Seabourne noted that the ship was experiencing moderate winds with fair weather and heavy southwest swells. However, the pumps had been running continuously, and the men were exhausted. That evening the crew went aft and asked permission to take to the boats, as their limbs were so sore that they could no longer operate the pumps. Captain McMahon refused. The heavy swells continued past midnight with otherwise clear and pleasant weather. The *Merrie England* made sixty-nine miles that day despite her deteriorating condition.

The pumps were still operating on Monday morning, and by evening the "ship was rolling and straining badly, making a deal more water."[157] At midnight a moderate breeze was blowing with constant rain; as night wore on, the wind backed to the northeast. Gamely they sailed on, making 106 miles that day.

On Tuesday morning, a passing barque appeared, and the crew hoisted a distress signal to bring her close. McMahon hove the *Merrie England* to at 1:15 p.m.; they put two boats overboard and abandoned ship with water in the hold at latitude 41°S, longitude 83°W (approximately 430 nautical miles off the Lagos Region of Chile). By then it was blowing a fresh gale with hard squalls and a short high sea, making it impossible for the crew to save anything but themselves. Fifteen years of hard duty at sea, a battering by the Calcutta cyclone of 1864, and one too many corrosive guano expeditions had finally caught up with the *Merrie England*. There was only one direction for her to go, and that was down.

Fortunately, the French barque *Amiral Jurien de la Gravière* rescued the *Merrie England*'s crew and deposited them safely at Valparaíso, Chile, on Saturday, March 11, 1871. This was approximately 650 nautical miles northeast of where they had abandoned ship. Here they were discharged after receiving from McMahon, by bills on William

Kelly, the full balance of wages owed them, as witnessed by the acting British consul.

### SHIPPING DISASTERS.
### LOSS OF THE MERRIE ENGLAND.

We learn by telegram from New York of the loss of the well-known Liverpool ship Merrie England, while on a voyage from the Chinchas Islands for Falmouth for orders, with a cargo of guano. She was abandoned off the coast of South America, near Cape Horn, and from the news of the loss coming from New York it is conjectured that part or all of the crew have been landed on the West Coast. The Merrie England had been a regular Liverpool trader for many years, having since she was built in Waterford in 1856, for Mr. Beazley, of this port, traded constantly between the East Indies, Australia, and Liverpool. Some time ago she was sold to a Mr. Kelly, of Liverpool, and was, we understand, his property when she was lost. She was a very fine vessel of 1,045 tons register, and a great favourite with passengers.[158]

Much like Kelly's previous horrible year of a decade earlier (1861), when the *Mary Carson*, the *Miles Barton,* and the *Hilton* were all lost, the year 1871 was off to a bad start. Regrettably, in just a few months, events would take an even nastier turn for William Kelly's wife. Martha's younger brother in New Orleans was about to confront the unthinkable on a hot summer's day in a city embroiled in a carnival of crime where murder was always just a fidgety trigger finger away.

## A Tragedy in New Orleans

In the summer of 1871, New Orleans was still grappling with the chaos and confusion provoked by post–Civil War Reconstruction. In the midst of this turmoil, Martha Kelly's younger brother, Sam Rainey, was himself coping with considerable personal distress.[159] The death of his wife, Maria, with child in 1869 had left him a widower and single parent supporting three children: Emma (age 13), William (age 11), and Eva (age 6). The child Maria was carrying when she died had not survived.

An independent cotton commissioner, Sam was a resourceful fellow who was continuously on the prowl for lucrative business ventures. Six years earlier, in happier times, Sam had received US Letters Patent No. 51,215 (dated November 28, 1865) for an ingenious folding nursery chair that he had designed and built for his son. He had also floated a plan to import Chinese immigrant laborers to New Orleans to ease the city's postwar labor shortages.[160] This was perhaps a local variation on the scheme that William Kelly had participated in when he transported indentured Indian laborers to Demerara a decade earlier. Kelly had visited New Orleans immediately after this trip and might have planted this immigrant labor scheme in Sam's fertile imagination. Sam held his seafaring brother-in-law in high esteem. Indeed, he had named his son after him: William Kelly Rainey.

Now, in the stifling summer of 1871, Sam was embroiled in a business arrangement run amok. In 1869, he had entered into a partnership with two friends and fellow Irishmen from County Antrim, brothers William and John Boyd. He had cosigned a loan with them to finance a crop of rice they had planted in Bayou Lafourche, south of New Orleans. With Sam distracted by the death of his wife, the Boyd brothers wrapped up their project, pocketed the money, and proceeded to roll every penny of it into their next venture—renting a cotton press in New Orleans—with no accommodation made with Sam Rainey. The Boyd brothers were hoping to emulate their uncle, Colonel Sam Boyd, the man William Kelly had brought to New Orleans as a boy on the *Ambassador* in 1840. This young lad was now a colonel (ex-Confederate army), very wealthy, and well on his way to cornering the lucrative cotton compression market in New Orleans. The Boyd brothers wanted a piece of this action.

Meanwhile, the note that Sam had cosigned with the brothers was coming due, and he had heard nothing from them. Fortunately, Sam had landed a job as head bookkeeper at the New Orleans National Bank at 54 Camp Street. This provided a steady income for him and his children, but he was still bitter about how the Boyds had treated him. He went about the city accusing them of being the damndest thieves in New Orleans, an accusation that was undermining the Boyds' plan to acquire their own cotton press. The feud between the men festered for months, growing daily more acrimonious until, on the hot and muggy morning of July 6, 1871, the Boyds made their way to the New Orleans National Bank and confronted Sam at his desk. After exchanging a few terse words, William Boyd shot Samuel Rainey dead in broad daylight at the height of the business day with a crowd of stunned citizen-witnesses looking on. When Boyd was arrested within minutes outside the bank, he obstinately claimed he had done it to vindicate his character.

The first Boyd trial was halted when one juror was found to be a wanted man himself, indicted for attempted murder in a neighboring parish. Then a second juror was discovered to be a convicted murderer who might (or might not) have been pardoned by New Orleans's military governor during the Civil War. The public was so perplexed by this ballyhoo over the jury that they lost sight of the original purpose of the trial. A key witness for both the prosecution and the defense—an emotionally conflicted man named Richard Mason Pasteur, who was himself teetering on the brink of madness—fled the city by train for Missouri, further confounding the trial.

Another force conspiring against justice for William and John Boyd and retribution for Sam was the powerful legal team representing the Boyds. This judicial juggernaut, probably financed by Colonel Sam Boyd, included Thomas Jenkins Semmes, who was ex-attorney general of Louisiana, ex-senator of Louisiana in the Confederate Congress, and a cousin of the Confederate naval hero Raphael Semmes. The Boyd brothers' legal counsel also included Henry C. Castellanos, a well-known criminal lawyer, man-about-town, and subsequently the author of *New Orleans as It Was*, an enduring little book that is still in print today. Finally, there was Alcé Aloysius Atocha, a rising legal luminary, ex-judge advocate, and provost court judge who was afterward appointed judge of the Superior Criminal Court of the parish of Orleans.

In the subsequent retrial of the Boyd case, much to the prosecutor's and the public's dismay, the jury acquitted the brothers. The trial judge, a garrulous Kentuckian named Edmund Abell who had been an active player in New Orleans legal and political circles for a quarter of a century, angrily declared the decision to be "the most illegal verdict rendered by any jury in some time."[161] There were suspicions of jury tampering. Three city dailies clamored for an overhaul of the criminal justice system in New Orleans, but justice and retribution were no longer on the public agenda; they had blown away like yesterday's newspapers in the street.

## A Letter to Mr. James Graham

Back in Antrim, Captain William Kelly was closely following the events that had devastated his wife's family. He and Martha had recently moved to a fine house called Bella Vista on the Antrim Road just outside Belfast. Sitting at his desk there on July 28, 1871, he penned a letter to his friend James Graham of Newpark, Antrim, expounding on his view of the astonishing tragedy that had engulfed his wife's family in New Orleans.[162]

> Bella Vista
> July 28th 1871
>
> My dear Mr. Graham:
> Since I last had the pleasure of seeing you, you have had a great bereavement in losing your dear wife. I assure you I deeply sympathize with you. And although you will know that it was impossible she could last long still when the blow came it came severe and heavy—You have the great consolation to know, she was well prepared for the great change. Would to God I could express myself in the same terms I heard her make use of when she was in Liverpool with us.

I returned some time ago from Liverpool, London and Holland, when I had been in a fruitless search after a ship to replace the one I have lately lost. It has been a serious loss to me, as ships have advanced in price, 25 to 30 per cent above what they were 12 months ago. This does not arise so much from the freights being so high but simply since iron ships and steamers have been so general. The builders in North America have quit building to a great extent, and as many ships are daily lost, it takes a considerable number to be built to make up for losses. I am sorry to say that Mrs. K is not well by any means, but time that great restorer of troubled mind will soon bring her round again.

You recollect or have heard of Tatty Boyd the lame schoolmaster who used to teach at Dunmaul. When I commanded the Ambassador twenty-eight years ago, I took out a boy, a son of Jack Boyd's, he was with Gwynn of Antrim. James Rainey took him into his house and in his service he is now a rich man. Some years ago, say 15 years, two sons of Tatty's went out, poor Sam Rainey, Mrs. K's younger brother, interested himself with the younger a good deal. Only last year I heard Johnny Stewart in Bangor relate how Sam, having heard that William Boyd was in great straits, having married very imprudently and being cast off by Sam Boyd. He and J. Stewart went on a Sunday afternoon, hunted him up, and found this Willy Boyd, and his wife in a most wretched hovel—his wife just confined—and not a second chair in the solitary chamber they occupied. They were in darkness, had not even a candle, poor Sam rushed out and soon returned bearing supplies—he paid his grocer's bill and also his butcher's bill for over 6 months, till he got him a situation.

Sam [Rainey] had but little money when the war was over. Three years ago Sam, whom I am told had about $5,000, and the two Boyds entered into a co-partnership to rent an old sugar plantation, and take a crop of rice off it. The Boyds had not their share of cash requisite, but gave their notes at long dates, which were endorsed by Sam and cashed. When the rice was being reaped and getting sent to market poor Sam was obliged to bring his sick wife to town, she lingered there a week or two and died leaving 3 children behind.

On Sam's return to the Plantation all was cleared off, and no explanation given. Sam walked about in vain looking for a situation, and about 6 or 8 months ago only got the situation of Head Book Keeper in the National Bank, a position he was well qualified to fill. These notes were in the meantime coming round to maturity and Sam was telling me he expected nothing else but the Boyds would not pay a cent of it if they could help it. It turned out as anticipated and he was not silent on the subject and you may observe by the printed matter I enclose that they had rented the Merchants Press. Now this fact shows that they must be each of them possessed of at least fifteen thousand dollars each to enable them to carry out such an undertaking. Had they done what was right and honest, the dreadful end would never have happened. Poor fellow to be shot down like a dog at his desk, it is dreadful to think.

As poor James his brother remarks in his letter, "What an awful event to think of his being ushered into eternity, without having given any evidence of faith in the Saviour, through whom alone we can be saved. God's judgments are upon us we ought to learn that true wisdom, by what having an interest in Christ we may be Saved."

The Murderer confesses his guilt, and in fact seems to glory in it. He done it he says to "vindicate his character." If he had tried to prove that Sam Rainey was a Liar, it would have been a far greater proof of his being a Gentleman, as he calls himself. I don't believe a hair of his head will fall for his great crime; the state of society is such in that land that he will have plenty of admirers.

I had a very high opinion of poor Sam Rainey. He was strictly honest, and was possessed of high principles. His ideas of honesty were, as I told him, completely out of place in the community among which he lived. They were bad enough in my time but I believe they are much worse now.

Hoping that this will find you well, I am Dear Sir truly yours,
William Kelly

Quite apart from the fascinating Rainey-Boyd backstory (as well as Kelly's opinion about the murder in New Orleans), this letter also considers the broader ramifications of the tragedy. Poor Martha—"Mrs. K"—was understandably shattered by the murder of her younger brother, but Kelly stoically opines that "time that great restorer of troubled mind will soon bring her round again." He also touches on the other recent calamity in their lives—the loss of the *Merrie England* four months earlier—and his fruitless search to replace his ship in the face of high prices, the decline of wooden vessels in the age of iron ships and steamers, and the reduced output of the North American shipyards that had built so many vessels in the past.

Kelly displays extraordinary prescience in his confident prediction that not a hair of William Boyd's head would fall for his great crime. He suspected that the tattered social fabric of the Reconstruction era in New Orleans would likely produce a travesty of justice, and the subsequent courtroom shenanigans proved him right.

After their acquittal, the Boyd brothers relocated to Galveston, Texas. There William Boyd served for two years as a city alderman. He became a pillar of the community and a prominent member of the Knights of Pythias, a benevolent men's organization, ironically in his case, dedicated to honor, friendship, and the chivalrous protection of defenseless women and orphaned children. He was a founding member of the Galveston Rowing Club and supported his large family of four boys and four girls, first as a cotton weigher, then as a builder. He eventually moved to Houston, where his construction company paved the city streets for the first time. He also built and operated one of Houston's first horse-powered street railway systems.

Not to be outdone, William Boyd's brother John (who had also taken a shot at Sam in the bank but missed) received numerous patents for a portable "house with no nails" that was displayed in the Texas exhibit at the World's Industrial and Cotton Centennial Exposition held in New Orleans in 1884-85.

When word of the Boyd brothers' attack on Samuel Rainey followed them to Texas, the murder was likely chalked up to youthful indiscretion and shrugged off with a knowing wink, just as William Kelly's letter predicted.

## Revisiting the *Sterling*

While the Boyd trials were playing out in New Orleans, Kelly's ship *Sterling*, still under the command of Clement Bowen, departed from London on November 16, 1871, on a globe-girdling voyage to Uruguay (January–February 1872) and across the Pacific to Burma (May–June 1872), returning to Liverpool on December 1, 1872.[163]

On her next voyage, Kelly replaced Bowen with Captain John Vines Seabourne of King Stanley, Gloucestershire. Seabourne had previously served as first mate under Captain Robert McMahon on the *Merrie England*'s final voyage. Kelly moved officers and crew around his small fleet, providing opportunities for advancement not only for his sons but also for other seamen who proved their worth in his employ.

The *Sterling* next departed Liverpool on January 4, 1873, bound for Valparaíso, Chile (where Seabourne and the rest of the *Merrie England*'s crew had been dropped off after abandoning the ship in 1871). The *Sterling* arrived there in May 1873, spent the summer cruising about Iquique in northern Chile and Callao, Peru, and then departed for home in October, arriving back in Falmouth in early March 1874 and Dunkirk on March 21, 1874.[164]

The *Sterling* continued under Kelly's ownership until about 1876—the last year the ship is listed in the US Lloyd's Register of Shipping with Kelly as her owner. I know that the *Sterling* meant a great deal to Kelly because he commissioned an oil painting of the ship (painter unknown), which went to Kelly's son John by Martha's will in 1884. The ultimate fate of the painting is unknown.

The fate of the ship *Sterling* is also a mystery. The *Liverpool Mercury* of July 18, 1877, reported that "the American barque Sterling dragged her anchors at Salt Pond on the 19th June, drifted on shore, and broke up in a few hours, the beach being strewn with driftwood for a considerable distance in the neighborhood." Salt Pond was on the coast of what is now Ghana, virtually an east-west coastline. A strong southerly gale could have driven the ship onto the beach. However, this might not have been Kelly's *Sterling*. The *Portland Daily Press* of July 20, 1877, reprinted a clarifying statement (datelined London, July 19) that might be useful in any future investigation into the fate of William Kelly's *Sterling*: "It was the American bark Sterling, Captain Tufts, last reported at Accra that was wrecked June 19th at Salt Pond, not the ship Sterling." If the Salt Pond casualty was not Kelly's *Sterling*, perhaps the "ship *Sterling*" referenced here was his ship and still afloat somewhere.

## William Kelly's Acquisition of the *Princess Alexandra*

As a replacement for the *Merrie England*, William Kelly purchased the ship *Princess Alexandra* (Official Number 46141) on January 12, 1872. Built in 1863 at Saint John, New Brunswick, by brothers Francis and Joseph Ruddock, the ship was a 1,294-ton vessel with a female figurehead, two full decks, and a half poop steering deck. The ship was named after Princess Alexandra of Denmark, who had married Queen Victoria's son and heir, Albert Edward, in 1863. The vessel measured 188 feet long × 39 feet beam × 24 feet depth of hold.

William Kelly's ownership of the *Princess Alexandra* is complicated by the fact that she was previously commanded by Charles William Kelley of Yarmouth, Nova Scotia, from 1863 to 1868. This Charles Kelley is not related to William Kelly of Antrim as far as I know. In the 1860s the ship was variously owned by Lamport & Holt of Liverpool and her builders, F. & J. Ruddock of Saint John. The following three masters followed Captain Charles Kelley: Edward James Shaw of Falmouth, Nova Scotia (1868–1869); John Williams of Wales (1870–1871); and John Alfred Barrett of Devon (1871). Under these men, she sailed primarily as a timber ship out of Belfast.[165]

In 1872 familiar Antrim surnames begin to appear among the ranks of the *Princess Alexandra*'s masters including Robert McMahon, ex-*Merrie England* (1872–1873); Samuel Molyneux (1872–1873); Archibald Darroch, ex-*Merrie England* (1872–1873); William Kelly Jr., ex-*Sterling* and ex-*Merrie England* (1875–1877); and Nathan Kellett (1877). These names indicate that this is the era when William Kelly of Belfast owned the *Princess Alexandra*. There is also a noticeable shift in the ship's sphere of activities from North American timber operations to the Indian, Australian, South American, and Chincha Islands trades.

The *Princess Alexandra* was primarily associated with William Kelly Jr. during the years of his father's ownership in the 1870s. It does not appear that William Kelly Sr. ever sailed her as master on a major voyage, but his youngest son saw plenty of onboard service as boatswain, third mate, second mate, and first mate between 1872 and 1875—and as her master (without credentials) between 1875 and 1877. The crew agreement and partial log of one voyage in the early 1870s cast some light on an eventful trip when William Kelly Jr. learned some valuable lessons about ship and crew management.

Figure 17: The ship *Princess Alexandra*, watercolor on paper, approximately 20" × 30", artist unknown, date unknown. Image credit: David and Anne Burton, Wolfville, Nova Scotia.

In Figure 17, the ship *Princess Alexandra* flies the Red Ensign at her stern. Popularly known as the "Red Duster," this was the standard flag flown by British merchant ships in the nineteenth century. The five multicolored flags flying from the ship's mizzen topgallant mast are signal flags based on Marryat's Commercial Code of Signals. The top flag is the third distinguishing pennant, and the four flags below it represent the numbers 8375, which signified the *Princess Alexandra* in Marryat's code.[166]

## Cardiff to Rio, Calcutta, Bombay, and Dundee: An Inauspicious Voyage

The *Princess Alexandra* departed Cardiff for Rio de Janeiro on January 12, 1872, under Captain Robert McMahon, the same master who had presided over the demise of the *Merrie England* a year earlier. The ship's first mate was Archibald Darroch, another veteran of the *Merrie England*. The crew list records William Kelly Jr. as having previously served on the *Sterling*. His name is penciled in as "boatswain" with a line drawn through "second mate." In the official log, however, he is consistently described as "second mate."[167]

Problems with a couple of crewmen emerged in the South Atlantic on their way to Rio de Janeiro. On Wednesday, February 14, a month after leaving Cardiff Bay, McMahon, Darroch, and Kelly cosigned the following entry in the ship's log: "On Tuesday Charles Miller & Wm. Connery commenced beating Frederick Malmbury, striking him with marlin spike & threatening to rip him open with a knife. When mate interfered Miller wounded him with marlin spike & has at a former time threatened to take his life."

The three ship's officers documented another incident on March 20 at 5:30 p.m. at Rio de Janeiro: "Charles Miller noisy and very insolent towards the officers, doing all he can to insult the officers, and when I call him down, he spoke in a very insolent manner to me & afterwards [said] he would cut the mate's stuffen' out of him."

Needless to say, Miller and Connery were both discharged on March 22 at Rio de Janeiro. Miller had received "middling" grades for general conduct and ability in seamanship in the ship's log; Connery received "middling" for conduct and "good" for ability. (Along with the majority of the crew, William Kelly Jr. was rated "very good" in both categories.)

The *Princess Alexandra* departed Rio on May 3, 1872, and went on to Calcutta, where she remained for about a month and a half. The ship's departure from Calcutta and onward passage to Bombay would not be an easy journey. On August 30, three days after departing, Henrik (Henry) Kullman, a twenty-one-year-old seaman from Finland, fell overboard while working on the bowsprit and drowned in the Hooghly River.

Then, on September 11, mates Darroch and Kelly made another grim entry in the ship's log off Chennai in the Bay of Bengal: "At 7:30 a.m. Captain Robert McMahon died from the effects of a Paralytic Stroke received on the 10th at 4 p.m. Previous to his death he had been ill with jaundice but was recovering. During his illness he prescribed for himself." The unfortunate McMahon was only thirty-two years old.

Now it would be up to First Mate Darroch and Second Mate Kelly to get the *Princess Alexandra* through to Bombay. Two days later, in the middle of the Bay of Bengal, twenty-year-old seaman Charles Engberg, another Finn, died from diarrheal disease (which to this day still kills four to six million people a year globally). The crew agreement states that Engberg left behind "2 singlets, 4 jackets, 3 prs trousers, 3 shirts, 1 Gurnsey frock, 2 jumpers, 1 table cloth, 2 mufflers, 3 prs socks, 1 pr boots, 1 pocket book, 1 chest, 1 canvas bag and 1 hat, all very old."

When the *Princess Alexandra* dropped anchor at Bombay in early December, Darroch and Kelly learned that

William Kelly Sr. had arranged for Captain Samuel Molyneux of the ship *Goshawk* to take charge of the *Princess Alexandra* for the return trip to Calcutta and subsequent passage home. The twenty-five-year-old Molyneux came aboard on December 7. He immediately took the ship from Bombay back to Calcutta, where they completed their business in a week and departed for the United Kingdom on January 31, 1873.

The Bay of Bengal would dampen the crew's spirits with one more adverse turn of events. On April 6, while still in Indian waters, Molyneux noted in the ship's log that August Segren, a twenty-five-year-old Swedish seaman, was sick with heart disease and "would be of little use for the remainder of the voyage." On May 7 at 2:45 a.m., after they had rounded the Cape of Good Hope and were beating northward, Segren's heart gave out. The young Swede was the last of four crew members, including the ship's captain, to be consigned to the waves during this ill-fated voyage.

The *Princess Alexandra* arrived at Dundee, Scotland, on April 16, 1873. Mates Archibald Darroch and William Kelly Jr. were probably grateful that, with the expulsion of Miller and Connery at Rio, at least no one had been murdered on their watch. Both mates and Captain Molyneux likely received the warm thanks of William Kelly Sr. for bringing his ship and most of his crew safely home through a welter of challenging circumstances.

CHAPTER SEVEN

# Standing Over

(1873–1877)

> STAND OVER: A maritime term meaning to leave one shore and sail towards another.
>
> *The Shorter Oxford English Dictionary*

Green's 1870 Directory of Liverpool and Birkenhead lists Captain William Kelly as the owner of two houses at numbers 18 and 35 Upper Parliament Street, Toxteth, Liverpool. Kelly appears to have retired, a wealthy man of property, sometime in the early 1870s.

Returning to the land of his birth, he moved first to a house grandly named Bella Vista in the rapidly developing north end of Belfast[168] (possibly near Cave Hill/Greencastle Park[169]). An 1877 real estate listing describes the house as "beautifully situated on the Antrim Road commanding a full view of Belfast Lough and surrounding scenery and within 15 minutes of the tram cars." The house had two reception rooms, five or six bedrooms, and servants' and other necessary apartments with hot and cold running water. The property included a substantial yard with a two-stall stable and coach house, a well-stocked garden and grounds, and an adjoining acre and a quarter of grazing land.[170]

Bella Vista might have been located close to where Old Cavehill Road and the Antrim Road intersect, in the neighborhood of Blessed Trinity College today (previously Saint Patrick's College Bearnageeha). As a named property, the house was almost certainly an imposing place that might have put a strain on Kelly's finances, especially after his loss of the *Merrie England* and acquisition of the *Princess Alexandra* in 1871.

Kelly's son-in-law John Moore and daughter Fanny took over Bella Vista in the summer of 1874 when William and Martha moved to more modest accommodations at 14 Abercorn Terrace (now Brookvale Avenue). This property was a good-sized terrace house with three floors off the Antrim Road. It stood a mile or so closer to town in another rapidly developing suburb of the city. Abercorn Terrace was William's primary residence in Belfast until sometime in 1876, when he and Martha moved just a few hundred yards northeast into 6 Richmond Crescent, now part of the Antrim Road.

Figure 18: William Kelly's home at 6 Richmond Cres., Belfast.
It is likely the center house with two white bays flanking the door.
Image credit: Dr. Bob Foy, 2013.

## Mr. Plimsoll's Shipping Bill

Despite his health issues, William Kelly's retirement years were wholeheartedly active and vigorous. He remained a well-known master mariner and the managing owner of two ships, the *Sterling* and the *Princess Alexandra*. He remained a close associate and friend of James Beazley, as well as a respected member of the Liverpool and Belfast shipping communities. As such, he was also an active lobbyist for ship owners' interests. This understandable proclivity brought him, along with many like-minded businessmen and politicians, into disagreement with a fascinating man who was hailed by the press as "the seaman's friend." This was the inimitable Mr. Samuel Plimsoll (1824–1898), the Liberal Member of Parliament for Derby.

Plimsoll was an ardent campaigner against unseaworthy merchant vessels, those overloaded and often equally overinsured "coffin ships" in which some unscrupulous ship owners risked the lives of their crews for quick financial gain. In 1873 he published an influential book, *Our Seamen: An Appeal*, which shocked the public with documentary evidence about the scale of the problem. Approximately one thousand sailors a year were drowning off the coasts of England, with many deaths attributable to unseaworthy ships.[171]

As part of this campaign, Plimsoll provided a free copy of his book to every Member of Parliament. Of course, at that time a large number of these men were ship owners themselves. Probably even a larger number owed their seats to the backing of wealthy ship owners in their home districts. Those who opposed Plimsoll's initiative to improve the seaman's lot believed government should not restrict the freedom of ship owners to run their businesses as they saw fit. For this reason, Plimsoll's whistleblowing generally met stony walls of silence in the halls of Westminster. However, in 1873 he finally succeeded in getting a Royal Commission appointed to look into the matter. A draft Merchant Shipping Bill addressing his concerns was read in the House of Commons later that year.

This is where I caught a fleeting "glimpse" of William Kelly in a newspaper clipping where his name appears among a deputation of Belfast ship owners who were meeting with their Members of Parliament to discuss Plimsoll's bill.[172] The meeting was polite, but the businessmen's lack of enthusiasm for the bill as written is all too evident. They expressed their sympathy with the intention of preventing casualties and saving lives and property at sea, but "they did not think the Bill...was calculated to do much in these respects, while, if enacted, it would be very detrimental to British mercantile interests...and would be very unfair to ship owners....The disorganization of the merchant shipping trade which would follow from the licensing system proposed was shown to be disastrous. The difficulty of establishing the load-line scale of the Bill was fully explained, and the deputation very earnestly impressed on both members (by whom they were cordially received) the importance of deferring legislation...till after the report [of] the Royal Commission."

Plimsoll fought hard against this rising tide of opposition and eventually succeeded in securing safer working conditions for Britain's sailors. In 1875 Prime Minister Benjamin Disraeli first threw his support behind the new Merchant Shipping Bill but then caved in to the opposition, whereupon Plimsoll accused his opponents of villainy. He even shook his fist in the face of the Speaker, for which he was expelled from the House, until he eventually relented and apologized. This incident culminated in the 1876 passage of the Unseaworthy Vessels Bill, which, among other things, required lines to be painted on the sides of ships to show their maximum loading point. These lines came to be known as the Plimsoll marks (or lines).[173] They were the "load lines" Kelly and the other Belfast ship owners complained about in 1873. Once instituted, these lines probably saved many lives by preventing the overloading of vessels—although nothing is straightforward in the legislation of human activity. Unfortunately, the 1876 act allowed ship owners to paint the lines wherever they wanted on the sides of their ships. Some defiantly and nonsensically painted the lines on their steamship funnels, where they served no purpose at all. It was not until 1890 that the Board of Trade applied the regulations as Plimsoll had intended them.[174]

This small episode in William Kelly's life begs the question: Was Kelly a coffin ship owner? Two of his ships, the *Express* and the *Merrie England*, foundered at sea during a time of rising national concern about heavy ship losses due to overloading and shoddy maintenance. Plimsoll's campaign for improved safety at sea addressed a very real need, and sailors and the public at large enthusiastically supported his legislative efforts. Kelly, on the other hand, appears to have aligned himself with the cadre of wealthy ship owners who did everything in their considerable power to halt Plimsoll's well-intentioned and popular call for safer ships.

Despite these problematic appearances, I have found no evidence that William Kelly was an unscrupulous ship owner. After all, the *Express* sank while carrying sand ballast as a direct result of encountering gales and a hurricane after six months at sea. She was a twelve-year-old ship nearing the end of her useful life. Likewise, the *Merrie England* was a fifteen-year-old ship and fifteen months into a circumnavigation of the globe when she sank approaching Cape Horn during her return passage to the United Kingdom. Carrying a load of guano in her hold, the ship encountered heavy swells, hard squalls, and high winds, causing her to spring a leak that her pumps could not contain. If any fault attaches to Kelly for the foundering of these ships, his attention to their maintenance and the upkeep of their equipment might be worthy of consideration, but even these are impossible to prove without a deeper understanding of the norms of upkeep and maintenance for older merchant vessels at this time. In any event, these possible shortcomings pale in comparison with the act of deliberately overloading and over insuring a ship, and sacrificing her passengers and crew for financial gain—the true touchstone of the nineteenth-century coffin ship.

Kelly threw in his chips with the owners because he shared their interest in close and careful scrutiny of Plimsoll's shipping bill before it became the law of the sea. He was a cautious man, probably with a conservative bent. His career as seaman, mate, master, and managing owner of ships at sea made him leery of rushing legislation into law without first considering all its ramifications for the shipping industry at large and everyone involved.

Kelly's own officers and seamen cast the greatest vote of confidence in the man as a conscientious ship's master and managing owner. His crews teem with men who signed up to sail with him more than once—John Peterson, Henry Green, Thomas Dodd, Hugh Wisnom, James Annandale, Clement Bowen, Robert McMahon, Nathan Kellett, and Archibald Darroch, to name just a few.

The career of Captain John Vines Seabourne reflects especially well on Kelly as a managing owner. After serving as first mate on the *Merrie England* in 1871, Seabourne went on to command Kelly's ships *Sterling* in 1873 and *James Beazley* in 1877.

The surviving crew lists tell us something about Kelly as a businessman, but what about his life as a family man? For insight into this, I turned to the Kelly letters in our family history archive. Though few and far between, these notes are revelatory of the man and his family interests.

## A Letter to Miss Elizabeth McFerran

William Kelly seems to have been a confirmed, perhaps even a prodigious, letter writer. The fact that two of his letters to family in North America have survived into the twenty-first century indicates how much the recipients of these letters (and their descendants) valued them. His correspondence went into our family archive and has stayed there, passed dutifully from one generation to the next for over 140 years. Along with the Old Bailey Criminal Court transcript of 1848 (see "Charlie Richmond's Mattress" in Chapter 1), the letters offer a muffled echo of William Kelly's voice.

Kelly probably wrote the undated letter below to his niece Elizabeth McFerran (my great-grandmother) in the summer of 1875. I can date the letter to this timeframe because it references a book of hymns published by the nineteenth-century missioner Ira D. Sankey. Kelly writes that he had sent this hymn book to the McFerrans two weeks earlier. The book is inscribed: "Wm. Kelly to Elizabeth MacFerran, Antrim Lodge, Kemptville, May 1875."[175]

# Standing Over

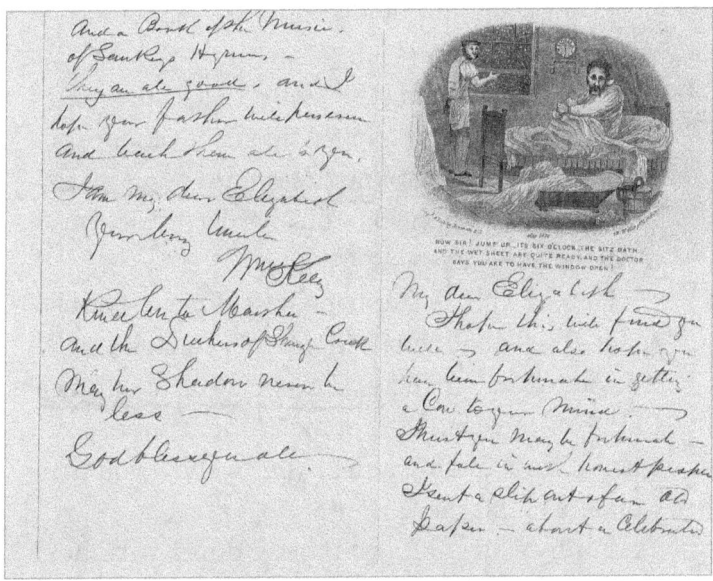

Figure 19: The first page of William Kelly's letter to his niece, Elizabeth McFerran in Kemptville, Ontario, possibly 1875. Image credit: Bradley archive.

The cartoon on the notepaper shows an unhappy, rather rumpled gentleman sitting up in bed while his trusty manservant stands at the window cheering him on, "Now sir! Jump up. It's six o'clock. The sitz bath and the wet sheet are quite ready, and the doctor says you are to have the window open!" Without a doubt, Kelly's comical stationery opens a window into his whimsical sense of humor.

> My dear Elizabeth –
> I hope this will find you well—and also hope you have been fortunate in getting a [cow?] to your mind. I trust you may be fortunate—and fall in with honest people.

I sent a slip out of an old paper—about a celebration a [farmer?] had.

I hope that among the lambs that Esther and [she?] gets—she may happen upon one or more of that sort—5 lambs at one time; must soon make you all rich—I expect you won't hardly speak to me if I come out again.

I hope I will have the happiness of seeing you all again. If so—I will stop at Montreal—and telegraph for you to join me there, give you a run about the City. You know but little of the World. I often wish when I am alone I just had you to show you the wonders of this place.

Fanny—Mrs. Moore is now down with her Baby and Nurse—and Agnes is along—Mary is here, ready for a start for France as soon as I hear of the ship's arrival.[176] She will return back with her brother William.

My health thank God is good, but this horrible fat is killing me.

There is no news I can send that would interest you. Your father [sits?] over the News Paper I suppose—I sent a fortnight ago Hymn Book pieces and a Book of the Music, of Sankey's Hymns—they are all good, and I hope your father will persevere and teach them all to you.

I am my dear Elizabeth,
Your loving Uncle,
Wm. Kelly
Remember [me?] to Martha—and the Duchess of Shingle Creek—May her Shadow never be less—God bless you all.

Kelly's letter to his niece exhibits gentle humor and chatty candor. He writes that he has sent them a newspaper clipping about a farmer and his lambs, because it brought to mind Elizabeth's younger sister, Esther, who had a flock of her own. Also, he has sent them a book of hymns with the hope that her father would teach them to his daughters. It appears that Kelly wrote frequently to the McFerrans. He even visited them from time to time when his travels took him to Montreal and he had time for a side trip to Ontario. He also dabbled in property speculation with the one-hundred-acre McFerran property in Kemptville, purchasing most of the lot from his brother-in-law John McFerran in 1863 and then gifting the property back to his sister, Mary McFerran, in 1873.[177]

Continuing with his letter, Kelly confesses that, when traveling alone, he often wished that Elizabeth was with him so he could show her the wonders of the world. Then there is news of his daughters—Fanny visiting with Kelly's first grandchild, along with Agnes and Mary. His own health is good, Kelly says, "but this horrible fat is killing me"—a prescient comment if ever there was one. Finally, there is a parting nod to Elizabeth's older sister, Martha, and an obscure reference to the "Duchess of Shingle Creek" whose aristocratic shadow has sadly long since vanished, along with Shingle Creek.[178] All in all, the letter is a rather touching note to a twenty-two-year-old woman in Kemptville, Ontario, from her grizzled, sixty-four-year-old uncle in Belfast.

Figure 20: The glittering McFerran sisters, about 1875: Elizabeth (left), Esther (right), and Martha (seated with child). This black-and-white photograph does not show the manual colorization in the original—gold rings, gold brooches, and hints of pink highlighting the sisters' cheeks and neckwear. Image credit: Bradley archive/undated.

## The *Princess Alexandra*: A Problematic Passage from France to Callao

In his 1875 letter to Elizabeth McFerran, William Kelly wrote, "Mary is here, ready for a start for France as soon as I hear of the ship's arrival. She will return back with her brother William." The *Princess Alexandra*, now commanded by William Kelly Jr., would arrive soon in Belfast, making it possible for his sister Mary to travel to the ship's next port of call, Le Havre in northwestern France. There William Kelly Jr. would provision the *Princess Alexandra* for her next extended voyage: "Havre to Callao for orders, from thence to any port, ports or places in the Guanape Islands to load, thence to Callao if required and back to a final port of discharge in the United Kingdom or on the continent of Europe with liberty to call at a port or ports for orders; voyage not to exceed eighteen months."[179]

On July 3, 1875, twenty-four-year-old William Kelly Jr. mustered a diverse crew at Le Havre: first mate Nathan Kellett (age 37) of Carrickfergus, County Antrim (certification no. 24685); second mate James Collins (age 29) of New Ross, County Wexford; carpenter Friedrich Free (age 32) of Germany; steward Ramond Lavendo (age 41) of Martinique; cook Carl Nielsen (age 36) of Norway; and a mixed group of nineteen able-bodied seamen from all over the place—Holland, Sweden, Austria, Greece, Trieste, and Finland. There was even a twenty-three-year-old sailor from Constantinople named John Christian serving as boatswain.

William Kelly Jr. was three years younger than the average age of his crew, and nine years younger than the average age of his first and second mates. Of course, he was the son of the vessel's owner, but how much credibility and respect would that buy him on a polyglot ship of all nations run by three Irishmen when the inevitable difficulties cropped up? When the *Princess Alexandra* departed Le Havre on July 5, 1875, there would indeed be stormy days ahead, literally and figuratively.

## Murder on the High Seas (1): The Bloodied Capstan Bar

It took only three weeks for a capital offense to overwhelm the *Princess Alexandra*. On Thursday, July 29, 1875, somewhere in the middle of the Atlantic, there was an altercation between second mate James Collins and boatswain John Christian. According to subsequent newspaper articles, Collins had the watch that morning. About eight a.m., Christian asked Collins for orders, whereupon Collins took offense at something Christian said, or perhaps it was his tone of voice or demeanor. Collins flew into a rage, shouting: "Oh, you're an [expletive] of a boatswain!" Christian turned to walk away. Collins picked up a capstan bar[180] and struck Christian a violent blow on the back of the head, dropping him to the deck. Some of the crew carried Christian to his berth, where he died four hours later.

This extraordinary incident implicating the ship's second officer in the death of a crewmate must have thrown the ship into considerable turmoil and put young Captain Kelly and first mate Kellett on the spot to regain control of ship and crew. As the *Princess Alexandra* pushed on around the Horn, Collins was likely confined in whatever passed for a brig on a merchant trader in those days (perhaps the cabin storeroom or the sail room). They eventually arrived at

Callao, Peru, on October 21, 1875. Here Collins was handed over to the British consul, who arranged for his return to Liverpool on the Pacific Steam Navigation Company steamship *Iberia* (Captain J. W. Shannon) to stand trial in the United Kingdom. Three crewmen were also returned as witnesses— A. Lindstrom (age 38) of Sweden, Ferdinand Tezzia (age 34) of Austria, and R. Natalias (age 23) of Trieste—with their wages paid by bills on William Kelly of Belfast.

With these formalities handled, the *Princess Alexandra* commenced trading up and down the west coast of South America, filling her hold with guano from the newly discovered deposits at Pabellón de Pica and Huanillas in northern Chile. Reporting on the deposits at both these places in 1875, the British consular agent wrote:

> I will venture to say that there exists in Pabellon de Pica about 800,000 tons of guano, all of which is covered with sand and stone varying from 3 to 15 metres in depth, and running up to the slope of the hill which is semi-circular to a height of 400 feet. The deposits cover a distance of 1,500 metres in length, but it is an utter impossibility for any person to make an exact estimate of the amount of guano at Pabellon de Pica...The guano [at Huanillas] is of excellent quality and free from sand and stone...It will be a very difficult and tedious job to ship guano at this place. Quantity, I calculate, at about 150,000 tons.[181]

The *Princess Alexandra* remained in these waters for almost a year. They departed Huanillas for the United Kingdom on September 13, 1876.

## A Letter to Mr. W. J. McFerran

It would be interesting to know when and how William Kelly Sr. first heard of the murder committed on his ship. As the owner of the vessel, he must have found out relatively quickly, especially once the British consul in Callao was involved—and there were wages to pay for Collins and the three witnesses who were returned to the United Kingdom.

Two months after the *Princess Alexandra* arrived at Callao, William Kelly Sr. wrote another letter to his family in North America, this time to William J. McFerran, his thirty-three-year-old nephew in New York State (the older brother of Kelly's niece Elizabeth McFerran, to whom he had previously written, probably in the summer of 1875, as referenced above).[182]

> Belfast, December 13th, 1875
> Mr. W. J. MacFerran
>
> My dear Nephew—
> On looking over last week's Witness [a Belfast newspaper], I happened to observe an article among others relative to Methodism in old Lisnagarry or Lisburn, as it is called now. This is six miles from Belfast and a very ancient place. To this place flocked the poor Flemings or Protestants from the Netherlands to escape from that horrible wretch the "Duke of Alva," the Spanish Governor, under Ferdinand & Isabella of Spain—in the 16th century they and the Flemish Protestants settled at Lisnagarry and were the founders of the linen and damask trade in this country.

Your great grandmother's name was Wolfenden, and I remember often hearing her speak of her brother Robert who was the friend of Wesley. Your great grandfather, John Paterson, was also one of the early Methodists—he was also a descendant of the Flemings—or Belgians as they are called at the present day. Both were strong Methodists. John Paterson is buried at Mattewan, 60 miles above New York, opposite Newburgh. I thought you might take an interest in this, and that is why I sent it. Uncle Sam knew your great grandfather and grandmother well.

The weather here, strange to say, is the finest for this time of year I ever remember. No snow, the young ones had ten days skating, but today it is as warm and balmy as in May. We have much better weather than they have had in Spain and the South of France. I send you also a Northern Whig. It is called "The Liberal Paper" here, not so strong orange as the "News Letter", but a loyal paper, and far more cleverly conducted than the N. Letter. There is a first-class article on the present state of Europe in the leading article.

Give my kind love to Uncle Sam, and your wife. I had a letter from your poor mother lately and I fear she will never be able to walk in this world, all this through ignorance and stupidity in not changing her clothes when wet.

I am in a great hurry as I am writing down to William at Calla and the mail closes in a couple of hours. I expect to get a letter from John, 1st proximo. I expect to go on to India, and very likely to N. York, then across to Liverpool.

>   Hoping this will find you in good health, I am
> my dear nephew,
> Wm. Kelly

Kelly's letter to his nephew reveals his interest in the Antrim newspapers of his day, in the history of Antrim and his family, as well as current events. He connects the McFerrans with the Wolfenden family and John Wesley, the founder of the Methodist movement. The Wolfendens of Lambeg, a village located between Belfast and Lisburn, now absorbed into greater Belfast, were generally thought to have been French Protestant Huguenots from the Low Countries. Some claim that they arrived in Ireland from Yorkshire in the late seventeenth century. Abraham Wolfenden built a house on the old Belfast–Dublin road near the River Lagan crossing, a place he called Lambeg House (now Chrome Hill).

A local yarn claims that Wolfenden entertained King William III in this house when William's carriage was damaged while crossing the Lagan on the way to the Battle of the Boyne in 1690. Another story recounts a visit John Wesley made to Lambeg House in 1787 when he is said to have twisted together two beech saplings to illustrate the effect of bringing together the Anglican and Methodist Churches. Apparently, the conjoined trees flourish to this day, still entangled at the entrance to the house at Chrome Hill.[183]

Along with history and religion, family was also much in William Kelly's mind as he wrote to his nephew. After sending his love to his nephew's wife and uncle, Kelly mentions a troubling letter he had recently received from his sister, Mary McFerran of Kemptville, Ontario, the mother of William and Elizabeth McFerran (Figure 21). He laments that Mary will probably never walk again as a result of an unexplained illness that he attributes to her own folly "in not changing her clothes when wet." Kelly's explanation of Mary's paraplegia, blaming damp clothing, is not particularly persuasive—although Sir Samuel Wilks, M.D., F.R.S., cited the following case in a lecture on diseases of the nervous system that he published in 1878:

> CASE—A young man walked about in his wet clothes, and afterwards slept in them. On the following day he felt very unwell, with aching pains all over him. On the third day he was obliged to keep his bed, on account of the weakness and numbness in the legs. It was then found that there was complete paraplegia of motion and sensation as high as the pelvis....These symptoms increased, and on the 10th day he was excessively ill, with febrile symptoms; abdomen tympanitic; breathing quick and interrupted....On the twelfth day he died....The post mortem showed acute inflammation of the bladder and kidneys, and to this death was attributed.[184]

Fortunately, Mary McFerran's illness was not as dire as that of Wilks's anonymous young man. In fact, she would live another twenty years before passing away on February 1, 1895 in her eighties. Her obituary states, "For over a score of years deceased had been unable to walk and consequently confined to the house."[185]

William Kelly concluded his letter to William McFerran with the conventional plea that time was pressing. He had to mail a letter to his son William at "Calla" (Callao, Peru) before the post office closed. I wonder what advice Kelly gave his son in this letter. He must have had something to say about the appalling murder committed on the *Princess Alexandra*.

Figure 21: Mary (Kelly) McFerran (c.1813–1895).
Image credit: Bradley archive/undated.

## Murder on the High Seas (2): A Perfectly Friendless Man

On Christmas Eve 1875, eleven days after William Kelly wrote to William McFerran, the steamship *Iberia* delivered a manacled James Collins and the three witnesses from the *Princess Alexandra* to the authorities in Liverpool. On Christmas Day, the story of the high-seas murder broke with a nationwide flurry of newspaper articles in the *Belfast News-Letter*, the *Liverpool Mercury*, the *Bradford Observer*, the *Bristol Mercury*, the *Manchester Times*, and elsewhere.

> SERIOUS CHARGE AGAINST THE MATE OF A SHIP.—Yesterday, James Collins, second mate of the British ship Princess Alexandra, was taken into custody by the Liverpool police on a charge of having caused the death of the boatswain, John Christian. It is stated that about the 29th July, whilst the vessel was on a voyage from Havre to Callao, the prisoner became enraged at something the boatswain said to him, and thereupon he struck Christian with a handspike and knocked him down; Christian was so severely injured that he died a few hours afterwards. When the vessel arrived at Callao, Collins was arrested, and, by the direction of the British consul at that port, sent to this country by the Pacific Steam Navigation Company's steamship Iberia. Yesterday, on the arrival of the prisoner at this port by the Iberia, he was taken to the detective office by River-police Constable No. 10 (Pegler), and locked up on the charge.[186]

If William Kelly Sr. had not known about the incident before this (which is unlikely), he certainly knew about it now, along with fresh details of the accused seaman's arrival at Liverpool. River Police Officer Pegler, who took charge of Collins on the *Iberia*, quoted the seaman as saying, "I am guilty, but what I did was in self-defense. I am to blame, but I have always been a harmless and inoffensive man."[187] When brought before Mr. Raffles at the Liverpool Police Court, Collins said that he had already endured considerable punishment. He told the judge he was perfectly friendless, said he would like several of the ship's passengers to be called as witnesses in his favor, and requested a solicitor. Raffles declined to engage a solicitor for him and said that he would be committed for trial at the assizes soon enough.

With his son's difficulties now common knowledge, William Kelly Sr. was likely inundated with concerned inquiries from friends and business acquaintances, especially those in Belfast's close-knit shipping community.

## A Meeting of Belfast Ship Owners

As demonstrated by his participation with other ship owners in the Plimsoll delegation three years earlier (see "Mr. Plimsoll's Shipping Bill" earlier in this chapter), William Kelly played an active role in the Belfast Ship Owners' Association during his retirement. Indeed, just a couple of months after the "friendless" James Collins arrived back in Liverpool from Callao, Kelly attended a meeting of this organization held at the Belfast Chamber of Commerce on Saturday, February 19, 1876.[188] The purpose of the meeting was to receive committee reports on two parliamentary bills related to Samuel Plimsoll's merchant shipping legislation. The following exchange at the end of the meeting features a brief appearance by William Kelly.

Belfast steamship agent Henry Gowan read an extract from a speech delivered by Wilhelm Adolf von Freeden (1822–1894)[189] dealing with the inconsistent and potentially dangerous systems of steering then used by the international shipping community. A number of collisions had recently occurred as a result of ships going to sea with sailors of various nationalities who "in the method of steering attached a diametrically opposite meaning to the same command—one when ordered to 'port' going to port, and another at the same order steering in an exactly opposite direction," said Gowan. ("Hear, hear," shouted the assembled owners.)

The chairman alluded to a recent collision at Dover,[190] which had resulted in loss of life and property as an example of this lack of uniformity in steering, whereupon Captain Kelly expressed his opinion "that the continental plan of steering, by which the vessel went to port when port was ordered, and to starboard when starboard was ordered, [was] a much better plan than the British method, which he thought had come down unaltered and unimproved from the days when ships were guided by means of rudders." ("Hear, hear," affirmed the owners again.)

In Kelly's day, it was common for steering orders on British ships to be given as Tiller Orders. The tiller, typically found in smaller sailing boats, is a stick or pole attached to the top of the rudder. The helmsman uses the tiller to steer the boat by moving the rudder from side to side. However, since the tiller is forward of the rudder pivot point, the tiller's movement is reversed at the rudder. In larger sailing vessels, the ship's wheel, which was mechanically connected to the rudder, replaced the tiller—with the same reversal taking place. For example, if a ship's captain used British Tiller Orders to turn his ship to port (left), he would order "hard a-starboard." The ship's helmsman would then turn the wheel to starboard (right), which moved the rudder to the vessel's port side, resulting in a leftward turn.

A different steering system applied in France, where "hard a-port" meant turn to port and "hard a-starboard" meant turn to starboard. Austria and Italy used the British system. Scandinavian steering practices varied from ship to ship. Clearly there was confusion at sea when it came to the important responsibility of changing a ship's direction.

Returning to the meeting of the Belfast Ship Owners' Association, Mr. Wright moved, Captain Kelly seconded, and it was resolved "that the attention of Mr. Corry should be drawn to the speech of Herr Freeden, with a view of having measures taken for the securing of an assimilated international system in the steering of ships."[191]

It was said of Kelly: "He was of such a retiring disposition that he rarely came before the public, but when his opinion was asked for it was freely and judiciously given."[192] Kelly's historical insight into something as rudimentary as the steering of a ship was one of those occasions when his opinion was sought and cheerfully given. In fact, in 1876, he was sixty years ahead of his time in recommending a standardized international steering system. Although many maritime nations had abandoned the British steering convention by the end of the nineteenth century, the United Kingdom retained the system until 1933[193] and the US merchant marine until 1935. Why was this? The old "indirect" system of steering was a long-established maritime tradition and provided consistency. Regardless of whether a vessel was steered directly by tiller or mechanically by wheel, they all had a vestigial tiller of some sort, so Tiller Orders were the same for all *when they were observed and understood*. The problem was they were *not consistently observed and understood*, which all too often resulted in near collisions, even catastrophes at sea.

## Murder on the High Seas (3): William Baliol Brett

Five weeks after the Belfast Ship Owners' Association meeting, on Wednesday, March 29, 1876, while the *Princess Alexandra* was still sailing off the coasts of Peru and Chile, James Collins was finally granted his day at the Liverpool assizes. With His Lordship Justice William Baliol Brett presiding,[194] Mr. McConnell prosecuting, and Mr. Foard defending, the seamen who had been removed from the *Princess Alexandra* along with Collins described what they had seen and heard when Collins allegedly struck and killed John Christian.

The Swedish seaman Lindstrom stated that on the morning of the incident, Collins had asked Christian if he had anything for the men to do, and Christian replied that he was awaiting Collins's orders. Collins then swore at Christian, picked up the capstan bar, and hit the boatswain on the head with it.

"When he struck him, the deceased was doing nothing," said Lindstrom.

Justice Brett asked if any of the men had quarreled with the second mate during the voyage.

"No, sir, only a man named Fred," replied Lindstrom (possibly referring to the carpenter, Friedrich Free).

"And did the crew dislike Collins? Had he been a bad officer?" asked the justice.

Lindstrom said he could not say, but none of the sailors were armed when they approached Collins.

Speaking for the defense, Mr. Foard asked another member of the crew, an American named Frank Smith,[195] if he had heard any of the crew threatening the second mate.

"No sir. The greatest part of the crew was afraid of him," replied Smith.

"It was a scratch crew picked up at Havre, was it not—all foreigners except two?" asked Foard.

"Yes," replied Smith, "but the captain would not have Englishmen any way."

"What nationality was the captain?" asked Foard.

"An Irishman," replied Smith.

The Austrian crewman Ferdinand Tezzia confirmed that the crew was a multinational mix with only two men who spoke English.

Foard reiterated that when the river police at Liverpool charged Collins with the offense, he had admitted his guilt but stated, "Until this happened, I had always been a harmless and inoffensive man." Foard also reminded the jury that when Collins had appeared before Mr. Raffles at the police court, he had said he only intended to hit Christian on the hand "to protect the property he was in charge of in the absence of the captain and first officer"—and that Collins also said he had been threatened by the crew on previous occasions. In his conclusion, Foard said that there was no evidence of malice on the part of Collins; that the crew or part of them, being foreigners, were possibly disaffected; and that the prisoner, in a moment of passion—whether well- or ill-founded—had struck John Christian a blow that proved deadly.

Mr. Justice Brett summed the case up for the jury, reminding them that if they found that Collins had intended to kill Christian, even if the intention came into his head on the spur of the moment, they would have to find him guilty of willful murder. He pointed to the weapon as a critical aspect of the case. The capstan bar used by the prisoner was no doubt formidable, but unless he struck the man on the head with it, it was hardly a weapon likely to kill him. The jury would need to carefully weigh the prisoner's selection and use of the capstan bar in considering whether he intended to kill Mr. Christian with it.

Interestingly, Justice Brett also expressed his dissatisfaction that none of the officers or men, except the foreign witnesses, had been sent home to give evidence. The makeup and nature of the crew were also key elements in the case, he told the jury. The men were a motley crew from everywhere picked up at Le Havre, and they were under the command of Irish officers. Brett wished that the court might have had the benefit of testimony from Collins's fellow officers to better understand their view of the conduct of the crew and the feelings between the officers and crew. In addition, the judge had only seen a part of the ship's log. He wished he had seen the whole of the log so that he could assess what had transpired between the officers and crew in the days before the murder. Brett then carefully went through the evidence, and the jury, after a short deliberation, returned a verdict of manslaughter.

In sentencing James Collins, Justice Brett said:

> The jury has saved your life. If you had been found guilty of murder, nothing could have prevented the law taking its course, and you must have been executed. I am one who has a strong opinion that the officers of merchant ships are to be supported in maintaining the discipline of the ship. But I am also of opinion strongly that the crew of a merchant ship are entitled to ample protection against the tyranny of their officers; and although, if the crew attempt to withstand the officer, I will go a long way in the defense of these officers, at the same time, when an officer of a merchant ship gives way to brutal passion, and does such a violent act as you have done, it must be shown that the crew are to be protected; and if an officer give[s] way to such violence, thereby causing the death of one of the crew, he cannot expect to escape a most severe punishment....That you had a difficult crew to deal with I feel inclined to believe; although for that reason you were bound to be firm, you should also have been more forbearing. You had great power.... You were bound to exercise that power properly.... I cannot help thinking that there was a reluctant obedience, almost amounting to disobedience, on the part of some of the crew of this ship; but that is no justification for what you did, and it is an act which must be severely punished.

Brett then sentenced Collins to fifteen years' penal servitude. On leaving the dock, Collins thanked the jury for saving his life and reiterated that the crew had threatened to kill him if they could.[196]

This was a difficult and stressful period in the lives of William Kelly Jr. and William Kelly Sr. The young ship's master had to deal with a problematic crew that might have been testing his leadership, while his second mate was a fragile link in the chain of command. The testimony in James Collins's trial is largely devoid of references to the ship's master beyond the fact that he was an Irishman with a preference for foreign crewmen over "Englishmen," and Collins himself testified that he was "protect[ing] the property he was in charge of in the absence of the captain and first officer." Even Justice Brett picked up on this conceivable executive vacuum when he grumbled that he wished he and the jury could have heard from the ship's officers.

The murder of John Christian had tarnished the *Princess Alexandra* with unwelcome notoriety while also subjecting William Kelly Sr. and his family to the harsh and unwelcome light of public scrutiny. I wonder if Kelly might have regretted putting his ship in the hands of his youngest son, even on a routine trade and guano run to South America.

In any event, Kelly did not have the luxury of dwelling for long on the trials and tribulations of the *Princess Alexandra*. In the spring and summer of 1876, a lovely new ship had appeared on the horizon, one requiring his close attention.

## The Barque *James Beazley*

Weary of the challenges presented by outdated, second-hand wooden ships like the *Express*, the *Merrie England*, and the *Princess Alexandra*, William Kelly had prudently overseen the construction of a new vessel designed in accordance with his own specifications, using the latest materials and state-of-the-art technology. She was a beautiful iron barque, the kind of ship he needed if he was going to compete seriously in a shipping industry that was rapidly moving away from wooden ships. Iron-hulled vessels were more economical and efficient. They were easier to build and maintain. They also offered much-improved carrying capacity. Kelly must have started this huge project many months earlier, but the first mention of it in the press is the following announcement from June 1876.

> ADDITION TO BELFAST SHIPPING.—On Thursday last, 8th inst., there was launched from the yard of the well-known iron shipbuilders, Messrs. Osborne, Graham & C., of North Hylton, near Sunderland, an iron clipper barque of 860 tons register, and about 1,300 tons burthen [carrying capacity], built to the order of Captain William Kelly, Belfast. Her dimensions are—195 feet by 33 feet beam and 19.9 depth of hold. She has been built under special survey, and is classed 100 A at Lloyds. On leaving the ways she was named by Miss Mary Kelly, daughter of the owner, the James Beazley, in compliment to the well-known Liverpool ship owner of that name. She will be commanded by Capt. J. Seabourne, late of the ship Stirling [sic], belonging to the same owner.[197]

The *James Beazley* (Official Number 74533) was built for clipper-like speed with a sharply raked stem, knife-like cutwater, and lengthened bow above the water. Her distinctive black-and-white bichrome hull accentuated her sleek and graceful lines. She had iron fore and main masts, bowsprit, lower topsail yards, and wire rigging. Kelly had equipped her with all the latest improvements, including William Harfield's patented steam-powered windlass (1874).

As soon as his vessel was fitted out, Kelly wasted no time dispatching her on her maiden voyage to the East Indies. The *James Beazley* departed Sunderland on Tuesday, July 25, 1876, for Madras and Calcutta in the capable hands of Captain John Seabourne. With this important milestone passed, Kelly moved to another matter that required his immediate attention. He had felt for some time that his energy was not what it used to be, and his doctor confirmed that his chronic heart disease was entering a worrisome phase. The stress of managing two aging ships at sea, one of them tainted by manslaughter, while also designing, building, and launching a third vessel, must have taken its toll on Kelly. What was most perturbing: there was little to do beyond preparing for the inevitable.

## "The Mariner Hath His Will"

As Shakespeare's Julius Caesar pragmatically proclaims: "Of all the wonders that I have heard, / It seems to me most strange that men should fear; / Seeing death, a necessary end, / Will come when it will come."[198] With this stoical mindset, Kelly set about putting his affairs in order, while also reducing the size of his fleet. He still owned the *Sterling* when the *James Beazley* first appeared in 1876. However, there is no mention of the *Sterling* in Kelly's will. He probably sold the older ship to help defray the cost of the *James Beazley*.

On November 11, 1876, Kelly signed his last will and testament at 14 Abercorn Terrace, Belfast.[199] Two executors also signed the will: Kelly's business associate Thomas Scott of Sydenham, Belfast; and William Moore, a Belfast ship and insurance broker. William Moore was the brother of Kelly's son-in-law John Moore, who had married Fanny Kelly in 1872.

The will valued Kelly's effects within the United Kingdom at under £18,000 (which would provide purchasing power of approximately £2.3 million in 2022). The ship *Princess Alexandra* was to go to his sons John and William, with William to be the ship's master. However, if the sons could not agree on this, the ship was to be valued either by someone appointed by the sons or by Thomas Scott, and William was to pay John his half of the value of the ship. If William was unable to pay the amount due in cash, William was to give a mortgage to John for the ship and during its existence pay John his remaining money after expenses in account of the principal. Also, William was to insure the ship for at least £3,000 in the name of the executors and provide them with the policy. Daughters Agnes, Fanny, and Mary were to receive £1,000 each. His wife, Martha, was to receive the *James Beazley* plus all railway shares, bank shares, his real estate, and personal estate for as long as she remained his widow.

By far the greater part of Kelly's will was given over to sorting out the ownership and management of the *Princess Alexandra*, with various scenarios and constraints laid out involving his sons, John and William Jr. Despite his youngest son's uncertain handling of the Collins fiasco, Kelly seemed intent on bequeathing the ship to William, or at least giving him right of first refusal. In any event, his oldest son, John, was by now fully engaged in his own career, having recently returned from Australia and India in command of the ship *Amyone*.

When Kelly signed his will, the *Princess Alexandra* was finally homeward bound from Callao. William Jr. brought her into London on March 6, 1877, enabling father and son to sort out together the many lessons learned during the ship's difficult voyage to South America and back.

While the *James Beazley* was loading at Calcutta, Kelly made three decisions related to the *Princess Alexandra*. The ship's next assignment would be less demanding; another promising officer would assume his first command; and his son would take some time off to ponder his future.

Accordingly, on April 24, 1877, the *Princess Alexandra* departed London for a trans-Atlantic excursion to Wiscasset, Maine, and the east coast of North America with Nathan Kellett (ex-first mate) in command, supported by first mate Thomas Skinner (ex-*Amyone*). As for William Kelly Jr., he took a spell of shore leave to rest and recover from his calamitous voyage to Peru.

## Pilfered Geraniums

What a strange, incongruous, and startling interlude this was. The *Belfast News-Letter* of Tuesday, July 10, 1877, reported on a heavy penalty for flower thievery meted out by a Belfast court with the enthusiastic support of an aggrieved Captain William Kelly Sr.

Samuel Workington and Robert McDonald, two "respectable-looking young men," were charged by sub-constable Larkin with stealing a quantity of flowers from the garden of Captain Kelly, Richmond Crescent, Antrim

Road. Mr. McLean Jr. prosecuted and Mr. Harper appeared for the defense.

The sub-constable deposed that between two and three o'clock on Sunday morning, he observed the prisoners emerging from Captain Kelly's garden. They each had a bunch of geraniums, and when the sub-constable approached them, Workington dropped his flowers and ran away. The sub-constable gave chase and, with the assistance of another policeman, arrested both men.

Captain Kelly's gardener said the flowers produced by the sub-constable were similar in every respect to those growing in his master's garden. Furthermore, Captain Kelly had instructed his gardener to request that the judge deal sternly with the prisoners, as he was much annoyed by people breaking into and plundering his garden.

Judge O'Donnell said he had power to sentence the prisoners to six months imprisonment. "This system of robbing and destroying gardens is becoming too prevalent," he said. Workington admitted the offense but said McDonald had taken none of the flowers. Judge O'Donnell fined Workington £5 and costs or two months' imprisonment, and McDonald £2 or a month's imprisonment.

Kelly's request that the judge deal harshly with the mischief-makers is a sign that he loved his garden and disliked the persistent incursions into it. In some respects, this episode hearkens back to the Old Bailey case of Charlie Richmond's mattress some thirty years earlier, when Kelly pressed charges against a seaman who had walked off the *Belinda* with bedding that did not belong to him. Kelly was not averse to bringing the full weight of the law down upon the heads of young men who strayed from the straight and narrow, whether it was for a mattress or a bouquet of geraniums.

Figure 22: The back garden at 6 Richmond Crescent, Belfast, where highly coveted geraniums once bloomed.
Image credit: Dr. Bob Foy, 2013.

## The Last, Long Voyage

On August 7, 1877, William Kelly Sr. was buoyed up by the safe return of the *Princess Alexandra* to Cardiff following a happily humdrum voyage to the East Coast of the United States with Nathan Kellett in command.

Perhaps thinking twice about his youngest son's ability to manage the ship successfully, Kelly executed a codicil to his will on August 21, transferring his property to Martha and stating that his ships should be sold with Martha receiving the interest. The remainder of the proceeds were to be divided equally among their children with the exception of £2,000, "which my wife shall have the power to settle on my sons should she think them worthy of it." For some reason, the codicil also stipulated that any daughter of Kelly who married without Martha's consent should receive only £50. This requirement would only have applied to their youngest daughter, twenty-four-year-old Mary McConnel Kelly, who would subsequently marry John Orr Wallace (1847–1917) two years later. Martha must have consented to the marriage because she hosted the wedding at her home, 6 Richmond Crescent, Belfast.[200]

Interestingly, William Kelly Jr. obtained his Certificate of Competency as ship's master after special application to the London Local Marine Board on September 1, 1877. Now, with his accreditation as a master mariner finally in hand (certificate no. 03,542), William was no longer dependent on his father for sailing opportunities. At age twenty-five, he was his own man. The certification came not a moment too soon.

Just two weeks later, on the morning of Wednesday, September 12, 1877, following his usual routine, William Kelly Sr. wrote some letters at home and then went for a drive in his horse-drawn gig, but feeling unwell and noting ominous thunderheads in the sky above, he returned to Richmond Crescent. There, on a squally and boisterously windy day, perhaps with the pungent scent of moist earth and geraniums redolent in the air around him, a rising tide of exhaustion engulfed the sixty-six-year-old mariner. Suddenly overwhelmed, he gave himself up to the deep and everything "changed"—in the nineteenth-century British sense of the word as signifying the final passage from the world one knows to "that unknown and silent shore."[201]

In a curious synchronicity, Kelly died on the eleventh anniversary of the day he had settled with the families of Captain Roland Savage and the drowned crew of the *Express*, which had disappeared into the North Atlantic in 1866 (see Chapter 6, "The Disaster of the *Express*").[202]

Only six years earlier, in his 1871 letter to James Graham, Kelly had remarked upon the recent death of Graham's wife, writing, "You have the great consolation to know, she was well prepared for the great change. Would to God I could express myself in the same terms I heard her make use of when she was in Liverpool with us."

William Kelly, a dyed-in-the-wool Presbyterian descended from Irish handloom weavers, had spent his entire adult life either at sea or otherwise engaged in maritime business. I imagine he seldom found himself at a loss for words. Yet when contemplating the inevitability and finality of death, he struggled to express himself, even though he had already plotted a lifetime of courses, always knowing where he had come from and where the winds and currents would take him. His many diligent comings and goings over many years at sea must have prepared him, at least to some extent, for this final departure and its unfathomable journey's end.

A stanza from Tennyson's self-proclaimed final poem, "Crossing the Bar," (1889) comes to mind (although the poem would not be published for another twelve years).

> Twilight and evening bell,
> And after that the dark!
> And may there be no sadness of farewell,
> When I embark...

There was sadness on Richmond Crescent but business as usual at sea. Unaware of his father's passing, Kelly's oldest son John was commanding the *Boyne*, a square-rigger that had departed Southampton for Calcutta just four days earlier. William Kelly Jr. was also back at sea, serving as first mate on the Belfast schooner *Twin Sisters*. Pushed by a fresh, strong breeze blowing under leaden skies above a rain-washed Irish Sea, William was delivering coal to the Scottish port of Ayr.

Both of Kelly's sons were in their element, doing what they loved, employing the skills he had taught them, and learning new competencies in deep-sea voyaging. William Kelly had launched them on their own careers in the British merchant service where he had served with distinction for over forty of the sixty-four years comprising Queen Victoria's reign.

> DEATH OF CAPTAIN WILLIAM KELLY.— In our obituary column today we record the death of this gentleman which took place at his residence Richmond Crescent on Wednesday. His death, though not unexpected, was sudden. Capt. Kelly had attended to his letters as usual in the morning, and gone out to drive, but, feeling unusually weak, returned to his house, where he expired in a few minutes, the immediate cause of his death being heart disease from which he has suffered for a lengthened period. The deceased gentleman was born in Antrim and at an early age adopted a seafaring life. He rose rapidly to the position of captain in the mercantile marine and for many years was one of the most successful men sailing

to our different colonies during the rush to Australia. The ship which he commanded was a great favourite, and many a North of Ireland man today now located in Australia, will hear of his death with deep regret. Capt. Kelly was for many years associated with Mr. James Beasley [sic], of Liverpool, in shipping business, and when he retired from the sea was shore manager for that gentleman till he came to reside in his native country. A short time ago when building a new iron ship for himself, out of compliment to his old friend and employer he named her the James Beasley. Although closely connected with the shipping trade of the North of Ireland, he was of such a retiring disposition that he rarely came before the public, but when his opinion was asked for it was freely and judiciously given. In accordance with his own request, the funeral, which takes place this morning will be strictly private. The remains of the deceased gentleman will be interred in the family burying ground at Muckamore near Antrim - his native town. The funeral will arrive at Muckamore cemetery about 1 o'clock.[203]

Figure 23: The Kelly plot at Muckamore burial ground (tall obelisk, center background and nearby stones). Image credit: Dr. Bob Foy, 2013.

Kelly's daughters Mary and Fanny were also well acquainted with the Belfast shipping community. Mary had presided at the launch of the *James Beazley* in 1876. Fanny had married John Moore of Moore Bros., ship brokers and agents for the Northern Steam Towing Company and the Belfast and Bangor steamers. During the summer months, the Moore steamers—the *Erin* and the *Bangor Castle*—carried thousands of passengers back and forth from Belfast to the seaside resort of Bangor on the south side of Belfast Lough. An article in the same issue of the *Belfast News-Letter* that published William Kelly's obituary announced the end of the season for these popular steamers that were closing down for the winter, stating, "The Messrs. Moore deserve every credit for the spirited manner in which they catered to the convenience and enjoyment of the public."[204] Even after William Kelly's death, vessels of all types, sail and steam, would continue to loom large in his family's thoughts and imaginings, as John and William Jr. remained master mariners for the rest of their lives.

The *James Beazley*, the sleek, new vessel that particularly bore Kelly's stamp of approval, was still at sea on her maiden voyage when Kelly died. His lovely clipper barque was now poised to veer off in a different direction—to the other side of the world and many more years at sea with a new name, different owners, and an astonishing last hurrah.

## From *James Beazley* to *Bankfields*

Rounding out her maiden voyage, the *James Beazley* had departed Calcutta in the summer of 1877 and sailed on to New York. There she offloaded 10,454 bags of linseed and other cargo in early October. On October 15, she set out from New York still under the command of John Seabourne with a cargo of grain for the United Kingdom. The barque arrived back in the Mersey on November 9, 1877, two months after William Kelly's death.

In December 1877, in accordance with Kelly's wishes, his wife, Martha, and William Moore of Belfast sold the *James Beazley* to William Just, a Liverpool ship and insurance broker who resided at a house called Bankfields in Eastham (Hooton), Cheshire. The new owner renamed his barque the *Bankfields* after his residence and registered the ship under this new name at Liverpool. The *Bankfields*'s new captain would be Thomas Venus of North Shields (certificate no. 03,520).

The beautiful barque that William Kelly had built would go on to sail the seas for thirty-five years, dispelling the old nautical superstition that renaming a ship brought bad luck. For many of those years, Samuel Wakeham & Sons of Liverpool sent the *Bankfields* on numerous voyages to the west coast of South America. Eventually, the ship's operations shifted to Australia and New Zealand. In 1903, the Adelaide Milling Company purchased the *Bankfields* for use in the South Africa trade. In 1907 to 1908, Messrs. A. H. Turnbull & Co. of Christchurch operated the ship as a guano trader before shifting it to various intercolonial trade routes between New Zealand and Australia.

Finally, in 1911, Turnbull & Co. sold the *Bankfields* to the Adelaide Steamship Company who converted the barque to a coal hulk for use in Fremantle harbor, Western Australia. Here she remained, diminished but still serviceable, for another thirty-nine years until wear, tear, and time finally lowered the boom on her in a truly dramatic fashion.

On Wednesday, June 7, 1950, the *Bankfields* rendered her last service to the nation that had adopted her. Stripped of her coal-handling gear, she was towed twenty-seven miles from Fremantle to the "Ships' Graveyard," southwest of Rottnest Island.[205] Here she absorbed an onslaught of sixty-pound, high-explosive bombs delivered by three diving, 400-mile-per-hour Mustang aircraft from the No. 25 City of Perth Fighter Squadron. With the *Bankfields* listing as a result of these direct hits, the Mustangs looped lazily around in the cloudless sky and finished the barque off with consecutive machine-gun strafing runs that sent her splintered and broken beneath the waves at approximately 1:10 p.m. Overall, the Royal Australian Air Force considered it "a satisfactory exercise."[206]

In an interesting timeline, William Kelly's daughter Mary had launched the *James Beazley* in County Durham, England, on June 8, 1876. The ship disappeared beneath the waves as the *Bankfields* off the coast of Western Australia on June 7, 1950—seventy-four years later, almost to the day, and just thirteen days before the author of this book was born.

The local West Australian papers covered the sinking of the *Bankfields* in detail, with the *Perth Daily News* highlighting the personal reminiscences of Mrs. R. Harkess, whose late husband had skippered the ship for many years. Mrs. Harkess had raised four children on the *Bankfields* when the handsome windjammer was popularly touted as "the glamour ship of Fremantle."[207]

Figure 24: The barque *Bankfields* moored (and mirrored) at Port Pirie, South Australia, about 1887. Image credit: State Library of South Australia, A. D. Edwardes Collection, PRG 1373/9/84, public domain.

Figure 25: The *Bankfields*'s last passage to the Ships' Graveyard off of Fremantle, Australia. Image credit: *Perth Daily News*, June 7, 1950, 1.

## When All Is Said and Done

The *Bankfields*'s survival until June 1950 is a testament to her design, durability, and upkeep for over seven decades. Thirty-five years under canvas and almost forty years of stationary service as a coal hulk is no mean feat. William Kelly had built a glamour ship that turned into a toughie, outlasting him and several generations that followed him.

Martha Kelly died on February 21, 1884, at her daughter Fanny's residence, 1 Wellington Park, Belfast, leaving an estate of just over £600. Her son Captain John Kelly of 4 Haverstock Terrace, Hampstead, London, and daughter Agnes Kelly of 1 University Terrace, Belfast, validated her last will and testament. The will referenced William Kelly's codicil stating that Martha should have the power to settle on their two sons £1,000 each, "should she think them worthy of it," and this she did in her own will.

Martha's will distributed William Kelly's remaining personal belongings among their five children.[208] John Kelly received his father's gold watch and chain along with his painting of the ship *Sterling*. William Kelly Jr. took his father's gold-headed cane, his silver snuffbox (which would find its way to the Moore family), and the painting of the ship *Mary Carson*. Fanny (Moore) received Joseph Heard's painting of the ship *Miles Barton*. Mary (Wallace) took Samuel Walters's painting of the ship *Merrie England*,[209] and Agnes Kelly inherited an oil portrait of William and Martha together (current disposition unknown).

Martha also passed on many household possessions to the family. Two figures on the parlor mantelpiece went to John, a silver salver to William. The best bedroom furniture, a diamond ring, and a short sealskin jacket went to Agnes. The dining room table, a silver dish with an oval top, the claret jug, a box of silver fruit knives and forks, and white lace curtains went to Fanny. The best china cups and saucers, two silver dishes with covers, a gold ring with one stone, and the drawing room chandelier went to Mary. A gold and black iron bedstead with a hair mattress and bedding, along with a marble-top dressing table, went to granddaughter Martha Florence Moore (age 10). A silver biscuit canister, twelve silver teaspoons, a silver soup ladle, two large gravy spoons, and two silver salts went to granddaughter Edith Mary Moore (age 6).[210]

This dealing out of prized possessions and humble everyday items sheds light on artifacts of the Kelly household. It also reminds us that William and Martha had lived in a different age with strict, gender-driven expectations and restrictions delineating their roles. The houses and children had been Martha's domain, as the ships were William's. For forty years, Martha had managed their properties in Antrim Town, New Orleans, Belfast, and Liverpool. She raised their children with little assistance from a husband who was absent for long stretches at sea. In their early days, William and Martha might have sailed together on occasion. She certainly presided over the *Merrie England*'s launch at Waterford in 1856, with William and John Kelly applauding along with other dignitaries as she smashed a bottle against the vessel's bow. However, as the family grew and William moved his base of operations to Liverpool, "Mrs. Captain Kelly"[211] had settled into the role expected of her. She had been the head of household and primary caregiver for their five surviving children first in the Townhead section of Antrim Town; next at 21 Pilot Street, Belfast; then at 52 Upper Stanhope Street and 18 Upper Parliament Street, Liverpool, until Kelly retired and returned with Martha to Belfast.

Martha shouldered this tremendous responsibility against the black crape backdrop of three deceased children—John (1839) in New Orleans, then Fanny (1845) and James (1847) in Belfast. Later there was the appalling 1871 murder of her brother Samuel Rainey in New Orleans. This last calamity had left Martha (in William's words) "not well by any means," but he also opined that her native resiliency would bring her round again in due course—and I can only hope it did.

When all is said and done, William and Martha stayed the course after their 1837 wedding at Craigmore, but it could not have been an easy life with William's lengthy absences and no guarantees that he would return from his hazardous assignments at sea. This book addresses the vulnerability of those in peril on the open ocean—the burning of the *Dalriada*, the catastrophe of the *Hilton*, the conflagration of the *Mary Carson*, the destruction of the *Miles Barton*, the disaster of the *Express*, the foundering of the *Merrie England*. It is a testament to William's seamanship (along with a pinch of Irish luck, perhaps) that he survived the loss of the *Belinda* in 1848 and then moved on to a lengthy and rewarding seafaring career. He became a successful ship owner, and his sons followed in his wake.

Sadly, William Kelly Jr. would die just two years after his mother on September 9, 1886, at 44 Botanic Avenue, Belfast. The young man succumbed to typhus after a long and arduous voyage from London to Brisbane and back to Liverpool via Portland, Oregon, in command of the barque *Inglewood* (Official Number 63886) with his wife, Annie, at his side. William broke his right arm and shoulder blade when a heavy sea swamped the ship on the way into Brisbane. He eventually brought the *Inglewood* back to Belfast but was worse for wear afterward. He was only thirty-four when he died. The flags of the ships in Belfast harbor flew at half-mast out of respect for the popular young seaman.[212]

After serving as master of the sailing ships *Amyone* and *Boyne* from 1875 to 1879, William Kelly Sr.'s oldest son, John, transitioned from sail to steam. Between 1879 and 1902, he commanded the SS *British Crown*, SS *British King*, SS *Koh-i-Noor*, SS *Tyrian*, SS *Horatius*, and SS *Hudson*. John's career ship was the *British King*, which was built at Belfast's Harland and Wolff shipyard in 1881 (where RMS *Titanic* was launched in 1911). As master of the *British King* between 1882 and 1889, John accumulated approximately 400,000 nautical miles on four voyages as a pioneer of direct steam service from the United

Kingdom to New Zealand and on over forty round trips between Liverpool and Philadelphia. While taking the British Standard Oil steamer *Hudson* from New York to China and Japan, John died at Colombo, Ceylon, on September 1, 1902, at age fifty-five. The cause of death was recorded as apoplexy (possibly a stroke). His crew buried him at Colombo, and the *Hudson* proceeded eastward with the first mate in command.

## The Fate of the *Princess Alexandra*

The *Princess Alexandra* remained in Kelly's extended family under the ownership of John and William Moore for fifteen years after Kelly's death. Nathan Kellett served as her captain from 1877 into the 1880s, with Captains Hollywood (1886) and Kain (1888) succeeding him. The ship made numerous trips to Pensacola, Pascagoula, Quebec, Rio de Janeiro, and other ports of call until the twenty-nine-year-old vessel, sailing in ballast from Belfast to Saint John, New Brunswick, foundered during a fearsome, five-day North Atlantic hurricane in October of 1892. Captain James McGonnell, his wife, and seventeen crewmen were rescued by the Swedish barque *Jacob Rahners* of Gothenburg and brought safely to Dover. As fate would have it, the Moore brothers had previously sold the *Princess Alexandra* to Mr. William R. Rea and others of Belfast who had established a consortium to manage the ship. Thus, the Kelly family had no business connection with the *Princess Alexandra* at the time the ship was lost. However, they would certainly have had vivid memories of the past controversies related to this noteworthy family ship.[213]

Figure 26: Captain William Kelly (1811–1877).
Image credit: Bradley archive/undated.

*Arising from a good education, sound sense, and a cultivated understanding will be that self-possession and self-confidence which are so necessary for a shipmaster....A master in possession of these qualities is like a man walking in the broad daylight, who can see everything around him, and who knows where he is going and what he is doing.*

—James Lees, *A Manual for Shipmasters (1851), 3-4*

## CHAPTER EIGHT

# Trail's End

### (2023)

When it comes to seamanship and ship ownership, Captain William Kelly was the genuine article. He appears to have been an able sailor—steady, thoughtful, and principled in command—well known, successful, and respected within his business circles. However, his apparent aversion to the limelight held lasting fame at bay. My father thought Kelly was an important man but knew little about him. Even in Northern Ireland, when Dr. Bob Foy gave a talk on Kelly at the Belfast Family History Society in 2013, no one in the audience had heard of this sea captain.[214]

Beyond the eroding effects of time and tide, one reason history has forgotten Kelly might be that he was never a grandstander. He was the antithesis, for instance, of James "Bully" Forbes, the braggart shipmaster of James Baines's speedy Black Ball clippers *Marco Polo*, *Lightning*, and *Schomberg* who flew his own personal flag at the foremast of the ships he commanded. It was Forbes who famously shouted, "Hell or Melbourne," during one run from Liverpool to the Australian goldfields. On another occasion, he took it up a notch, boasting, "Ladies and Gentlemen, on my last trip I astonished the world. This trip I intend to astonish the Almighty." Forbes and others like him drove their ships mercilessly through fair weather and foul, with lee rails drenched for weeks on end. They showed little consideration for crew or passengers, striving only for breakneck speed in their all-consuming race to be first to Melbourne. At the end of his career, Forbes lost some ships, and his reputation sank. By the 1860s, the press was describing him as "a seedy, broken-down skipper with the forced joviality of a broken-hearted man."[215]

Kelly was another type entirely: an unassuming gentleman-mariner who, without creating a cult of personality around himself, still racked up a solid reputation for fast passages without terrifying his passengers and alienating his crews in the process. Numerous passenger testimonials are evidence of this, as is the fact that many of his officers and sailors chose to remain with him from ship to ship, voyage to voyage, and season to season.

Our family photographs of Kelly in retirement (Frontispiece and Figure 26) depict a sturdy man accustomed to authority with a steady gaze fixed on a distant point. One senses there was little that could rattle him. In thirty years at sea, he had experienced just about everything nature could throw at him, including explosive Hatteras storms with forty-foot waves and hurricane winds; freezing spray in the wintry North Atlantic; impenetrable sea fog shrouding the Grand Banks of Newfoundland; gray Garúa drizzle obscuring the parched coasts of Peru and northern Chile; the boiling black clouds of an approaching squall line in the Indian Ocean; chaotic thunderheads with heavy rain and lightning in the South China Sea; sparkling, razor-sharp drift ice in the South Atlantic; and the ship-stopping calms of the equatorial doldrums. He might even have sailed through the bioluminescent glow of a milky sea on a moonless summer night in the Gulf of Aden. Every day he faced new challenges (and incredulities) with the lives and hopes of many—passengers, crew, and shareholders alike—hanging on the decisions he made.

"Bully" Forbes died before he was fifty, a broken man with a celebrated past, an intolerable present, and an uncertain future. William Kelly ended his days in full stride—still engaged with others (his letter writing the morning he died), still with a destination in mind (his last carriage ride), still tending to his surroundings (his garden), and still girdling the globe with his beautiful new clipper barque smartly carving the waves between Calcutta and New York in the capable hands of Captain John Seabourne.

In the golden age of sail, before the elegant wooden clippers gave way to iron, steel, and steam, William Kelly's career undoubtedly swung high and low. The *Belinda*'s 1846 passage to Quebec was fraught with smallpox and death, especially afflicting the children, yet the passengers—a quarter of them workhouse paupers—still found words to mention Kelly's kindness and attention to the sick.

Then there was the *Merrie England*'s 1860 run to Demerara overloaded with indentured laborers from India bound for the sugar plantations of British Guiana. Along with many ships that departed Calcutta for the West Indies that season, the *Merrie England* had a significant death toll. If Kelly managed this trip with the same compassion he had displayed fourteen years earlier during the *Belinda*'s disease-ravaged passage to Quebec, he might have earned similar accolades in 1860. However, the indentured Indian workers in Demerara faced "a new system of slavery" that was far removed from the freehold opportunities of Canada.

The Kelly brothers chose the same career, and their ships frequently traversed the same waters, sometimes simultaneously. They sailed together on the *Margaret Johnson*'s 1836 trip to New Orleans, on the *Merrie England*'s triumphant maiden voyage to Australia, India, and China in 1856. From this, I infer that the brothers were close. Certainly their parallel careers imply that they were kindred spirits with a shared taste for seafaring and "doing business in great waters." However, the hit-and-miss records pulled together here also suggest that they might have diverged in fundamental ways. As the British novelist, playwright, and Zionist leader Israel Zangwill (1864–1926) might have written, "It takes two men to make one brother."[216]

William emerges as a recognizable, almost familiar character thanks to our surviving photographs of him, his press clippings, and especially his letters, which contain approximately two thousand words describing his interests and concerns in his last years. In contrast, John, tragically lost with all hands in the sinking of the *Hilton*, remains a shadowy, fascinating figure, forever one with the unpredictable and unforgiving sea. With John, there are more questions than answers. What was he doing in California between 1848 and 1856? Was he, in fact, there at all? Why did he step down the chain of command from master to mate, while William remained a commander of ships throughout his career—"Master under God," as the old insurance policies characterized him?

John might have preferred overseeing the working interests of ships, leaving the executive functions to the ship's master. In line with this idea, I imagine a tragic but good death for John. In the dark, chaotic waters of an Indian Ocean hurricane, he likely strove mightily to save the *Hilton*, her men, and himself, but in the end he could do only one thing. When the ship capsized and sank, he played the hand he had been dealt, joining his captain and crew in their breathless, brotherly drift to the bottom.

The wreckage of John's last voyage raised the specter of similar situations of doubt, difficulty, and danger for William. Two of his career ships (the *Mary Carson* and the *Miles Barton*) sank just a month and a half after the *Hilton*—and within a month of each other. Eventually William's heart disease ended the active seafaring stage of his career. He would live out his final years, first overseeing James Beazley's interests at the port of Liverpool, then managing his own small fleet of commercial sailing vessels while entrusting them to the care of others at sea.

How do I characterize the relationship between William and John Kelly? How do they stack up in this mid-Victorian family seafaring saga? Given the incomplete information that has come my way, questions like this are certainly ponderable, but they are ultimately unanswerable with any degree of confidence. In spite of this, the brothers' paper trail suggests that each man possessed the expertise, tenacity, confidence, and strength of character to shape his particular seaward predisposition into a glorious, lifelong adventure, each according to his own inclinations.

As Villiers puts it, "Command in sail was exacting and its demands were immense and endless. They were not always met by any means, for they were, above all, demands upon character, and the man without real integrity of spirit had no hope of lasting success. But, granted that, and good qualities of leadership, and indefatigable energy, skill, and determination, the rewards for the true spirit were immense and endless, too. If many were called and few were chosen, those few had a glimpse of glory. There was no other career comparable with it, nor is there likely to be again."[217]

Villiers's praise for the true-spirited master mariner might bathe the Kelly brothers in its warm, reflected glow. However, real insight into their careers depends on the facts at hand, which are admittedly sparse, at least when compared with the richness, depth, and nuance of lives as lived. The trickle of sourced information in this book might offer only an incomplete and therefore possibly distorted reflection of the Kelly brothers. Nevertheless, I hope the stories collected here have at least rescued them from oblivion.

There might be much more to learn about them, especially if descendants emerge with new details to flesh out their lives—family perhaps in Northern Ireland, the Republic of Ireland, England, South Africa, Canada, the United States, or elsewhere. In the meantime, I continue to dream of a dusty old sea chest stamped with the name "William Kelly" in someone's attic somewhere. My reverie even conjures the contents of this imaginary trunk—a hoard of historic ships' logs, diaries, letters, photographs, and other ephemera that would allow me to expand on the stories collected in this book.

The trunk in the attic is only a pipe dream, the whimsy of a determined family historian. Yet current events make me wonder if the present and the future (along with the past) might draw me closer in spirit to my nineteenth-century seafaring forebears. A recent accomplishment far above Earth's oceans—indeed, in Earth orbit—makes me wonder if my Victorian mariners might still be relevant today within the context of twenty-first-century space exploration.

As noted in the introduction to this book, William Kelly was born in the same year that the Great Comet of 1811 streamed impressively by Earth. This transitory, icy visitor had emerged from the constellation Argo Navis (the Ship Argo), a remarkably nautical neighborhood of our Milky Way galaxy.

During their years at sea, William and John Kelly used the moon, planets, stars, and constellations as important reference points for ocean navigation. Today we can imagine actually traveling to and exploring these distant rocky and gaseous objects. However, many questions arise: First and foremost, how will we travel sustainably within our solar system, let alone through interstellar space?

Rocket fuel has been the propellant of choice for decades. It has taken humans to the moon and robots to Mars, but it is also heavy, unstable, hazardous, and requires continuous replacement. Chemical fuel will not take us to the stars. Fortunately, a new, recently demonstrated propulsion method might offer an alternative approach for deep space travel. This new development also has interesting implications for the legacy and relevance of my Victorian master mariners.

In the summer of 2019, the Planetary Society launched its citizen-funded LightSail 2 spacecraft into Earth orbit.[218] After successfully deploying the nanosatellite's 344-square-foot silver Mylar sail, ground-based engineers succeeded in raising the spacecraft's orbit by holding the sail at a constant 90-degree angle to the sun—much as a sailing ship tacks into the wind to move in a straight line. Sure enough, the sun's radiation pressure slowly pushed LightSail 2 into a higher orbit, establishing the feasibility of sailing on sunlight.[219]

Figure 27: Artist's concept of LightSail 2 in Earth orbit.
Image credit: The Planetary Society.

Solar sails leverage a peculiarity of photons. What these elementary light particles lack in mass, they make up for in momentum. When photons emanating from the sun or a laser array contact a satellite equipped with a light-reflecting solar sail, their momentum transfers to the sail, providing a gentle push. As the photons bounce off the sail, they give it another slight push. In the vacuum of space, this impetus accelerates the satellite in a direction away from the light source. Powerful lasers might someday accelerate sail-driven payloads through space, allowing them to "ghost" on photons, perhaps even achieving speeds of approximately two hundred kilometers per second.[220]

The winds and ocean currents that drove the *Miles Barton*, the *Merrie England*, and other sailing ships seaward in the nineteenth century were driven by the sun heating Earth's surface. LightSail 2 raises the possibility that sunlight might someday push compact containers of human creativity and curiosity beyond the heliosphere where charged particles from the sun encounter interstellar space—like the curling bow wave of a ship at sea. These sparks of sunlight might portend a new sun-jamming epoch that would have astonished my wind-jamming ancestors—or perhaps they would not have been surprised. The LightSail 2 project team cites an intriguing seventeenth-century quotation that hints at the possibility of modifying ships and sails to leverage heavenly breezes.

> Provide ships or sails adapted to the heavenly breezes, and there will be some who will brave even that void.
> JOHANNES KEPLER TO GALILEO GALILEI, 1610

What's past is prologue. Everything old is new again. From the milky sea to the Milky Way, a new golden age of sail might be in the offing, helping to make the Kelly brothers and their nineteenth-century seafaring cohort still relevant in the twenty-first century. Looking back and looking forward become complementary undertakings in a sun-driven technological continuum that straddles historic periods. White sails at sea. Silver sails in space.

After many years of diligently chasing my family's lost mariners, I have learned more about them than I ever thought possible. I have discovered a sizable trove of records, studied the world in which they travelled, and achieved a greater awareness and appreciation of their seafaring knowledge and know-how. William left behind a substantial semblance of himself. John left more the shadow of a semblance. In the absence of family stories and letters pertaining to John, and with no photograph of him, I struggle to envisage and comprehend him as I do William. While evidently knowing the ropes and exhibiting good leadership skills as a shipmaster in the 1840s, John served primarily as a first mate in the 1850s. Was he perhaps just not as ambitious as William?

Fortunately, a few words at the beginning of this book offer at least a metaphoric glimpse of John and countless other forgotten seamen of the golden age of sail—"when oceans were the lifeblood, sea lanes the arteries, ships the muscle, and mariners the heartbeat of a global impulse to move people and goods around the world." Indeed, these words capture the essence of John (and of William too). They embody the raw physicality and sheer determination that steered the Kelly brothers along separate but similar routes to different destinies. Tennyson's poem, "The Lotos Eaters," possibly touches upon the inevitable end of the seafarer's life.

> *Surely, surely, slumber is more sweet than toil, the shore*
> *Than labour in the deep mid-ocean, wind and wave and oar;*
> *O, rest ye, brother mariners, we will not wander more.*

Some mariners, like William, ended their days with a gradual winding down in retirement; others, like John, died of illness or accident at sea. Thinking of the last days of my great-great granduncles takes me back to my first days researching their lives—and to my reasons for writing this book. I first cut my teeth in genealogy with my family's English ancestors. They were mostly farm laborers and domestic servants, and before long I had plenty of grist for my genealogical mill—births, baptisms, occupations, weddings, deaths, and interments galore, but I discovered little about the lives they lived *between these life changing events*. Family stories were few and far between.

Then I remembered our family photo album with Captain Kelly, snug in his Victorian armchair, as if gazing out to sea. He was "an important man," according to my father. "Imagine the stories he would have told." The haunting Uilleann pipes of Ireland figuratively drew me across the Irish Sea to the shores of Lough Neagh. Here the clouds parted, the sun broke through, and I set about chasing my master mariners across oceans far and wide. I was amazed, delighted, and overwhelmed by the stories that emerged from the paper trail they left behind—especially the Shipping News in historic newspapers.

I recognize that the nineteenth-century "golden age of sail" was not golden everywhere, in every way, for everyone. The Kelly brothers were master mariners at the height of the British Empire and active participants in the Industrial Revolution, the Irish famines, the Australian gold rush, even a problematic indentured labor scheme. As strong Presbyterians, they would probably have espoused a robust work ethic and the profit motive in business and commercial ventures. The brothers' maritime activities are forever entangled in the historical context of their time, for better or for worse. Finding just a few of their stories has nudged me closer to a deeper and more nuanced understanding, not only of them, but of the Victorian era in which they lived.

I have written *Seaward* to lift William and John Kelly out of the obscurity that has for so long eclipsed them. I also hope that the book will inspire readers who are curious about their ancestors to dig deep, find the stories, and celebrate their own family history and heritage, as only they can do.

Someday soon I will revisit the rugged Sonoma Coast north of San Francisco. There on a windblown, sun-drenched headland festooned with Pacific reed grass, yellow bush lupine, and whitetip clover, I will squint out to the thundering sea. Shutting my eyes against the dazzling sun, I will imagine the Kelly brothers and their ships running before the wind—sparkling sails on the horizon, flashes of reflected sunlight moving purposefully within that narrow band of discernibility where the sea touches the sky.

Figure 28: Trail's End, The Sea Ranch, Sonoma County, California. Image credit: Paul Kozal (www.paulkozal.com).

# Sources

## Historic Newspapers

*American and Commercial Daily Advertiser*
*Amsterdam Algemeen Handelsblad*
*Army and Navy Gazette* (London)
*Augusta Chronicle*
*Belfast Commercial Chronicle*
*Belfast Morning News*
*Belfast News-Letter*
*Belfast Northern Whig*
*Belfast Protestant Journal*
*Belfast Telegraph*
*Boston Herald*
*Bristol Mercury*
*Caledonian Mercury* (Edinburgh)
*Colchester Essex Standard*
*Colonial Times* (Hobart, Tasmania)
*Cornwall Chronicle*
*Courier de la Louisianne* (New Orleans)
*Glasgow Herald*
*Hampshire Advertiser & Salisbury Guardian* (Southampton)
*Hobart Colonial Times*
*Hobart Courier*
*Hull Packet and East Riding Times*
*Kemptville Weekly Advance*
*Leeds Mercury*
*Liverpool Albion*
*Liverpool Daily Post*

*Liverpool Mercury*
*Liverpool Weekly Courier*
*Lloyd's Weekly Newspaper*
*London and China Telegraph*
*London Daily News*
*London Evening Standard*
*London Morning Chronicle*
*London Morning Post*
*London Public Ledger and Daily Advertiser*
*London Times*
*Manchester Times*
*Melbourne Age*
*Melbourne Argus*
*Moreton Bay Courier*
*Newcastle Courant*
*New Orleans Bee*
*New Orleans Commercial Bulletin*
*New Orleans Times-Picayune*
*New York Daily Tribune*
*New York Herald*
*New York Spectator*
*New York Times*
*North China Herald*
*Northern Daily Times*
*Perth Daily News* (Australia)
*Providence Evening Press* (Rhode Island)
*Public Ledger and Daily Advertiser* (London)
*Quebec Gazette*
*Reynold's Newspaper* (London)
*Singapore Straits Times*
*Sydney Morning Herald*
*Waterford News*
*York Herald*

## Other Sources

A. Green & Company's Directory for Liverpool and Birkenhead, 1870: https://archive.org/details/agreencosdirect00cog00g

British Newspaper Archive: www.britishnewspaperarchive.co.uk

CLIP Crew List Index Project: www.crewlist.org.uk

Documenting Ireland: Parliament, People and Migration (DIPPAM): https://www.dippam.ac.uk/

GenealogyBank: www.genealogybank.com

Google News Archive: www.news.google.com/newspapers

JSTOR: https://www.jstor.org

Lennon Wylie, Belfast Street Directories: https://www.lennon-wylie.co.uk/index.htm

Lloyd's Captains' Registers, National Archives (UK): www.nationalarchives.gov.uk/help-with-your-research/research-guides/officers-merchant-navy

Lloyd's Registers of Shipping (UK): www.maritimearchives.co.uk/lloyds-register.html

Lloyd's Registers of Shipping (US): https://onlinebooks.library.upenn.edu/webbin/serial?id=amlloyds and https://research.mysticseaport.org/item/l0237571883/

*Post-Office Belfast Annual Directory for 1843–44*: https://books.google.com

Proceedings of the Old Bailey, 1674–1913: www.oldbaileyonline.org

TROVE, National Library of Australia: www.trove.nla.gov.au

UK and Ireland, Masters and Mates Certificates, 1850–1927: www.ancestry.com

# Publications of the Hydrographic Office, Admiralty London

*The Australia Directory, Volume 1:* Comprising South and East Coasts, from Cape Leeuwin to Port Jackson including Bass Strait and Tasmania, 1897

*The Bay of Bengal Pilot: Including Southwest Coast of Ceylon, North Coast of Sumatra, Nicobar and Andaman Islands*, 1887

*The China Sea Directory, Volume 1: Directions for the Approaches to the China Sea and to Singapore by the Straits of Sunda, Banka, Gaspar, Carimata, Rhio, Varella, Durian and Singapore*, 1867

*The China Sea Directory, Volume 3: Comprising the Coast of China from Hongkong to the Korea; North Coast of Luzon, Formosa Island and Strait; the Babuyan and Bashi Groups, and Pratas Island. Yellow Sea, Gulfs of Pe Chili and Liau Tung. Also the Rivers Canton, West, Yung, Yang Tse, Yellow, Pei Ho and Liau Ho*, 1894

*Eastern Archipelago, Part I (Eastern Part): Comprising the Philippines, Sulu Sea, Sulu Archipelago, N.E. Coast of Borneo, Celebes Sea, N.E. Coast of Celebes, Molucca and Gillolo Passages, Banda and Arafura Seas, N.W. and West Coasts of New Guinea and North Coast of Australia*, 1902

*The Gulf of Aden Pilot: Sokótra and Adjacent Islands, Somáli and Arabian Coasts in the Gulf of Aden and the East Coast of Arabia*, originally compiled by Commander C. Y. Ward, R.N., from Memoirs by Officers of the Indian Navy, 2nd ed., with additions, 1882

*The St. Lawrence Pilot: Comprising Sailing Directions for the Gulf and River*, 1860

# Bibliography

Abbott, Clare. *Faithful of Days: The Story of Robert Crighton, Master Mariner*. Nottingham, UK: YouCaxton, 2014.

Baird, Patricia Stavely. *An Unlettered Girl: Her Life on the Goldfields*. Maddigan Press, 2002.

Beaumont, Joseph. *The New Slavery: An Account of the Indian and Chinese Immigrants in British Guiana*. Coventry, UK: Caribbean Press, 2011. First published 1871.

Briggs, L. Vernon. *History of Shipbuilding on North River, Plymouth County, Massachusetts. With Genealogies of Shipbuilders and Accounts of the Industries upon Its Tributaries. 1640 to 1872*. Norwell, MA: Norwell Historical Society, 1976. First published 1889 (Boston).

Bullen, Frank Thomas. *The Men of the Merchant Service: Being the Polity of the Mercantile Marine for Longshore Readers*. London: Smith, Elder, 1900.

Cunningham, Scott. *Sea Kayaking in Nova Scotia*. Rockport, ME: Down East Books, 2000.

Davidson, A. S. *Marine Art & Liverpool: Painters, Places & Flag Codes, 1760–1960*. Wolverhampton, UK: WAINE Research Publications, 1986.

Davis, R. H. "Disaster of the Ship *Express*." October 29, 1942. https://www.dippam.ac.uk/ied/records/51854.

Ellison, Thomas. *The Cotton Trade of Great Britain: Including a History of the Liverpool Cotton Market and of the Liverpool Cotton Brokers' Association*. London: Effingham Wilson, Royal Exchange, 1886.

Finch, Roger. *The Pierhead Painters: Naïve Ship-Portrait Painters, 1750–1950*. London: Barrie & Jenkins, 1983.

Flint, Timothy. *The History and Geography of the Mississippi Valley*. Cincinnati, OH: E. H. Flint and L. R. Lincoln, 1832.

Forwood, William Bower. *Recollections of a Busy Life: Being the Reminiscences of a Liverpool Merchant, 1840–1910*. Liverpool, UK: Henry Young & Sons, 1910.

Fox Smith, C. *There Was a Ship: Chapters from the History of Sail*. Hartford, CT: Edwin Valentine Mitchell, 1930.

Foy, Robert H. *Dear Uncle: Immigrant Letters to Antrim from the USA, 1843–1852: The Kerr Letters with Accompanying Notes on Their Background*. Antrim, UK: Antrim and District Historical Society, 1989.

———. *Remembering All the Orrs: The Story of the Orr Families of Antrim and their Involvement in the 1798 Rebellion*. Newtownards, UK: Ulster Historical Foundation, 1999.

Garratt, Dena. *Précis of the Wrecks in the Ships' Graveyard, Rottnest*. Report No. 148. Department of Maritime Archeology, Western Australian Museum, 1999.

Great Britain Foreign Office. *Reports from Her Majesty's Consuls on the Manufactures, Commerce, etc. of their Consular Districts*. Part II. London: Harrison and Sons, 1879.

Haines, Robin. *Life and Death in the Age of Sail: The Passage to Australia*. Sydney, Australia: UNSW Press, 2006.

Haldane, Charlotte. *Daughter of Paris: The Life Story of Celeste Mogador*. Hutchinson, 1961.

Hamilton, William B. *Place Names of Atlantic Canada*. Toronto: University of Toronto Press, 1996.

Harland, John. *Seamanship in the Age of Sail*. London: Adlard Coles, 1984.

Hastings, David. *Over the Mountains of the Sea: Life on the Migrant Ships, 1870–1885*. Auckland, NZ: Auckland University Press, 2013.

Hidy, Ralph W. "The Organization and Functions of Anglo-American Merchant Bankers, 1815–1860." In "The Tasks of Economic History." Supplement, *Journal of Economic History*, 1 (December 1941): 53–66.

Hopkins, Manley. *The Port of Refuge; or, Advice and Instructions to the Master-Mariner in Situations of Doubt, Difficulty and Danger*. London: Henry S. King, 1873.

House of Commons, Great Britain. *Papers Relative to Emigration to the British Provinces in North America*. London: William Clowes and Sons, 1847.

Hunter, Frederick Mercer. *An Account of the British Settlement of Aden in Arabia*. London: Trübner, 1877.

Irish, Bill. *Shipbuilding in Waterford, 1820–1882: A Historical, Technical, and Pictorial Study*. Dublin, Ireland: Wordwell, 2005.

Jackson, Robert. *Ocean Passages for the World: Compiled for the Use of Seamen, as an Aid for Ascertaining the Route to Be Followed in the General Navigation of the Several Oceans*. 1st ed. Printed for the Hydrographic Department, Admiralty, London, 1895.

Jung, Moon-Ho. *Coolies and Cane: Race, Labor, and Sugar in the Age of Emancipation*. Baltimore: Johns Hopkins Press, 2006.

Kemp, P., ed. *The Oxford Companion to Ships and the Sea*. Oxford: Oxford University Press, 1976.

Kenny, James G. *As the Crow Flies over Rough Terrain: Incorporating the Diary 1827/1828 and More of a Divine*. Ballymena, Antrim: J. G. Kenny, 1988.

Kotsch, William J. *Weather for the Mariner*. 2nd ed. Annapolis, MD: Naval Institute Press, 1977.

LaGrange, H. & J. *Clipper Ships of America and Great Britain, 1833–1869*. New York: G. P. Putnam's Sons, 1936.

Lees, James. *Dana's Seamen's Friend: Containing a Treatise on Practical Seamanship, with Plates; a Dictionary of Sea Terms; and the Customs and Usages of the Merchant

*Service; with the British Laws Relating to Shipping, the Duties of Masters and Mariners, and the Mercantile Marine.* London: George Philip & Son, 1862.

———. *A Manual for Shipmasters in a Series of Letters, Addressed to Them on Their Qualifications, Duties, Powers, Responsibilities, etc. Arising during the Course of a Voyage.* London: George Philip & Son, 1851.

Lubbock, Basil. *The Colonial Clippers.* Glasgow, UK: Brown Son & Ferguson, 1948.

MacGregor, David R. *Clipper Ships.* Watford, UK: Argus Books, 1979.

———. *Merchant Sailing Ships, 1850–1875: Heyday of Sail.* London: Conway Maritime Press, 1984.

Mackenzie, Joan Finnigan. *Witches, Ghosts and Loup-Garous.* Kingston, ON: Quarry Press, 1994.

Macmillan, Allister, ed. *Mauritius Illustrated: Historical and Descriptive; Commercial and Industrial; Facts, Figures and Resources.* Commemorative ed. New Delhi, Madras: Asian Educational Services, 2000. First published c. 1914.

Marcil, Eileen. *The Charley Man: The History of Wooden Ship Building at Quebec, 1765–1893.* Kingston, ON: Quarry Press, 1995.

Marshall, John J. "The Dialect of Ulster." *Ulster Journal of Archaeology* 10, no. 3 (1904): 121–30. http://www.jstor.org/stable/20608548.

Martin, Captain Henry Byam, R.N. *The Polynesian Journal.* Canberra: Australian National University Press, 1981. http://hdl.handle.net/1885/114833

McKenna, Joseph. *British Ships in the Confederate Navy.* Jefferson, NC: McFarland, 2010.

McKinstry, Robert. "Chrome Hill, Lambeg." *Lisburn Historical Society Journal* 6 (1986–87).

Mogador, Céleste. *Adieux au Monde: Mémoires de Céleste Mogador.* Paris: Locard-Davi et de Vresse, 1854.

Nicholson, Ian. *Log of logs: A Catalogue of Logs, Journals, Shipboard Diaries, Letters, and All Forms of Voyage Narratives for Australia and New Zealand and Surrounding Oceans* (3 volumes). Yaroomba, Queensland: The Author jointly with the Australian Association for Maritime History, [1990-1998].

Plimsoll, Samuel. Our Seamen: An Appeal. London: Virtue & Co., Ivy Lane, 1873.

Scoles, Sarah. "The Good Kind of Crazy: The Quest for Exotic Propulsion." *Scientific American*, August 2019.

Smith, W. S. *Historical Gleanings in Antrim and Neighborhood.* Belfast, UK: Mayne and Boyd, 1888.

Smyth, Alastair. *The Story of Antrim.* Antrim, UK: Antrim Borough Council, 1984.

Stevens, Robert White. *On the Stowage of Ships and Their Cargoes with Information Regarding Freights, Charter-Parties, etc.* London: Longmans, Green, Reader & Dyer, 1871.

Villiers, Alan. *The Way of a Ship.* New York: Scribner, 1970.

Walcott, G. (Secretary of the Colonial Land and Emigration Commission) to Chadwick, E. (Secretary of the Poor Law Commission); correspondence between September 11, 1846 and January 1, 1847; UK National Archives, Kew, Richmond, Surrey, Ref. HO 45 / O.S. 1615.

Wallace, Frederick William. *Wooden Ships and Iron Men: The Story of the Square-rigged Merchant Marine of British North America, the Ships, their Builders and Owners, and the Men Who Sailed Them.* Boston: Charles E. Lauriat, 1937.

Whidden, John D. *Ocean Life in the Old Sailing Ship Days from Forecastle to Quarterdeck.* New York: Little, Brown, 1908.

Wilks, Samuel. *Lectures on Diseases of the Nervous System Delivered at Guy's Hospital.* London: J. & A. Churchill, 1878.

# Notes

## Introduction

1 *The Kelly family monument:* Muckamore is a grange in the barony of Lower Massereene, County of Antrim, Northern Ireland. The graveyard is located on Oldstone Road, Muckamore, Antrim.
2 *Weavers in Islandreagh:* The search of the PRONI was undertaken by Dr. Bob Foy in the 1990s. Foy suggests that the Kelly family's relocation from Islandreagh to Antrim was an astute move, as handloom weaver incomes were declining in the late 1790s (Foy, personal communication).
3 *Penned this admiring poem:* The acrostic poem is dated "Antrim July 3rd, 1826" and signed "O. Kelly" (an as yet unexplored relative).
4 *The end of the line:* "September 16th (1828)...Last night John Kelly, Innkeeper, Townhead died; September 17th... attended John Kelly's funeral to Muckamore. He was aged 68 years." Extracted from Rev. Robert Magill's diary (1827–1828), as reproduced in Kenny, *As the Crow Flies over Rough Terrain*, 377. Robert Magill (1788–1839) was the Presbyterian minister of the Mill Row Congregation, Antrim. His diaries (1821–1837) offer fascinating glimpses into the daily life of a Presbyterian preacher who was deeply interested in the people of his congregation.
5 *TO INNKEEPERS. To be sold: Belfast Commercial Chronicle*, December 14, 1829, 3.
6 *CAUTION: Having seen an Advertisement: Belfast News-Letter*, December 22, 1829, 3. The PRONI appears to support William Kelly's contention that his father died intestate. A name search on the PRONI website (Pre-1858 Wills and

261

Administrations, Connor Diocesan Wills) lists John Kelly of Antrim died in 1828, with the following notation: "The original documents referred to in this index DO NOT exist. No further information, other than that recorded above, has survived."

7 *TO BE LET:* Belfast News-Letter, October 15, 1830, 3.
8 *Matson's Tenement:* Belfast Northern Whig, March 25, 1833, 3.
9 *Truly delightful to look upon:* Smith, Historical Gleanings in Antrim and Neighborhood, quoted in Smyth, The Story of Antrim, 56.
10 *White cedar for top timbers:* Wallace, Wooden Ships and Iron Men, 27–29.

## Chapter One

11 *Took to the sea early:* Kelly's obituary in the Belfast News-Letter (September 14, 1877, 3) says nothing about his formative years, merely stating that "the deceased gentleman was born in Antrim and at an early age adopted a seafaring life."
12 *Crisscrossing the Irish Sea:* The Belfast News-Letter (Belfast Ship News) reported, "February 16, 1836, arrived, *Hillsborough*, Kelly, Liverpool, salt—March 22, 1836, sailed, *Hillsborough*, Kelly, Liverpool, potatoes—April 25, 1836, arrived, *Hillsborough*, Kelly, salt—August 9, 1836, arrived, *Hillsborough*, Kelly, Copeland Island, oats—December 15, 1836, arrived, *Success*, Kelly, Liverpool, salt." The Copeland, Mew, and Lighthouse Islands are in the North Irish Sea off County Down. The Kelly listed in these notices might have been the William Kelly of this narrative, but this is not confirmed.
13 *The first mention:* The William Kelly mentioned in the advertisement is likely the subject of this narrative for the following reasons: First, the *Margaret Johnson* sailed a similar route to many that William Kelly would subse-

quently sail in the early years of his career (i.e., Belfast or Liverpool to North America with immigrants for the New World, then back with timber from Quebec or cotton from the American South). Second, the *Margaret Johnson*'s owner, David Grainger, also owned the *Dumfriesshire*, the *Belinda*, and the *Dalriada*, three ships that William Kelly would subsequently command. Finally, no other William Kelly is listed as a shipmaster in the Belfast papers of the late 1830s.

14 *Serving as a twenty-year-old apprentice seaman:* See the ship listing in Figure 11 (John Kelly's Claim for Certificate of Service).

15 *A beakhead bow:* This is the space in a sailing ship forward of the forecastle. Open to the sea, the beakhead was used as the seamen's lavatory and typically referred to as the heads.

16 *An artistic flourish:* For more information on the Liverpool or Watson's Code of Signals, refer to Davidson, *Marine Art & Liverpool*, 140–43.

17 *One of the prettiest and fastest-sailing vessels: Belfast Protestant Journal*, April 5, 1845, 2.

18 *Mr. William Kelly married Miss Martha Rainey: Belfast News-Letter*, March 28, 1837, 2. The wedding announcement also references the February 27 marriage of John Rainey's oldest daughter, Mary, to Mr. William Stewart of Duneane. The Rainey residence at Ballydunmaul was a townland northwest of Randalstown in County Antrim.

19 *Perched on a hill overlooking Lough Neagh:* Craigmore Presbyterian Church is located at 39 Clonkeen Road, Craigmore, Randalstown, Antrim. The Public Record Office of Northern Ireland does not have any baptism or marriage records for this church. It is not known if any exist.

20 *Timothy Flint commented:* Flint, *The History and Geography of the Mississippi Valley*, 271.

21 *Virulent yellow fever outbreaks:* There are two sources of information for the death of baby John Kelly: (1) the Muckamore monument, which states, "[His son John] who

died at New Orleans 5-10-1839 aged 18 mth.," and (2) the New Orleans Girod Street Cemetery Records, which state, "Kelly, John, died – September 5, 1839, aged one year, eight months, born at N.O. La. (In vault with his uncle James Rainey)." There is a discrepancy between the monument and the burial record, although not an insurmountable one. It makes sense to accept the date given in the New Orleans burial record, as this document is closest in time and place to the death of baby John Kelly.

22  *William Kelly to James Graham:* Foy, *Dear Uncle*, 100–102.
23  *Brought up from the Passes:* The Mississippi River delta is approximately 106 miles from New Orleans. Here the river divides into three major streams, or passes, that flow into the Gulf of Mexico.
24  *Breathes the air of authority:* Bullen, *The Men of the Merchant Service*, 240.
25  *As may have been saved:* Augusta Chronicle, April 17, 1845, 2.
26  *Miss Sarah Orr:* Per the *Belfast News-Letter* of July 4, 1845, 2, "On the 1st. inst., in St. Ann's Church, by the Rev. Mr. Oulton, John Kelly, Master of the late barque *Clio*, to Miss Sarah, fourth daughter of James Orr, Esq., Folly, Antrim." For more on Sarah's family, see Foy, *Remembering All the Orrs*.
27  *21 Pilot Street:* See listing for "William Kelly, ship-master" in the *Post-Office Belfast Annual Directory for 1843–44* (Google Books).
28  *A remarkably quick passage: Belfast News-Letter*, April 23, 1844, 3.
29  *Passengers and crew all well: Belfast News-Letter*, July 16, 1844, 3.
30  *Fanny, youngest daughter of Captain William Kelly: Belfast News-Letter*, April 17, 1845, 3.
31  *George H. Parke and David Grainger:* George Holmes Parke of Quebec and David Grainger of Belfast were brothers-in-law. George Parke was the son of James Parke (1772–1851) of Stewartstown, County Tyrone, Northern Ireland.

David Grainger (1799–1858) married George Parke's sister, Maria Belinda Parke, in 1829. Parke was a shipbuilder and merchant in Quebec who took delivery of the goods that Grainger's ships carried to Quebec. Parke subsequently loaded the ships with wood for their return to Belfast. Thanks to Dr. Bob Foy for this example of the importance of family ties in nineteenth-century transatlantic trade.

32  *A man named Lepan:* This was probably Henry Lepan (or Le Pan), certificate no. 43,546. Born in Belfast in June 1822, Lepan was active in coastal and foreign shipping around this time.

33  *Place where—at sea:* Belinda's crew agreement, BT98/583, UK National Archives, courtesy Clare Abbott.

34  *We, the passengers: Quebec Gazette,* September 1, 1845, 2.

35  *Passed the barque Sir Henry Pottinger:* The shipping section of Belfast's *Northern Whig* newspaper (October 18, 1845, 2) notes the three ships encountered by the *Belinda* in the Gulf of Saint Lawrence.

36  *Signed on in their place: Belinda's* crew agreement, BT98/583, UK National Archives, courtesy Clare Abbott.

37  *Almost half of them children: Quebec Gazette,* July 22, 1846, 2. In addition to her large passenger population, the *Belinda* also carried into Quebec a cargo of 280 tons salt, 3 bales calfskins, 75 mats cordage, and 97 mats canvas for G. H. Parke, as well as 36 mats cordage, 4 mats canvas, 1 box linen, and 1 box wearing apparel to order.

38  *Struck down by the same sickness: Belinda's* crew agreement, BT98/859, UK National Archives, courtesy Clare Abbott.

39  *All apparently willing to work:* Extracted from House of Commons, Great Britain, *Papers Relative to Emigration to the British Provinces in North America,* February 1847 for the period between June 27 and July 25, 1846 (hereafter *Papers Relative to Emigration*), 25.

40  *Sanctioned by the Poor Law Commissioners:* E. Chadwick, Secretary of the Poor Law Commission, to G. Walcott, Sec-

retary of the Colonial Land and Emigration Commission, January 1, 1847, UK National Archives, Kew Richmond, Surrey, Ref. HO 45/O.S.1615.

41 *Compared with those on English and German ships:* An immigration depot and quarantine station was established in 1832 on Grosse Isle in the Gulf of Saint Lawrence. Emigrant ships were not permitted to sail on to Quebec until they had assured the authorities that they were free of disease (fever, cholera, typhus, etc.). Grosse Isle is the largest Irish potato famine burial ground outside Ireland. It is estimated that approximately 500,000 Irish immigrants passed through the station on their way to Canada between 1832 and 1932.

42 *Only to admit seven to hospital:* Extracted from a letter written by G. W. Douglas, MD, medical superintendent of the Grosse Isle Hospital, dated at Quebec, November 20, 1846, *Papers Relative to Emigration*, 30–31.

43 *900 from Germany:* Extracted from *Papers Relative to Emigration*, 8.

44 *670 infants (under a year):* Extracted from *Papers Relative to Emigration*, appendix, table 2.

45 *Belinda's grieving parents:* The parents of Belinda and Alexander Hunter were William Hunter and Nancy McConay Hunter of County Down, Ireland. Belinda was baptized by Armine Wale Mountain (1823–1885), the son of George Jehoshaphat Mountain D.D. (1789–1863), who was the third Anglican bishop of Quebec, the founder of Bishop's College, and the first principal of McGill University. See Immigrants at Grosse Isle Quarantine Station, 1832–1937 (online database), Library and Archives Canada.

46 *The Chincha Islands:* Callao was a fortified port on the Pacific Ocean near Lima, Peru. One of the six districts of Callao is an area named Bellavista. In retirement in the early 1870s, William Kelly owned a house named Bella Vista off Belfast's Antrim Road. However, there is no proven connection between the name of this house and the district of Callao.

47 *Hailing the ship Ottawa:* Tuskar Rock, off the southeast coast of County Wexford, Ireland, is known for its famous lighthouse and numerous wreck sites.

48 *Hawaii, Tahiti, and the Society Islands: Belinda*'s crew agreement, BT98/1508, UK National Archives, courtesy Clare Abbott. The four *Belinda* crewmen were Robert Barclay, William Christie, Robert Halliday, and William Huxtable. For a description of the *Grampus*'s activities prior to her encounter with the *Belinda*, see "The Polynesian Journal of Captain Henry Byam Martin, R.N. In command of HMS Grampus, 50 guns, at Hawaii and on station in Tahiti & the Society Islands, August 1846 to August 1847," http://hdl.handle.net/1885/114833. Martin would subsequently be promoted to Rear Admiral in 1854 and appointed Knight Commander of the Order of the Bath (KCB) during the Crimean War in 1855.

49 *Kelly's clipped and somewhat brisk Ulster English:* The Proceedings of the Old Bailey, London's Central Criminal Court, 1674–1913, reference number t18480403-984, https://www.oldbaileyonline.org. See also Marshall, "The Dialect of Ulster." Ulster Journal of Archaeology 10, no. 3 (1904): 121–30.

50 *The cold Atlantic fog and winds:* Scott Cunningham, "Scatarie Island: 'Nova Scotia's Far East.'"

51 *Crew and materials saved: Acadian Recorder*, Halifax, July 1, 1848, 3.

52 *Along the dangerous Main-à-Dieu Passage:* The Main-à-Dieu Passage separates Scatarie Island from mainland Cape Breton, and the community takes its name from this sea feature. It is of Mi'kmaq origin and, ironically, is a French corruption of *menadou*, for "evil spirit or the devil." It was first rendered as Main-à-Dieu, "hand of God," by Joseph DesBarres during his survey of Cape Breton in 1786. The narrow channel separating Scatarie Island from the village of Main-à-Dieu is known locally as the Tickle. See Hamilton, *Place Names of Atlantic Canada*.

53  *Wildes, Pickersgill & Co.*: This was an Anglo-American merchant banking firm that specialized in financing the export of products from North America while also performing general financial, banking, and mercantile functions. See Hidy, "The Organization and Functions of Anglo-American Merchant Bankers, 1815–1860," 53–66.

54  *The story goes something like this:* The tale of the dripping sailor is paraphrased from Mackenzie, *Witches, Ghosts and Loup-Garous,* 64-65.

55  *Cabin passenger James Frenchy:* The 1850 US Census lists a James French (age 35), merchant, born in Ireland and rooming with an Irish gospel minister and family with four other Irish lodgers in New York (Ward 16, District 3). This might have been the *Belinda*'s conscientious letter writer, especially as he appears to be a man with the means to have paid for a cabin passage and with the education to serve as spokesperson for the passengers.

56  *A letter of commendation:* Philip John Davey (certificate no. 26,441) was born in Alderney, Channel Islands, about 1823–1825; he was a mate on the *Arethusa* from 1845 to 1849 (Great Britain, Masters and Mates Certificates, 1850–1927 database). By 1861 Davey was a ship's captain himself, married with three children, and residing in Aberdeen (1861 Census of Scotland).

57  *We are respectfully: Belfast News-Letter,* June 30, 1848, 1.

58  *Robert Dixon and lady: New York Evening Post,* November 14, 1848, 3.

59  *Captain of the Arethusa: Belfast News-Letter,* May 22, 1849, 4. The *Arethusa*'s next departure is Liverpool for Boston on May 18, 1849, under a Captain McDowell.

60  *Little to lose and everything to gain:* The assertion that John Kelly relocated to California is based on the annotation in his 1856 Claim for Certificate of Service (Figure 11): "Since the year 1848, Applicant has been residing in California." However, this note may not be correct, viz., the 1852 Belfast Street Directory that lists "Kelly, John; master

mariner" residing at 24 Caroline St., Belfast (Lennon Wylie Index). There are also intriguing references in the *Belfast News-Letter* to a vessel, the *Sarah* (Captain Kelly), clearing at Saint John, New Brunswick, on November 12, 1852, and arriving at Belfast with timber on December 22 with the ship being put up for sale on December 24. Why intriguing? John Kelly had married Sarah Orr in 1845.

61 *760 barrels flour: Belfast News-Letter*, June 26, 1849, 2.
62 *A married woman named Mary Hempl:* Schedule A Passenger List for ship *Dalriada* arriving at New Orleans from Liverpool, December 24, 1849, Ancestry.com.
63 *£10 a month: Dalriada's* crew agreement, BT98/2114, UK National Archives, courtesy Clare Abbott.
64 *The shipyard of Christopher Boultenhouse:* Boultenhouse was one of the principal shipbuilders in the Sackville area. His shipyard on the banks of the Tantramar River launched more than fifty ships between 1840 and 1875.
65 *Alexander Clyde and Henry Lewis: Mary Carson's* crew agreement, BT98/3004, UK National Archives, courtesy Clare Abbott.

## Chapter Two

66 *Launched from the shipyard of William and Richard Wright:* The Wright brothers' shipyard turned out thirty vessels between 1839 and 1855 including the *Constance* (built in 1852) and the *Star of the East* (built in 1853). The *Star of the East* appears later in this *Miles Barton* narrative and again in the *Merrie England* narrative.
67 *A wooden model of the Miles Barton:* The Bonhams catalog description reads: "The hull built up from the solid and finished bright with the planking lines drawn in, the topsides fitted with chain plates and at the bow a figurehead holding a rope. The decks are also finished bright with the planking lines scored in, and detailed with chocks, capstan, deck posts, pin and fife rails, deck house detailed with doors and windows and fitted with three boats lashed to the roof, two

additional boats on davits, one lowered by the boarding ladder, deck railings, ship's wheel and other details. Rigged with a bowsprit and three masts, cross spars, standing and running rigging. The entire model finished natural with many areas varnished bright. Displayed with mahogany framed glass case."

68 *According to Forwood:* Forwood, *Recollections of a Busy Life*, 44.

69 *Helps clarify the allusion:* Ellison, *The Cotton Trade of Great Britain*, 261.

70 *The Miles Barton's imminent departure:* Ads were placed in many newspapers, but these words appeared in the *Bristol Mercury* of February 19, 1853, 4.

71 *David Stavely's diary:* Thanks to David Stavely's great-granddaughter, Patricia Stavely Baird of Victoria, Australia, for providing me with a transcription of this diary. On April 12, 1860, David Stavely married Margaret (Maggie) McFadden, born in Ballyeasborough, Newtownards, County Down. Maggie had been a passenger with David on the *Miles Barton*'s 1853 passage from Liverpool to Melbourne. Patricia Stavely Baird has written a novel titled *An Unlettered Girl: Her Life on the Goldfield*, which tells David and Maggie's story. Patricia Baird's kindness in sharing the transcript of her great-grandfather's diary is greatly appreciated.

72 *The chief officer:* The officer mentioned here refers not to William Kelly but to his first mate, Mr. Tate.

73 *Blue or red flannel costume:* The year 1853 seems early for a nicety such as crew uniforms on a merchant ship. Discussion on the RootsWeb Mariners List suggested that the crew would only have been together a day or two at this time. The officers might have needed an effective way to tell the sailors apart from the emigrants until they got to know the men in their watches. They might have done this with rudimentary uniforms. The different colors might have denoted the port and starboard watches, or perhaps more likely, they distinguished the sailors (blue) from the carpenters, bakers,

cooks, and stewards (red). The red team would be required to turn out and haul canvas on occasion, but they didn't keep watches. After a few days, the officers would have become better acquainted with the crew, and the colored shirts would no longer be needed. Alternatively, Beazley might have mandated uniforms for his crews in an effort to instill some differentiating spit and polish into his ships.

74 *382 passengers (including 30 children):* First Report from the Select Committee on Emigrant Ships; with the Minutes of Evidence Taken before Them, ordered by the House of Commons, Great Britain, April 6, 1854, 181.

75 *The influence wielded by a ship's master at sea:* Naming a child born on a ship after the ship did not always end happily. As mentioned earlier, a child born on the *Belinda* during Kelly's difficult 1846 passage to Quebec died at the Grosse Isle Hospital with her name listed as Belinda Hunter, her age just twelve days.

76 *Arriving at their destination:* The distance from the Cape of Good Hope to Melbourne is reduced as ships move into the higher parallels of latitude. For example, maximum 40°S lat. equates to 5,988 miles; maximum 50°S lat. equates to 5,666 miles; and maximum 58°S latitude (the great circle route) equates to 5,592 miles. So traveling the great circle route could cut almost 400 miles off a trip versus traveling at 40°S lat. The lower latitudes north of 40°S offered a more comfortable passage with smoother seas—but a longer trip. The higher latitudes south of 45–50°S offered a shorter trip with steady winds that were, however, subject to sudden, violent shifts along with gales, hail, snow, and terrific seas. Clipper ships were built for speed. Shipmasters tended to nudge them south to make the fastest run possible.

77 *And death the journey's end:* John Dryden, "Palamon and Arcite," bk. 3, 1.887–8 (published 1700).

78 *Kelly recruited passengers to supplement his crew:* "Male migrants were always encouraged (if not ordered) to assist in the running of the ship and it was on the run in the Roar-

ing Forties that they were likely to be of the greatest assistance...more often they helped with the manually operated pumps to keep the hold free of water." Resource Package, "Southward Bound Display," South Australian Maritime Museum, Port Adelaide, Australia.

79 *Measured in terms of winds and weather:* Villiers, *The Way of a Ship*, 72.

80 *A complimentary letter: Belfast Northern Whig*, November 3, 1853, 2.

81 *The Miles Barton remained in Melbourne:* There is some indication that William Kelly's brother, John, might have been on board the *Miles Barton* during this voyage. A list of unclaimed letters at Melbourne's General Post Office dated August 31, 1853, includes the following name: "Kelly, John, ship *Miles Barton.*" See *Victoria Government Gazette*, No. 54, September 14, 1853.

82 *The courtly and stately chief of Haigh and Co.:* Forwood, *Recollections of a Busy Life*, 46.

83 *Relic of Miles Barton:* Letter to the editor, *Sea Breezes*, January 1928. The writer of the letter was William Gourley Moore, the son of William Kelly's daughter Fanny and her husband, John Moore. Fanny had inherited William Kelly's painting of the ship *Miles Barton*. William G. Moore and his brothers, James Kelly Moore and John Patrick Moore, all immigrated to South Africa. *Sea Breezes* magazine is still published today.

84 *A religious service:* Reprinted in the *Melbourne Argus*, August 12, 1854, 4.

85 *Not a single disturbance: Melbourne Argus*, July 24, 1854, 4.

86 *Frank Chalmer & Robert Birney:* In 1854, Frank Chalmer was a twenty-eight-year-old native of Liverpool and Robert Birney a thirty-four-year-old Irishman. Birney ended up farming near Romsey in the Lancefield District of Victoria where he grew wheat, oats, barley, and peas on 450 acres and was elected justice of the peace. Birney died aged sixty-three in 1883. Chalmer settled in Spring Gully, Bendigo, Victoria, where he served as auditor/valuator for the shires

of Strathfieldsaye, Marong, and Huntly. Chalmer wrote eloquent letters to the editor of his local paper over the years; hence, he might have been the primary author of the letter to Kelly. He died aged sixty-nine in 1895, leaving a widow, five daughters, and two sons.

87 *Tenement in the Town of Antrim:* Belfast Northern Whig, January 9, 1855, 3.

88 *A puzzling human tragedy:* See the *Courier* (Hobart, Tasmania), September 3, 1855, 3. The Welsh clergyman might have been fifty-six-year-old David Edwards, vicar of Ewenny, Glamorgan, near Swansea, born in 1799 (per the 1851 census of Wales). He is nowhere to be found in the 1861 census of Wales or England.

89 *Not satisfactorily ascertained:* Lloyd's Weekly Newspaper, June 3, 1855, 2.

90 *Flattering testimonials:* Cornwall Chronicle (Launceston, Tasmania), August 22, 1855, 4.

91 *Sauces, beer, and more:* Melbourne Argus, August 14, 1855, 4.

92 *Not one bag damaged:* Liverpool Daily Post, June 5, 1856, 3.

93 *Also one of Mr. Beazley's ships:* Liverpool Mercury, July 12, 1856, 4.

94 *The man who donated the revolver:* The Maritime Museum has confirmed that William Kelly Wallace donated the revolver to the museum in the mid-1960s (personal communication, March 23, 2018).

95 *Over two thousand miles from the nearest populated places:* The Kerguelen Islands are today a French Overseas Territory, part of the French Southern and Antarctic Lands.

96 *One of the two finest ship portraitists:* Finch, *The Pierhead Painters*, 62.

97 *A distant paddle steamer aids perspective:* Davidson, *Marine Art & Liverpool*, 52–57.

## Chapter Three

98 *Intended for the India and China trades:* Waterford News, July 4, 1856, 2.

99 *An exceedingly striking, yet graceful effect:* Liverpool *Albion,* July 7, 1856, 15.
100 *Profits of £14,692 for Beazley*: Irish, *Shipbuilding in Waterford, 1820–1882,* 38.
101 *Classed A1 at Lloyd's for ten years:* Lloyd's Register of Ships was created in 1764 to give ship underwriters and merchants an idea of the condition of the vessels they insured and chartered. Ship hulls were graded by a letter scale ("A" being the best), and ship fittings (masts, rigging, and other equipment) were graded by number ("1" being the best). Thus, "A1 at Lloyd's" was the best-possible classification for a vessel.
102 *The average duration of his future voyages: Hampshire Advertiser,* September 27, 1856, 3.
103 *Her complement altogether being 250:* Buck, "Last Hours on the Mersey," in the Forget-Me-Not, no. 77 (October 1856), 2–4, Liverpool Seamen and Emigrants' Friend Society, quoted in Irish, *Shipbuilding in Waterford, 1820–1882,* 38.
104 *900 tons of mixed merchandise: Melbourne Argus,* January 19, 1857, 4.
105 *Much interest is attached to the respective passages: Morning Chronicle* (London), October 22, 1856, 7.
106 *Details of her passage to Australia:* Merrie England's crew agreement and official logbook, BT98/5280, UK National Archives, courtesy Clare Abbott. Of special interest to John Kelly's career, the crew agreement lists his "previous ship served on" as the *Amelia* of Liverpool.
107 *She published her Mémoires:* Mogador, *Adieux au Monde.*
108 *I sat up until dawn:* Haldane, *Daughter of Paris,* 187–88.
109 *Thomas Manning and Moses Durant also deserted: Merrie England*'s crew agreement and official logbook, BT98/5280, UK National Archives, courtesy Clare Abbott.
110 *18,000 bags of rice: London Sun,* June 1, 1857, 8.
111 *Robert Jones was sent to Jail:* Signed by William Kelly and attested by Frederick Harvey, Vice Consul, on August 3,

1857, *Merrie England's* crew agreement and official logbook, BT98/5280, UK National Archives.

112 *Safflower, saltpetre, shellac, and more: The Public Ledger and Daily Advertiser* (London), February 22, 1860, 4.

113 *A new system of slavery:* "I am not prepared to encounter the responsibility of a measure which may lead to a dreadful loss of life on the one hand, or, on the other, to a new system of slavery." Lord John Russell to Governor Light, February 15, 1840, Parliamentary Papers, Volume XVI (No. 56).

114 *A monstrous, rotten system:* Beaumont, *The New Slavery*, 35.

115 *Did not care about them or their customs:* For more information on the Indian migration to Demerara, see Basdeo Mangru, "Indian Labour in British Guiana," *History Today* 36, no. 4 (1986).

116 *Before he smells the land:* Fox Smith, *There Was a Ship*, 103–4.

117 *After serving their indenture:* See "The Return to the Motherland," *Guyana Times International*, January 14, 2013, http://www.guyanatimesinternational.com/?p=21969.

118 *The scarcity of gangways: New Orleans Bee*, January 29, 1861, 1.

119 *A quantity of oil cake:* Oil cake was the solid residue left after certain oily seeds, such as cottonseed and linseed, had been pressed free of their oil. It was ground and used as cattle feed or fertilizer.

120 *186 boxes of shellac: London Public Ledger and Daily Advertiser*, January 30, 1862, 4.

## Chapter Four

121 *Mate on the Epaminondas:* The chronology for the ships *Flora*, *Epaminondas*, and *Hilton* comes from John Kelly's entry (certificate no. 72,262) in Lloyd's Captains' Registers BT 124/14; Recorded Service: 1851–1860, Certificate Numbers: 70,000-74,027, National Archives (UK).

122 *But the rate was refused: London Evening Standard*, June 7, 1861, 6.

123 *Safety of the Hilton:* Birmingham Daily Post, July 12, 1861, 4.
124 *Superheated areas of the tropical calms:* Macmillan, *Mauritius Illustrated*, 188.
125 *Near the S.W. part of the island:* Jackson, *Ocean Passages for the World*, 78.

## Chapter Five

126 *Burning furiously from stem to stern:* This section on the conflagration of the *Mary Carson* is summarized from "An Eventful Voyage," *Reynold's Newspaper* (London, England), February 10, 1861, 9 (reprinted from the *Liverpool Daily Post*).
127 *The gain to science would be immense:* Liverpool Daily Post, February 4, 1861, 5.
128 *A beautiful telescope:* Providence Evening Press (Rhode Island), April 15, 1861, 4.
129 *After the Second Opium War:* Two other detachments of the 3rd Buffs were accompanying the *Miles Barton*: 326 men under Lt. Col. Sargent traveling in the *Athlete* and 429 men under Lt. Col. Ambrose in the *Tasmania*. Army and Navy Gazette, April 6, 1861, 2.
130 *Between the Indian and Atlantic Oceans:* This write-up on the destruction of the *Miles Barton* is summarized from "Loss of the *Miles Barton*, from China," *London Evening Standard*, April 2, 1861, 6.
131 *Good Birkenhead order:* The newspapers subsequently compared the courage and discipline of the troops on the *Miles Barton* to that displayed by British soldiers when the steam frigate *Birkenhead* struck a submerged rock and sank near Cape Town in 1852. The phrases "Birkenhead drill" and "women and children first" were subsequently coined as rallying cries to honor these men who went stoically down with their ship in hopeless circumstances; many of them were new (and apparently impeccably trained) recruits heading to the Kaffir War against the Xhosa in South Africa.
132 *Did not survive his plunge into the sea:* Liverpool Daily Post, April 2, 1861, 5.

133 *Miles Barton Reef:* The following is an extract from the report of Mr. H. Wilson, assistant port captain and surveyor to the Liverpool Underwriters' Association, Cape of Good Hope, dated February 26, 1861, respecting the loss of the *Miles Barton* off Cape Agulhas:

> The general appearance of the land for many miles in all directions was low and undulated, and difficult to be distinguished at night, in smooth water, in the absence of any break on the beach; nothing but pure white sand as far as the eye can reach, both east and west of the ship. I would state here, for the information of whom it may concern, that this part of the coast to the eastward of Agulhas has not recently been surveyed, and its outlying dangers [are] little known. Had there not been a good look-out kept on board the Miles Barton, there cannot be a doubt that she would have gone right onto the Struys Bay Point Reef, which extends much further out than is marked in any of the published charts that I have hitherto seen. In steaming round the reef, the water was remarkably smooth, and broke at long intervals a long way out. All coasting vessels give this part of the coast a wide berth at all seasons of the year, owing to a well-known and dreaded indraught into those indentations of the coast.

134 *A public sale: London Evening Standard*, April 4, 1861, 7.

## Chapter 6

135 *The first voyage of the Express:* Crew Agreement No. 5585, *Express*, Maritime History Archive (hereafter "MHA"), Memorial University.

136 *A thirty-three-year-old sick seaman:* Crew Agreement, *Express*, MHA, Memorial University.

137 *Whether calm or with a breeze:* "The Gulf of Aden Pilot: Sokótra and Adjacent Islands, Somáli and Arabian Coasts in the Gulf of Aden and the East Coast of Arabia," originally

compiled by Commander C. Y. Ward, R.N., from *Memoirs by Officers of the Indian Navy*, 2nd ed., with additions (London: Printed for the Hydrographic Office, Admiralty, 1882), 9.

138 *Ostrich feathers from the Somali and Dankali coasts:* According to F. M. Hunter, the assistant political resident at Aden in 1877, harvesting ostrich feathers involved this technique: "A female domesticated bird is taken out by the hunter, and when another ostrich is seen in the distance, the man conceals himself as well as he can under the wing of the decoy, and endeavors to approach the wild bird, which usually displays no fear. When the hunter is sufficiently near, he shoots his game with a poisoned arrow, and plucks it immediately." See Hunter, *An Account of the British Settlement*, 109.

139 *Voyage not to exceed three years:* Crew Agreement, *Express*, MHA, Memorial University.

140 *Discharged by mutual consent:* Sanderson Brown died a little over a year after leaving the *Express*. See the *Hull Packet and East Riding Times*, September 23, 1864, 8: "Deaths: September 14, at Birkenhead, Mr. Sanderson Brown, late of Hull, of bronchitis, aged 42 years."

141 *Briggs Brothers Shipyard:* James Edwin and Harrison O. Briggs, *Boston Herald*, April 27, 1864, 2.

142 *Cushing Otis Briggs of Scituate, Massachusetts:* Briggs, *History of Shipbuilding on North River*, 282–325.

143 *William Kelly bought the ship:* "The following vessels have recently been sold in London: Ship *Sterling*, 700 T, built at Boston in 1864, £6,250." *New York Herald*, November 14, 1864, 8.

144 *A dramatic narrative:* The following events are extracted from Davis, "Disaster of the Ship *Express*." Captain R. H. Davis was chief of the Belfast Master Mariner's Club. In the 1940s, he gave many speeches and broadcast talks on Belfast's maritime history and heritage. See also Crew Agreement No. 2363½, MHA, Memorial University.

145 *Above the tweendeck*: This is the deck on a cargo ship located between the main deck and the hold space.
146 *According to Bill Irish:* Irish, *Shipbuilding in Waterford, 1820–1882*, 38.
147 *Wooden ceilings and planking:* See Stevens, *On the Stowage of Ships and Their Cargoes*, 248–49. This monumental and fascinatingly perusable book is often alliteratively abbreviated "Stevens on Stowage." Thanks to Piers Smith-Cresswell of the Mariners Mailing List for drawing this book to my attention.
148 *Oceangoing incubators for his sons:* See "UK & Ireland, Masters and Mates Certificates, 1850–1927," Ancestry.com, John Kelly, certificate no. 90,732.
149 *Captain Hugh Wisnom of Broadisland, Antrim:* Crew Agreement, *Sterling*, MHA, Memorial University (number not listed but author has the agreement).
150 *Second mate, Robert McAlpine:* Jane (McAlpine) Wisnom passed away fifteen years after this voyage. The *Belfast News-Letter* of Tuesday, October 21, 1884, contains her obituary: "WISNOM – Oct. 20 at Broadisland, Whitehead, County Antrim, Jane, relict of the late Captain Hugh Wisnom." Jane Wisnom was interred in the family burial ground at Glynn, a small village on Larne Lough, northeast of Belfast.
151 *Near the center of the Isle of Dogs:* Captain Davis's article "Disaster of the Ship *Express*" also has a paragraph on the *Sterling* that states: "Captain Hugh Wisnom, another well-known shipmaster of that day...made only one voyage in her, as on arrival at Queenstown, homeward bound, he was landed owing to illness and was succeeded by Captain Teague."
152 *A stroke of luck:* The following events are extracted from Crew Agreement No. M9100, MHA, Memorial University.
153 *Captain Teague came home:* See Davis, "Disaster of the Ship *Express*."
154 *Hope was entertained of his recovery: Glasgow Herald*, December 20, 1869, 4.

155 *As the Civil War roiled on:* McKenna, *British Ships in the Confederate Navy*, 36–37.
156 *At the islands to load guano:* Crew Agreement No. 21394, *Merrie England*, with partial log, MHA, Memorial University.
157 *Making a deal more water:* Partial log with Crew Agreement No. 21394, *Merrie England*.
158 *A great favourite with passengers: Liverpool Mercury*, April 11, 1871, 7.
159 *Considerable personal distress:* The following events are extracted from Bradley, Harold, "Chasing the Eye of the Storm," unpublished manuscript.
160 *The city's postwar labor shortages:* Sam's "coolie" scheme (and other similar proposals submitted by others at the same time) did not receive the federal government's seal of approval. See Jung, *Coolies and Cane*, 78.
161 *The most illegal verdict: New Orleans Times-Picayune*, December 2, 1871, 3.
162 *The astonishing tragedy:* William Kelly's letter to James Graham is reproduced in Foy, *Dear Uncle*, 100–102.
163 *A globe-girdling voyage:* Crew Agreement No. 60024, *Sterling*, MHA, Memorial University.
164 *Cruising about Iquique:* Crew Agreement No. 93382, *Sterling*, MHA, Memorial University.
165 *Sailed primarily as a timber ship:* These details regarding the *Princess Alexandra*'s masters (pre-William Kelly) are courtesy of MHA, Memorial University, as provided in various documents (crew agreements, official logbooks, vessel registries, etc.) solicited by Richard Bradley and forwarded to the author.
166 *Marryat's Code:* For more information on Marryat's Code, refer to Davidson, *Marine Art & Liverpool*, 140–67.
167 *Consistently described as "second mate":* The following events are extracted from the *Princess Alexandra* Crew Agreement No. 26690, January 12, 1872–April 16, 1873, MHA, Memorial University.

## Chapter 7

168 *A house grandly named Bella Vista:* "Belfast was expanding very rapidly in the nineteenth century, so new streets were being built and other grand houses biting the dust to make way. As a result it was common to have what appear to be separate streets (e.g., Richmond Crescent) embedded in a larger road (e.g., the Antrim Road). I think a builder put a group of houses up and gave them a name. Only later were more rigorous road and house numbering policies enforced." Dr. Bob Foy, personal communication, 2013.

169 *Near Cave Hill: Belfast News-Letter,* May 7, 1874, 1.

170 *A quarter of grazing land: Belfast News-Letter,* May 12, 1877, 2.

171 *Deaths attributable to unseaworthy ships:* Plimsoll, *Our Seamen: An Appeal,* 5.

172 *A deputation of Belfast ship owners:* See "Mr. Plimsoll's Shipping Bill," *Belfast Telegraph,* April 25, 1873, 3. The ship owners were identified as Messrs. James P. Corry, J.P.; Samuel Lawther, G.H. Carse, T.S. Dixon, Samuel H. Gowan, Wm. M. Barkley, Philip Wright, William Kelly, and William Porter, jun.

173 *The Plimsoll marks (or lines):* When rubber-soled shoes with canvas tops were introduced in England in the 1920s, they were referred to as Plimsolls because a dark line dividing the sole and upper canvas served the same purpose as the Plimsoll mark on a ship. If water rose above the line, you would have a wet foot.

174 *Applied the regulations as Plimsoll had intended them:* Sue Nicholson, "Samuel Plimsoll: Commemoration for the 'Sailor's Friend,'" BBC News, February 9, 2013. See also Geoffrey Moorhouse's review of *The Plimsoll Sensation: The Great Campaign to Save Lives at Sea* by Nicolette Jones, *The Guardian,* July 1, 2006.

175 *The book is inscribed:* Elizabeth's surname is generally spelled "McFerran" today (using the Irish spelling with "Mc"). William Kelly invariably wrote "MacFerran" (using the Scottish spelling with "Mac").

176 *Ready for a start for France:* The ship referenced here is the *Princess Alexandra*. William Kelly Jr. was functioning as her *de facto* captain at this time, even though he was not yet a certificated master mariner.

177 *Gifting the property back:* In August 1889, Mary McFerran (widow) passed the property to her son William John McFerran by grant for the sum of $1.00. Then, in 1891, the lot passed by grant of deed ("transfer in love and affection" plus $1.00) from the McFerrans to Martha McIntyre (William John McFerran's younger sister Martha married Albert McIntyre). Martha passed the property to her son Albert in her will dated August 15, 1903, just prior to her death on September 5, 1903.

178 *Duchess of Shingle Creek*: Shingle Creek was near Edwards in Saint Lawrence County, NY where the McFerrans lived before moving to Canada. The "Duchess" is probably a roguish reference to Elizabeth's mother, Mary (Kelly) McFarren.

179 *Voyage not to exceed eighteen months:* Crew Agreement No. 54332, *Princess Alexandra*, MHA, Memorial University.

180 *Collins picked up a capstan bar:* A capstan bar is a wooden lever used to turn a capstan, which is a rotating machine with a vertical axis that multiplies the pulling force of seamen when hauling ropes or cables on a sailing ship.

181 *About 150,000 tons:* Accounts and Papers of the House of Commons (44 volumes), 35, Commercial Reports, February 8–August 15, 1876, Vol. 76, 1876, https://google.com/books.

182 *Written, probably in the summer of 1875:* As previously noted, William Kelly invariably used the Scottish spelling, "MacFerran."

183 *The house at Chrome Hill:* The Battle of the Boyne and the beech sapling stories are both mentioned in McKinstry, "Chrome Hill, Lambeg."

184 *To this death was attributed:* Wilks, *Lectures on Diseases of the Nervous System*, 227–28.

185 *Confined to the house: Kemptville Weekly Advance*, Feb-

ruary 14, 1895. "McFerran, Mrs. Mary. Called away. On Friday last Mrs. Mary McFerran, widow of the late John McFerran, died at Beckett's Landing at the advanced age of nearly 90 years [sic]. For over a score of years deceased had been unable to walk and consequently confined to the house. Deceased was born in the County of Antrim, Ireland. She was married in her native land and there she buried her first husband. In the year '59 [sic] she came to the United States where she resided for some time, afterwards removing to this place. The funeral took place from the home of her son-in-law Albert McIntyre, to the South Gore cemetery Monday afternoon." Mary likely arrived in the United States around 1840, not in "the year '59." In 1841, she married John McFerran. They lived in Edwards, Saint Lawrence County, New York. Around 1854, they moved to Canada (north of Kemptville on the Rideau River near Beckett's Landing). Census records imply that Mary likely died in her early 80s, not "nearly 90."

186 *Locked up on the charge: Liverpool Mercury*, December 25, 1875, 6.

187 *A harmless and inoffensive man: Liverpool Weekly Courier*, January 1, 1876, 4.

188 *At the Belfast Chamber of Commerce:* See "Merchant Shipping Legislation," *Belfast News-Letter*, February 21, 1876, 4.

189 *Wilhelm Adolf von Freeden:* Freeden was a member of the German Reichstag for Hamburg (1871–1876), founder and first director of the Norddeutsche Seewarte (North German Hydrographic Office) at Hamburg, and one of the founders of the North German Lloyd Company.

190 *A recent collision at Dover:* This was likely the collision of the steamers *Franconia* and *Strathclyde* on February 17, 1876, which resulted in thirty-eight fatalities. The Glasgow steamship *Strathclyde* (Captain J. D. Eaton), bound from London to Bombay, was about two and a half miles from Dover proceeding at nine knots when she was overtaken by the German steamship *Franconia*. Captain Eaton turned

the *Strathclyde* to starboard, but at the same time the *Franconia* turned to port, and the two ships collided.

191 *An assimilated international system in the steering of ships:* Sir James Porter Corry (1826–1891) was 1st Baronet, JP, MP for Belfast, as well as a timber trader and ship owner.

192 *It was freely and judiciously given:* See William Kelly's obituary, *Belfast News-Letter*, September 14, 1877, 3.

193 *The United Kingdom retained the system until 1933:* "On January 1 the 'direct' system of helm orders came into use on all British vessels. For centuries the order to 'Starboard the helm, Port the helm' has caused the ship's head to go in the opposite direction, the practice having come down through the centuries when tillers were in use. Under the new regulations the order 'Starboard' will be given, when it is intended that the wheel, the rudder blade and the head of the ship should go to starboard, and the order 'port' will be given when it is intended that the wheel, the rudder blade and the ship's head should go to port. Though it is expected that little difficulty will be experienced in changing over from the 'indirect' system to the 'direct' system, for a time the orders will be given in the words 'Wheel to Starboard' and 'Wheel to Port' thus enabling the helmsman to adapt himself gradually to the new system." "The New Helm or Steering Orders," *Nature* (London) 131, no. 3297 (January 7, 1933): 20–21.

194 *William Baliol Brett presiding:* William Baliol Brett, 1st Viscount Esher PC, QC (1817–1899), known as Sir William Brett between 1868 and 1883, was a British lawyer, judge, and conservative politician. He was briefly solicitor general under Benjamin Disraeli and then served as a justice of the Court of Common Pleas between 1868 and 1876, as a Lord Justice of Appeal between 1876 and 1883, and as Master of the Rolls. He was raised to the peerage as Baron Esher in 1885 and was made Viscount Esher upon his retirement in 1897.

195 *An American named Frank Smith:* This seaman, identified in the newspaper accounts as Frank Ernest Louis Smith,

is a mystery man. No such name appears in the *Princess Alexandra* crew list for the 1875–1877 Callao voyage, and he is not named by the British consul at Callao as one of the crewmen sent back to the United Kingdom on the *Iberia* to testify at Collins's trial.

196 *The crew had threatened to kill him:* James Collins's court hearing is summarized from Liverpool Assizes, Before Justice Brett, "Charge of Murder on the High Seas. The Duty of the Officers of Ships," *Liverpool Mercury*, March 30, 1876, 8.

197 *Belonging to the same owner: Belfast News-Letter*, June 15, 1876, 2.

198 *Of all the wonders that I have heard:* William Shakespeare, "Julius Caesar," II, ii, 32–37. *The Mariner Hath His Will:* Samuel T. Coleridge, "The Rime of the Ancient Mariner."

199 *Kelly signed his last will and testament:* Public Record Office of Northern Ireland (PRONI), Mic15c/2/18, 146-151.

200 *Consented to the marriage:* "WALLACE-KELLY: At the residence of the bride's mother, 6 Richmond Crescent, Belfast, by the Rev. T. Y. Killen, John Orr Wallace, to Mary, youngest daughter of the late Captain Wm. Kelly." *Belfast Weekly News*, Saturday, February 1, 1879, 1. Wallace was a commission agent/broker working at No. 2 Skipper Street, Belfast.

201 *"That unknown and silent shore":* An extract from "Hester," a funeral poem by the English poet Charles Lamb.

202 *The beneficiaries of Captain Roland Savage:* "Savage, Rowland *(sic)*. Effects in England. Under £50. 4 Dec. The Letters of Administration of the Personal estate and effects of Roland Savage late of Tooshilly in the County of Down late Master of the Ship *Express* deceased who died in or about March 1866 at Sea granted 10 February 1868 at Dublin in Ireland to Rowland *(sic)* James Savage of Tooshilly aforesaid Farmer the Nephew and one of the Next of Kin of the said Deceased were sealed at the Principal Registry London." Irish Administrations Sealed. 1868. England & Wales, National Probate Calendar, Index of Wills and Administrations, 1858–1995, https://www.ancestry.com.

203 *Muckamore cemetery about 1 o'clock: Belfast News-Letter*, September 14, 1877, 3.
204 *Enjoyment of the public: Belfast News-Letter*, September 14, 1877, 2.
205 *To the "Ships' Graveyard"*: "Redundant vessels have been scuttled in the deep water SW of Rottnest Island since 1910. The ships' graveyard is encompassed within the area of Lat. 32° 00'S to 32° 05'S and Long. 115° 10'E to 115° 23'E at depth from 50 to 200m. Seabed of sand and shell with scattered rocky outcrops." See Garratt, *Précis of the Wrecks in the Ships' Graveyard*. Sea dumping of old vessels in deep water is now discouraged in Australia. It is only permitted if this is the only practical means of disposal.
206 *A satisfactory exercise*: "She'll Meet Old Friends in Davy Jones' Locker," *Perth Daily News*, June 7, 1950, 1.
207 *"The glamour ship of Fremantle"*: "Widow Weeps for a Glamour Ship," *Perth Daily News*, June 7, 1950, 1.
208 *Kelly's remaining personal items:* Public Record Office of Northern Ireland (PRONI), Mic15c/2/2, 25.
209 *Samuel Walters's painting of the ship Merrie England:* Bill Irish's book *Shipbuilding in Waterford, 1820–1882* contains a photograph of Walters's painting of the *Merrie England* (Plate 22). This is likely the painting that William Kelly commissioned, which was subsequently willed to his daughter Mary Wallace in 1884. The painting was sold at auction in 1969 by Phillips, Son, and Neale to the Caelt Gallery, Notting Hill, London. The painting's last known owner (per Irish's book) was Arthur E. Malabar of Liverpool.
210 *Two silver salts:* Thanks to Dr. Bob Foy for his research into the various iterations of William Kelly's will and Martha's will.
211 *Mrs. Captain Kelly:* The appellation "Mrs. Captain Kelly" appears in a newspaper article referencing William Kelly Sr.'s house in the Town of Antrim (see page 90, and n. 87).
212 *Out of respect for the popular young seaman: Belfast Northern Whig*, September 10, 1886, 5.

213 *Vivid memories of past controversies:* See the *Belfast Telegraph*, November 8, 1892, 3 (for list of crew rescued) and the *Belfast News-Letter*, November 9, 1892, 6.

## Chapter 8

214 *No one in the audience had heard of him:* Dr. Bob Foy, "Clipper Ships, 1840–1870: The Glory Days?" (a presentation to the Belfast Family History Society, November 7, 2013).

215 *A broken-hearted man:* Quoted in Cecil Johnson, "Hell or Melbourne: Exploits of the Notorious 'Bully' Forbes," *Melbourne Argus*, December 6, 1930, 2.

216 *It takes two men to make one brother:* This aphoristic assertion is widely attributed to Israel Zangwill. However, I have only found the statement used as a subtitle to Zangwill's 1893 romantic stage play, *Merely Mary Ann* (possibly appended by someone else).

217 *Those few had a glimpse of glory:* Villiers, *The Way of a Ship*, 209.

218 *The Planetary Society launched its citizen-funded LightSail 2 spacecraft:* Based in Pasadena, California, this organization was founded in 1980 by astronautics engineer Louis Friedman, planetary scientist Bruce Murray, and cosmologist Carl Sagan. The society's vision is "to know the cosmos and our place in it." Its mission is to "empower the world's citizens to advance space science and exploration."

219 *The feasibility of sailing on sunlight:* The LightSail 2 spacecraft makes two 90-degree turns during each orbit of Earth. The sail holds itself perpendicular to the solar photons for half of its orbit. During the other half, when the spacecraft is moving toward the sun, the sail turns parallel to the photons, essentially turning off the thrust, so that it does not negate the effect of moving to a higher orbit.

220 *Speeds of approximately two hundred kilometers per second:* Scoles, "The Good Kind of Crazy," 64.

# INDEX

In the index, figures and tables are indicated by *fig.* and *t*. Substantive information in the endnotes is denoted with an 'n' between the page number of the note and the endnote number. Where there is more than one endnote on a given page an 'nn' is used; a hyphen indicates sequential notes, whereas a comma separates non-sequential notes.

Vessels and captains mentioned in passing are listed under the headings "vessels mentioned in passing" and "master mariners."

Abell, Edmund (judge, New Orleans), 179–180
Adelaide Milling and Steamship Companies, 232
Aden: described, 152–154; *Express* voyages to, 153–155, 160*t*.; Ostrich feathers and eggs, 154–155, 278n138; *Sterling* voyages to, 169–170, 172
Africa, 22, 81, 103–104, 145, 151–152, 154
A.H. Turnbull & Co. of Christchurch, 232
Akyab, Burma (Sittwe, Myanmar), 120–121, 155, 159, 160
Albert White & Co. (ship builders, Waterford), 99, 109–110. See also *Merrie England*
*Ambassador* (ship, commanded by William Kelly Sr.), 19–21, 158*t*., 178, 181

American Civil War, 129, 130, 133–134, 171–172
American clipper ships (Briggs-built), 160–161
American Line shipping company, 165
Anchor Line shipping company, 165
Anderson, Robert, Major (Union officer), 134
Anjer, West Java (Banten), 95, 159*t*.
Annandale, James (seaman/carpenter), 156, 197
*Antiques Roadshow* (BBC) and painting of *Miles Barton*, 102–105
Antrim Town, Northern Ireland: and the Head Inn, 4–5; John Kelly Sr.'s property in, 9–12; "Queen of" (Fanny, sister of

John and William), 7–8, 24, 57; William Kelly Sr.'s property in, 90, 236
apprenticeship (British Merchant Service), 21–22
Arabian Sea, milky sea phenomenon in, 152–153
*Arethusa* (ship, Captain John Kelly): Belfast-New York trips with immigrants, 51–52, 53; cargoes on, 47, 48, 51, 52, 53; crossing paths with William and *Belinda,* 43, 52; description and ownership of, 47, 136; Great Gale of 1846, 47–48; New York-Liverpool with cargo, 53; Quebec-Liverpool trips with timber and salt cod, 47, 50–51
*Arethusa* (ship, Captain William Kelly), 27–28
Argo Navis (constellation), 5
*Argus* (Melbourne), 78, 88, 93–94, 116
artifacts and memorabilia: acrostic poem, 7–8; book of hymns, 198–199, 200; gold watch and chain, 78, 80, 235; letter about ostrich eggs, 154–155; letter to *Sea Breezes,* 82–83; Master's Certificates, 105–106, 107–108*figs*.; model of the *Miles Barton,* 64, 65*fig.*; oil painting of the *Mary Carson,* 235; oil painting of the *Merrie England,* 6, 235, 286n209; oil painting of the *Miles Barton,* 83, 101–105, 235, 272n83; oil painting of the *Sterling,* 186, 235; revolver, 100–101, 101*fig.*; silver snuffbox, 82–83; W. Kelly Sr. letters, 180–183, 198–201, 206–208; water color of the *Princess Alexandra,* 188*fig.*
A.T. Solling & Co. (merchant, Rotterdam), 98
Atkinson, Usborne & Co. (shipping agents, Quebec), 48–50
Atocha, Alcé Aloysius (lawyer, New Orleans), 179
Australia. *See* Melbourne, Australia

Baines, James (Black Ball Line of clippers), 240
Baird, Patricia Stavely, xvi, 270n71
Ballarat gold fields, 117
Bangor steamers, 230
*Bankfields* (clipper barque), 219–221, 231–233, 233*fig.*, 234*fig.* See also *James Beazley*
Barnett, James Drover, 41
Barr, Alexander (seaman/*Belinda* mate), 42
Bartoll, William Thompson (painter), 48*fig.*
Barton, Miles (Liverpool cotton broker), 65–66, 82
Bassein, (rice milling and export center in Burma), 167
Battle of the Boyne, 208, 282n183
Bay of Biscay, 62, 151
BBC *Antiques Road Show (Miles Barton* painting), 101–105
Beaufort, South Carolina, and the wreck of the *Clio,* 23
Beauregard, P.G.T. (Confederate General), 134
Beazley, James (Liverpool ship

owner): and the British Ship Owners' Company, 165; business associate of Thomas Haigh, 82; and *Merrie England,* 99, 109, 110; and *Miles Barton* passenger berths, 70–71; and the naming of *Miles Barton* (ship), 65; relationship with W. Kelly Sr., 57–58, 60, 63, 194, 229, 244; and *Star of the East,* 77, 147
*Bee* (New Orleans), 59, 129
*Belfast Commercial Chronicle,* 9–10, 13
Belfast Family History Society, 240, 287n214
*Belfast Mercantile Register* and *Weekly Advisor,* 24
*Belfast News-Letter*: about Belfast and Bangor steamers, 230; and *Belinda,* 44; on the burning of *Dalriada,* 123–124; compared with *Belfast Northern Whig,* 207; on J. Kelly's marriage to S. Orr, 264n26; on Jane Wisnom's interment, 279n150; passenger letter of commendation for J. Kelly, 51–52; on pilfered geraniums, 223; on *Rowena,* 15; on ship owners vs. Plimsoll, 281n172; and ship sailings and cargos, 230, 262n12, 268n59, 269n61; W. Kelly Sr. vs. Mrs. Frizzell, 10–11, 261n6; W. Kelly Sr.'s death and obituary, 26, 262n11, 269n60; on W. Kelly's marriage to M. Rainey, 15, 263n18
*Belfast Northern Whig* (on *Miles Barton*'s first voyage), 78–80
Belfast Seamen's Friend Society, religious services, 25
Belfast Ship Owners Association, 212–215
*Belfast Witness,* 206
*Belinda* (ship commanded by W. Kelly Sr.): Belfast-Quebec voyage and Irish famine emigration, 29–30, 32–38, 268n55, 271n75; builder, owner and description of, 26–27, 136, 263n13; cargoes, 27, 31–32, 38, 39, 265n37; and Charlie Richmond's theft of a mattress, 41–43, 224; Drake Passage-Cape Horn-Chincha Islands (Callao, Peru) guano trips, 39–41; first voyage and W. Kelly Sr. taking command at sea, 27–28, 47, 265n33; German emigrant passengers on, 43–44; North Channel-Atlantic-Gulf of Saint Lawrence via the Strait of Belle Isle, 29–30; voyages, routes, days at sea and nautical miles travelled, 158–159*t.*; wreck of, 44–46, 45*fig.*, 59, 164, 237
Bengal and Bay of Bengal, 62–63, 80–81, 89, 119–120, 125, 155, 156, 190–191
*Birmingham Daily Post,* 138
Birney, Robert (*Miles Barton* passenger), 88, 272n86
births onboard Kelly ships, 72, 74, 94, 114, 168
Board of Trade: Certificates of Service, 60, 61*fig.*, 105–106, 107–108*figs.*; and crewmen

deaths at sea, 140
Bombay (Mumbai): administered British settlement at Aden, 153; in Cardiff-Rio-Calcutta voyages, 189–191; cargo, crew and captain on *Dalriada* when it burned, 123–124; in Liverpool-Melbourne-Calcutta, 80–81, 118–119, 136, 147–148, 159*t.*; in Liverpool-Melbourne-Ceylon-India-Hong Kong-Shanghai voyages (*Miles Barton*), 113, 118–119, 121, 122*fig.*, 159–160*t.*
Boultenhouse, Christopher (ship builder), 58
Bowden, H.C. (ship owner), 22
Boyd, Jack (father of Sam Boyd), 181
Boyd, John, 177–178, 182–185
Boyd, Sam, 19, 178, 179
Boyd, Tatty (father of William and John Boyd), 181
Boyd, William: business ventures with and murder of Sam Rainey, 177–178, 181–183; relocation and life after acquittal, 184–185; trials and acquittal of, 179–180, 184
Boyle, William (seaman), 170
Brett, William Baliol (judge, Liverpool Assizes), 215–218, 219, 284n194
Briggs Brothers shipyard (Edwin and Harrison Briggs), 160–161. See also *Sterling*
Briggs, Cushing Otis, 160
brigs, 18, 21, 70, 106. See also vessels mentioned in passing
British colonialism, 5, 6, 22, 126
British consuls, 42, 170–171, 176, 205, 206, 211, 285n195
British Ship Owners' Company, 165. *See also* Beazley, James
British Standard Oil, 238
Brown, Sanderson (seaman), 157
Buchanan, Alexander C. (Quebec Superintendence of Emigration), 32–34
Buck, James (Rev.), 67–70, 83–87, 112
Buckler, Alexander, 41
Bullen, Frank Thomas, 22
Burma (Myanmar), Akyab, 120–121, 122*fig.*, 155, 159, 160
Burnet, D. (merchant, Quebec), 51

Calcutta (Kolkata): cargo from, 124–125, 135; crew desertions and a drowning, 119, 158; cyclone of 1864, 166, 175; and indentured laborers, 125–128, 138, 242; and *James Beazley*, 221, 223, 231, 242; and John Kelly (W. Kelly Sr.'s son), 228; in Liverpool-Melbourne-Bombay voyages, 80–81, 119, 159*t.*; and *Mary Carson*, 62–63, 159*t.*; and *Merrie England*, 113, 119–125, 132*fig.*, 160–161*t.*, 166, 175; and *Miles Barton*, 80–81, 89–90, 159*t.*; and *Princess Alexandra*, 190–191; and sinking of *Hilton*, 137–138. *See also* Hooghly River
Callao, Peru: and a murder onboard *Princess Alexandra*, 203–206, 210, 211, 212, 215, 223; and *Belinda*, 39–41,

159t.; and Bella Vista district, 266n46; and *Dalriada*, 57; and hailing of *Elizabeth George*, 73; and sinking of *Merrie England*, 174–176; and *Sterling*, 169–173, 185
Campbell, Henry Dundas (Governor of Sierra Leone), 22
Canada: demographics of immigrants from Ireland to, xii, 32–38; Elizabeth McFerran in Kemptville, Ontario, 199–201; Saint Lawrence River and Gulf of St. Lawrence, 25, 27, 28, 29, 30, 45, 59, 265n35, 266n41; salt cod industry, 50–51; Scatarie Island, 44–46, 45*fig.*, 59, 267n52; timber and flour shipments to British ports, 24, 27, 30–31, 38–39, 47, 54; and W. Kelly Sr.'s ostrich eggs, 154–155. *See also* New Brunswick; Nova Scotia; Quebec; ship building and builders; timber trade
Cape Finisterre, 62, 93, 151
Cape Horn, Chile: and *Belinda*, 39, 40; and *Northern Light*, 161; and *Sterling*, 173; and wreck of *Merrie England*, 173–176, 197
Cape l'Agulhas, 277n133
Cape of Good Hope: and *Express*, 151–152; and *Mary Carson*, 62; and *Merrie England*, 114, 116, 121, 125, 174; and *Miles Barton*, 73, 77, 81, 93, 145, 277n133; and *Princess Alexandra*, 191; variables determining distance to Melbourne from, 271n76

Cape Otway lighthouse, 74
Cape Verde, 62, 151, 169, 170, 171
capstan bar, 204, 215, 217, 282n180
Cardiff Port (Wales), 167, 169, 170, 174, 189, 225
cargoes. *See* cotton; guano; human migrations; specific ships; timber
Castellanos, Henry C. (lawyer and author, New Orleans), 179
Cathcart, Charles Murray (Governor General of Canada), 32
Certificates of Service for master mariners, 60, 61*fig.*, 105–106, 107–108*figs.*, 147, 226
Ceylon (Sri Lanka): British crown colony, 81; en route to Akyab, 155; Point de Galle/Galle, 113, 118, 119, 120, 122*fig.*, 155
Chabrillan, Céleste de, 117–118
Chabrillan, Gabriel-Paul-Josselin [G-P-J]-Lionel de Guigues Comte de, 116–117, 118
Chadwick, E. (Secretary of the Poor Law Commission), 33–34
Chagos Archipelago, 123, 124
Chalmer, Frank (*Miles Barton* passenger), 88, 272n86
children: and Australian migration, 71, 84, 271n74; born onboard ships, 72, 74, 94, 114, 168; of Indian indentured laborers, 127; and Irish migration on *Belinda*, 32–33, 34, 37–38, 242, 265n37; of the Kelly family, 2, 8, 18, 21, 26, 60, 225, 235–236; naming after ships, 38, 72; of the

Rainey family in New Orleans, 129–130, 177, 178, 182; raised on *Bankfields*, 233; "women and children first," 276n131. *See also* specific Kellys and Raineys

China: and British troops, Second Opium War, 144; clipper ship trade to, 2, 58, 99, 109, 243; James Beazley trade in, 58; in Liverpool-Melbourne-Bombay-Ceylon-India-Hong Kong-Shanghai trips, 2, 113, 119–121, 122*fig.*, 155, 159–160*t.*; oil steamer *Hudson* to, 238

China Sea, 2, 95, 120, 156, 241

Chincha Islands, 39–41, 173–174, 187, 266n46. *See also* Callao, Peru

Christian, John (murdered seaman), 203–204, 211, 215–217, 219

Clarence and Stanley Docks (Liverpool), 59

*Clio* (barque, Captain John Kelly), 22–24, 52, 106, 264n26

clipper ships: American (Briggs built), 160–161; for Australia, India and China trade, 2, 58, 99, 109; Black Ball Line, 77, 240; Fox Line, 91; *James Beazley*/*Bankfields* as, 220, 231, 242; *Merrie England* as, 109, 113; *Miles Barton* as, 63–66, 65*fig.*, 77, 78; *Star of the East* as, 147; W. Kelly Sr.'s reputation as a master of, 66, 77, 90, 98–99; White Star Line of Royal Mail Packets, 99, 111, 113. *See also James Beazley; Merrie England; Miles Barton*

Clover & Royle (Woodside, Birkenhead dry dock), 111

Clyde, Alexander, 63

"coffin ships," 36, 194, 196, 197. *See also* Plimsoll, Samuel

coincidence and synchronicity: W. Kelly Sr.'s birth, Great Comet, and Argo Navis, 5, 246; W. Kelly Sr.'s wedding and Queen Victoria's coronation, 16; W. Kelly Sr.'s Certificate of Service number, 60; W. Kelly Sr.'s death and drowned crew of *Express*, 227; scuttling of *Bankfields* and author's birth, 233

Collins, James: and the murder of J. Christian, 203, 204–205, 206, 211–212, 282n180; publicity, trial, witnesses and sentencing of, 211–212, 215–219; and W. Kelly Jr., 222

Collins, John (mutinous seaman), 115–116, 119

Colonial Land and Emigration Commission, 33–34, 260, 265n40

colonialism, 22, 32–34, 125–128

Confederate States of America, 129, 133–134. *See also* American Civil War

Connery, Rose (Irish workhouse emigrant), 38

Connery, William (problematic seaman), 189–190, 191

Connor, William (child emigrant), 38

*Cornwall Chronicle*, 110

Corry, James Porter (ship owner), 214, 281n172, 284n191

cotton and the cotton trade: and the Boyd brothers, 177–178, 184–185; brokers and brokering, 82, 84, 129; and conflagration of *Mary Carson*, 143; and Cotton Press King, 19–20; from New Orleans, 14, 17, 19–20, 25, 31, 39, 51, 52–53, 55–56, 131; and oil cakes, 131, 275n119; port of Mobile, Alabama, 25. *See also* Boyd, Sam

*Courier* (Hobart, Tasmania), 90

crew agreements: of *Belinda*, 27–28, 267n48; and births, marriages and deaths onboard, 168–169, 190; of *Dalriada* Captain W. Kelly Sr.'s salary, 56; of *Express*, 149, 150, 155–156, 157; and the Merchant Seamen's Act (1844), 40; of *Merrie England*, 114; and possessions of deceased crewman, 190; of *Princess Alexandra*, 188, 190; of *Sterling*, 167, 169; and W. Kelly Sr.'s illness at sea, 157

crew deaths at sea: on *Belinda*, 27, 32; on *Dalriada*, 56; on *Express*, 158, 163, 227; of J. Kelly (W. Kelly Sr.'s son), 238; on *Mary Carson*, 63; on *Merrie England*, 119; on *Princess Alexandra*, 190, 191, 204; on *Sterling*, 167–168

crew discipline: and attempted murder of captain, 169, 170, 171; consular role in crew discipline, 42, 120, 170–171, 176, 205, 206, 211, 285n195; and criminal trials of seamen, 41–43, 211–212, 215–218; and the mutinous J. Collins and J. Knox, 115–116, 119; refusal to obey orders or work, 120, 121; and theft of a mattress, 41–43; unruliness and assault, 114–115, 189–190, 191. *See also* Collins, James

crews: belongings and money allowed onboard, 41–43; desertions, 32, 56, 119, 168, 274n109; of *Express*, 150–151, 156–157, 162–165; first mate's/chief officer's duties, 112–113; illnesses, 27, 32, 56, 63, 151, 157, 167, 190, 191, 238; international character of, 151, 203–204, 217; loading guano, 39–40, 174, 205; management of unruly crews, 114–116, 189–190, 204, 211–212, 215–219; master/managing owner's duties, 150; officers and seamen loyal to W. Kelly Sr., 197–198; rescued at sea, 44–46, *45fig.*, 143–144, 145–147, 174–176, 238; sizes of, 71, 123, 145, 167; transfers, 27–28, 40, 136–137, 171–172, 173, 174; uniforms of, 68, 270n73; wages, 56, 140, 164, 175–176, 205, 206

"crossing the line" ceremony at equator, 72–73

Cunard Line, 165

currents: Antarctic Circumpolar, 77; in Arabian Sea, 152; around King Island, 74; around Scatarie Island, 45; in Bass Straight, 74; in Bay of Biscay, 62; at the Gulf of the

Saint Lawrence, 45; Mozambique and Agulhas, 81; near Mauritius, 139; near Scatarie Island, 45; in Palawan Channel, 95; in Torres Strait Passage, 94
*Cyclops* (steamer) rescuing *Miles Barton* crew and soldiers, 146–147

*Dalriada* (ship commanded by W. Kelly Sr.): burning of, 123–124, 148, 237; cargoes, 54, 56; deaths and desertions, 56; description and first voyage of, 54–55; Liverpool-New Orleans round trip, 55–56; spontaneous combustion and burning of, 123–124, 148, 237; voyages, routes, days at sea and nautical miles travelled, 159*t*.
Darnley, John and Mary (passengers), 114
Davey, Philip John (first mate of *Arethusa*), 51, 52, 268n56
Davis, R.H. (captain and Belfast maritime heritage authority), 169–170, 256, 278n144
deaths and illnesses at sea: of anonymous woman, 75–76; of children, 32–33, 36–38; of cholera, 167; of crew and Irish pauper emigrants, 32–38; of diarrheal disease, 190; by drowning, 137–140, 141*figs*., 146, 190; of heart disease, 157, 191; of Indian indentured laborers, 127–128; of J. Kelly (brother of W. Kelly Sr.), 137–140; of J. Kelly (son of W. Kelly Sr.), 238; of W. Kelly Sr., 157; in wreck of *Express*, 163–165. *See also* epidemic diseases; human migrations; shipwrecks and disasters
Demerara, Guiana (Guyana), 2, 125–128, *132fig*., 138, 160, 177, 242–243, 275n115
Diego Garcia, 123–124
Disraeli, Benjamin (British Prime Minister), 195, 284n194
Dixon, Robert and Lady (passenger), 53
Dodd, Thomas (seaman, cook), 151, 197
Douglas, George W. (medical superintendent of Grosse Isle Hospital), 35–36
Dover collision, 213, 283n190
"dripping sailor" story, 49–50, 164–165
Dryden, John (English poet), 76
"Duchess of Shingle Creek," 200, 201, 282n178
Dumas, Alexandre (Sr. and Jr.), 117–118
*Dumfriesshire* (ship commanded by W. Kelly Sr.): cargoes and passengers, 25; description, ownership and voyages of, 24–26, 28, 57, 263n13; voyages, routes, days at sea and nautical miles travelled, 158*t*.; wrecked under captain Alexander Davis, 46
Dunbar's Dock (Belfast), 25, 31
Durant, Moses, 119

Edington, Stewart (captain of barque *Rowena*), 15, 16

Ellison, Thomas (author), 65
Elmer, James (seaman), 167
*Epaminondas* (ship): builder, owner and description of, 136–137; charcoal drawing of, title page, iv, 137; John Kelly (brother of W. Kelly Sr.) on, 136–137, 275n121
epidemic diseases: cholera, 167, 266n41; measles, 127; smallpox, 33, 37–38, 242; typhus, 6, 36, 237, 266n41; yellow fever, 18, 22, 263n21
equatorial doldrums, 242n6
*Express* (ship, W. Kelly Sr., master/managing owner): acquisition of, 149–150; Aden-Singapore-London voyage, 153–155, 160*t*; cargoes, 154, 155, 162, 164; description and registration of, 149, 219; disaster of, 161–165, 196–197; first mate H. Wisnom, 167; J. Kelly (son of W. Kelly Sr.), as apprentice on, 151, 166; Liverpool-Aden voyage, 150–153, 160*t*.; R. Savage Captain and crew shipwrecked, 162–164, 196–197; signing-off on deceased crew's wages, 227; Sunderland-Calcutta-London voyage, 156–158, 160*t*.; voyages, routes, days at sea and nautical miles travelled, 151–153, 155, 160*t*.

Filles, Emilia Barton (child passenger), 72
Finch, Roger (author and nautical painter), 104–105, 257, 273n96
Fitzgerald, Augustine (passenger/merchant), 20
Flaugergues, Honoré (astronomer), 5
Flint, Timothy (American pioneer/missionary/author), 17
Foard, Mr. (defense, Liverpool Assizes), 215–216
Forbes, James "Bully" (captain), 77, 240–241, 242, 287n215
Fort Ross, Sonoma County, 5, 7
Fort Sumter (South Carolina), 134
Forwood, William Bower (English merchant, ship owner, politician), 65, 82, 257
Fox Line (of Henry Fox), 91
Fox Smith, Cicely, 127–128, 257, 275n116
Foy, Bob, Dr. (local Antrim historian and author): Family History Society talk, 240, 287n214; Kelly, Kerr and Orr family research of, xv, 257, 261n2, 264n31, 281n168; photos taken by, 141*fig.*, 193*fig.*, 225*fig.*, 230*fig.*; and search for *Miles Barton* painting, 102
Franco-Prussian War, 118
Free, Friedrich (seaman/carpenter), 203, 216
Freeden, Wilhelm Adolf von (mathematician and navigation expert), 213, 214, 283n189
French Consul to Melbourne and his wife, 117–118
Frenchy, James (passenger),

51–52
Frizell, Eleanor, 9–12, 16
Furious Fifties, 77, 114

Galilei, Galileo (astronomer), 248
Galle, Point de, Ceylon, 113, 118, 119, 120, 122*fig*., 155
George H. Parke & Company (Quebec shipbuilder and merchant), 26–27, 28, 54, 136, 264n31, 265n37
geraniums, pilfered, 223–224
Germany/German immigrants, 37, 43–44. See also *Belinda*
*Glasgow Herald*, 38–39
gold, 8, 53, 64, 76, 117, 240–241
"golden age of sail," xiii, 1, 242, 248, 249
*The Gold Robbers (Les Voleurs d'Or)*, 117, 118
Gowan, Henry (Belfast steamship agent), 213
Gowan, Samuel H. (Belfast ship owner), 281n172
Graeber, Charles (seaman), 173
Graham, James and his wife (friends or W. Kelly Sr.), 19, 180, 227
Grainger, David (Belfast ship owner): and *Arethusa*, 27, 47–49, 50–53; and *Belinda*, 29, 31–32; business relationships, 264n31; and *Conqueror*, 29; and *Dalriada*, 54–58; and *Dumfriesshire*, 24–26; and *Epaminondas*, 136–137; family ties in transatlantic trade, 264n31; and *Jessie*, 22, 106; and *Margaret Johnson*, 14, 22, 106. See also *Belinda*;

Parke, George Holmes
Grainger, Maria Belinda (wife of David Grainger), 27
Great Comet of 1811, 5
Great Gale of 1846, Marblehead, Massachusetts, 47–48, 48*fig*.
Green, Henry (seaman/steward), 150, 156, 197
Grogan, Rose (maid), 59
Groom, William (seaman/captain), 14
Grosse Isle Hospital, 33, 35–36, 37, 266nn41-42, 271n75
Groundwater, Isaac (seaman/carpenter), 167–168
Guañape Islands, 173, 174, 203. *See also* Callao, Peru
guano, xii, 14, 39, 152, 166, 173–176, 197, 205, 219, 232, 280n156
Gulf of Aden, 152–153, 155, 242, 255, 277n137
Gulf of Saint Lawrence, 29, 30, 44, 45, 265n35, 266n41

Haigh, Thomas (English cotton broker), 82, 83, 272n82
Halhead, Fletcher & Co. of Liverpool (owner of *Hilton*), 137
Harkness, Mrs. R. (*Bankfields*), 233
Harland and Wolff shipyard (Belfast), 237
Harper, Mr. (defense attorney), 224
Hawes, Maria Louise (wife of Sam Rainey), 59
Hazlett, Thomas (Irish merchant), 59
Head Inn, Antrim Town, 4–5, 7,

8, 9–11, 16
Heard, Joseph: painting of *Margaret Johnson*, 14, 15*fig*.; painting of *Miles Barton*, 70, 83, 101–105, 235, 272n83
Hempl, Mary (deceased passenger), 56
*Henry Brigham* (ship) rescue of *Mary Carson* crew, 142–143
Hester, James (surgeon superintendent on *Miles Barton*), 92
*Hilton* (ship): cargoes, 137–138; and J. Kelly (brother of W. Kelly Sr.), 137; lost at sea with all hands, 137–140, 141*figs*., 148; as one in a series of catastrophes, 147–148; tombstone inscription, 138–139; in W. Kelly Sr.'s life and thoughts, 142, 155, 176, 244
Hobson's Bay, 88, 89, 93
Hong Kong, 2, 89, 113, 119, 121, 122*fig*., 144, 155, 159–160*t*.
Hooghly River (Bengal), 62, 80–81, 89–90, 158, 190. *See also* Calcutta
human migrations: and colonial authorities in Canada, 32–36; emigration to Australia, 64, 67–71, 84–87, 271n74; German emigration to the USA, xii, 43–44; Indian indentured laborers, xii, 125–128, 138, 242–243, 275nn113-114; and the Irish famine, 6, 29–30, 32–38, 242, 265n37
Hunter, Alexander (deceased child), 38
Hunter, Belinda (deceased child), 38, 266n45, 271n75
Hunter, William and Nancy (parents of Alexander and Belinda), 266n45

indentured laborers: from Calcutta to sugar plantations at Demerara, xii, 125–128, 138, 242; and Chinese immigrants to New Orleans, 177; indenture as "a new system of slavery," 126, 242–243, 275n113-114; passenger deaths on way to Demerara, 127–128
India Docks (London), 40, 41, 42, 43
India trade. *See* Bombay (Mumbai); Calcutta (Kolkata)
Indian corn/cornmeal, 35–37, 39, 52
Indian Ocean: currents, winds and storm hazards in, 73–74, 76, 81, 118–119, 139–141; and the death of J. Kelly (W. Kelly Sr.'s brother), 4, 137–140, 244; and fire on *Dalriada*, 123–124; and first voyage of *Mary Carson*, 62–63; and loss of *Hilton*, 137–140; Roaring Forties and Furious Fifties, 73–74, 77, 114; routes through, 62–63, 80, 119–120; Seychelles Islands, 152, 167
Indonesia, 2, 94, 94–98, 96*fig*., 97*fig*.
Ireland, 6, 29–30, 32–38. *See also Belinda*; *Dumfriesshire*; *Mary Carson*
Irish, Bill (author), 165, 258, 286n209

Jackson, Robert (captain, Royal Navy), xvi, 139, 258, 276n125
*James Beazley* (clipper barque): renamed *Bankfields*, 219–221, 231–233, 233*fig.*, 234*fig.*; design, construction and first voyage of, 219–221; and Mary Kelly, 220. *See also* Beazley, James (Liverpool ship owner)
jibing, 145
Jones, A. (seaman/second mate), 171
Jones, Robert (seaman/sent to jail), 120
Jones Wharf, Saint Charles River, 25
Just, William (owner of *Bankfields*), 231

Kala Pani (Hindi/"black water"), 126–128
*Kate Stewart* (Captain Teague), 171–172
Kellett, Nathan (seaman/commanded Kelly ships), 187, 197, 203–204, 223, 225, 238
Kelly, Agnes (daughter of Martha and W. Kelly Sr., possible twin of James), 18, 21, 26, 60, 133, 200, 222, 234, 235
Kelly, Annie (wife of William Kelly Jr.), 237
Kelly, Eleanor (mother of W. Kelly Sr. and John), 4, 8, 17–18
Kelly, Fanny (first daughter Fanny of Martha and W. Kelly Sr., deceased in childhood), 24, 26
Kelly, Fanny (second daughter Fanny of Martha and W. Kelly Sr.), 57, 60, 82, 102, 133, 193, 200, 222, 230, 272n83. *See also* Moore, Fanny
Kelly, Fanny (sister of W. Kelly Sr. and John Kelly), 7–8, 57
Kelly, James, (son of Martha and W. Kelly Sr., possible twin of Agnes), 18, 21, 26, 41
Kelly, John (brother of W. Kelly Sr.), life: overview of, 3–4, 6–7; marriage to Sarah Orr, 23–24, 264n26; relationship and comparison with W. Kelly Sr., 105–106, 243–244, 248–249; death, 4, 135, 137–140, 141*figs.*
Kelly, John (brother of W. Kelly Sr.), career: *Amelia*, 274n106; apprenticeship, 21–22; and the California gold rush, 53; Canadian-built ships, 12; as captain of *Arethusa*, 47–49, 50–53; Certificates of Service, 105–106, 107–108*figs.*; and *Clio*, 22–24, 52, 108*fig.*, 264n26; and the "dripping sailor," 49–50; early career on *Margaret Johnson*, 14, 158*t.*, 243; on *Epaminondas* and *Flora*, 136–137; as *Hilton* first mate, 137–140; sailing with William on *Miles Barton*, 272n81; sailing with William on *Merrie England*, 106, 112–113, 136, 155, 243. *See also Arethusa; Hilton*
Kelly, John (second son John of Martha and W. Kelly Sr.): birth and childhood, 41, 60, 133; apprentice on *Express*,

151; second mate on *Sterling*, 166; survived the wreck of *Miles Barton*, 147; commanding *Boyne*, 228; master mariner, 228, 231, 237–238; in *Sea Breezes*, 83; gold watch and *Sterling* painting, 186, 235; in W. Kelly Sr.'s will, 222–223, 225, 234; death, 238

Kelly, John (first son John of Martha and W. Kelly Sr., died in childhood), 18

Kelly, John Sr. (father of W. Kelly Sr. and John Kelly), 4–5, 9–12

Kelly, Martha (*née* Rainey, wife of W. Kelly Sr.): Kelly family in 1851 and 1861 censuses, 59, 133; children of, 2, 18, 21, 26, 40–41, 60, 82; marriage and wedding, 16–17, 236; Rainey family in New Orleans, 17–18, 129–130; family life and role in the business, 236–237; impact of her brother's and her children's deaths on, 181, 183–184, 236; and *James Beazley*, 222, 231; death and last will and testament of, 234–236

Kelly, Mary McConnel (daughter of Martha and W. Kelly Sr., married J. Orr Wallace), 82, 133, 200, 220, 222, 226, 230, 235, 286n209

Kelly, Mary (W. Kelly Sr.'s sister, married J. McFerran, mother of William and Elizabeth), 8, 201, 207, 208–210, 210*fig.*, 283n185

Kelly, William Jr. (son of Martha and W. Kelly Sr.): birth, 63; UK census 1861, 133; early career of, 156–157, 166; assessment of seamanship, 190; transferred to *Sterling* from *Merrie England*, 173; as first mate on *Twin Sisters*, 228; master of *Princess Alexandra*, 187–191, 203–204; and J. Collins's murder trial, 219; Certificate of Competency as Master Mariner, 226; in W. Kelly Sr.'s will, 222–223, 225–226; family heirlooms and, 235; final voyage and death, 237

Kelly, William Sr., career at sea: *Ambassador*, 19–21, 158*t.*, 178, 181; certificates of service and master's certificate, 60, 61*fig.*; clipper master on *Miles Barton* (ship)'s maiden voyage, 66; and *Dalriada*, 54–58; and *Dumfriesshire*, 24–26; early career, 13–14, 158*t.*; and *Margaret Johnson*, 13–16; and *Mary Carson*, 58–60, 62–63; overview, 2–3, 158–160*t.*, 228–229; passenger recognition and gifts, 78–80, 82, 88–89, 93; personality, professionalism and reputation as a seaman, 2, 33, 43, 77, 90, 98–99, 111–112, 240–241, 242–243; retirement from active seafaring, 192, 194; salary (*Dalriada*), 56. See also *Belinda*; *Express*; *Margaret Johnson*; *Merrie England*; *Miles Barton*

Kelly, William Sr., as ship owner: acquisition of *Princess Alexandra*, 186–187, 193; design and construction of *James Beazley* (clipper barque), 219–221; of *Express*, 149–150, 156–158, 161–165; of *Merrie England*, 165–166, 174–176; and Plimsoll's Unseaworthy Vessels Bill, 194–198; of *Princess Alexandra*, 186–188, 193, 203–205, 211–212, 215–219; retirement from seafaring and other business, 157–158, 200–201; as shore manager for J. Beazley's fleet, 165; a standardized international steering system for ships, 212–215; of *Sterling*, 160–161, 167–173, 173, 186. *See also* specific ships

Kelly, William Sr., personal and family life: birth, siblings and early education, 4, 8, 12; dispute with Mrs. Frizell over Head Inn, 9–12; marriage, 16–17; children, 18, 21, 24, 26, 40–41, 57, 60, 63, 82; as a family-man, 2–3, 198–201, 199*fig*., 202*fig*.; demographics and census data of, 4, 59, 133*t*.; relationship and comparison with his brother John, 105–106, 244–245, 248–249; and the loss of his brother John, 138–140, 142; letter to J. Graham about the Sam Rainey murder, 180–183; letter to Elizabeth McFerran, 198–200, 199*fig*.; letter to William J. McFerran, 206–210, 210*fig*.; health of, 157–158, 200, 201, 221, 228, 244; and ostrich eggs, 154–155; and pilfered geraniums, 223–225, 225*fig*.; synchronicities of his life, 5, 60, 227, 233; attitude toward death, "the great change," 180, 227; death of, 225–231, 230*fig*.; will and testament with codicil, 102, 222–223, 225–226

Kelly, William Sr., residences: at 14 Abercorn Terrace, Belfast, 193; at 21 Pilot Street, Belfast, 24–25, 236; at 6 Richmond Crescent, Belfast, 193, 193*fig*., 225*fig*., 226, 285n200; at 18 Upper Parliament Street, Toxteth, Liverpool ("Cemetery View"), 131, 133*t*.; at 35 Upper Parliament Street, Toxteth, Liverpool for investment, 192; at 52 Upper Stanhope Street, Toxteth, Liverpool, 60; at *Bella Vista* on Antrim Road, Belfast, 180, 192–193; in Townhead section of Antrim Town, 60, 90

Kepler, Johannes (German astronomer), 248

Kerguelen Archipelago (Desolation Islands), 103, 115–116, 273n95

Knights of Pythias (men's organization, New Orleans), 184

Knox, James (mutinous seaman), 115–116

Kotzebue, Otto von (Russian officer/explorer), 6–7

Krakatoa (Indonesian volcano),

97–98
Kullman, Henrik (seaman), 190

Lamport & Holt (British merchant shipping line), 187
Larkin (Belfast sub-constable), 223–224
Lavendo, Ramond (seaman/steward), 203
Lees, James (British maritime author), 239, 259
Lewis, Henry (seaman), 63, 269n65
LightSail 2 spacecraft, 246
Lindstrom, A. (seaman), 205, 215–216
*Liverpool Albion*, 109
Liverpool Cotton Brokers Association, 82
*Liverpool Daily Post*, 143–144
Liverpool Exchange, 65
Liverpool 'Man-catchers' (thieves), 92
*Liverpool Mercury*: on American Civil War, 133–134; on California gold rush, 53; on charges against James Collins, 211; on *Clio* shipwreck, 23; on *Express*, 151, 155; on *Merrie England*, 99; on *Miles Barton*, 67–70, 84–85, 90, 95, 98; on *Sterling*, 186
Liverpool Seamen's Friend Society and Bethel Union, 67, 87. *See also* Buck, James (Rev.)
Liverpool Underwriters' Association, 277n133
Lloyd's Captains Register, 138, 138–139, 141, 141*fig.*
Lloyd's Register of Shipping, 149, 161, 167, 186, 274n101
*Lloyd's Weekly Newspaper*, 92
*London Evening Standard*, 137, 276n130
London Local Marine Board, 226
*London Sun*, 119
London, West India Docks, 40, 41, 42, 43
Long, John (seaman), 56
Louisiana, Ordinance of Secession, 129

McAlister, Duncan S. (agent, New Orleans), 20–21
McAlpine, Robert (seaman), 167–168
McCauley, Neil (captain), 14, 29
McConnell, Mr. (prosecution, Liverpool Assizes), 215
McDonald, Robert (geranium thief), 223
McFerran, Elizabeth (niece of W. Kelly Sr., sister of W. J. McFerran), letter from William Kelly Sr., 198–200, 199*fig.*, 202*fig.*
McFerran, Esther (Elizabeth McFerran's sister), 199, 200, 202*fig.*
McFerran, John (W. Kelly Sr.'s brother-in-law), 154–155, 201, 283n185
McFerran, Martha (Elizabeth McFerran's sister), 200, 201, 202*fig.*
McFerran, Mary (W. Kelly Sr.'s sister, mother of William and Elizabeth McFerran), 8, 201, 203, 207, 208–210, 210*fig.*
McFerran, William J. (nephew of

W. Kelly Sr., brother of Elizabeth McFerran), W. Kelly Sr.'s letter to, 206–208
McGonnel, James (last captain of *Princess Alexandra*), 238
McLean, Jr. (geraniums prosecutor), 224
McMahon, Robert (commanded Kelly ships), 174–175, 189, 190, 197
Macmillan, Allister (English author and editor), 139, 259
Macnamara (soldier, deceased in *Miles Barton* wreck), 146
Magee, William (seaman/steward), death, 119
Mahan, Mary (domestic in Sam and Maria Rainey household), 130
Main-à-Dieu Passage (Cape Breton), 45*fig.*, 46, 267n52. *See also* Scatarie Island
Malacca, Strait of, 119–120, 155
Malay Peninsula, 119–120, 155
Mangru, Basdeo (Guyanese historian), 127
Manila, 91, 94, 95, 96–97*figs.*/maps., 98, 159*t.*
Manning, Thomas (seaman/deserter), 119, 274n109
*A Manual for Shipmasters* (Lees), 239, 259
*Margaret Johnson* (barque commanded by W. Kelly Sr.): abandoned at sea, 14–15; cargoes, 13–14; description of, 13–15, 15*fig.*; J. Kelly's early career on, 21, 106; Kelly brothers sailing on, 13–14, 158*t.*, 243, 262n13; New Orleans, 17, 21; voyages, route, days at sea and nautical miles travelled, 158*t.*
marine art. *See* paintings and marine art
Marryat's Commercial Code of Signals, 188
Martin, Henry Byam (captain, HMS *Grampus*), 40, 259, 267n48
Martin's Wharf, Quebec, 48
*Mary Carson* (ship, commanded by W. Kelly Sr.): cargoes, 58, 59, 143; description, builder and ownership of, 58; Liverpool-India trip, 62–63; Liverpool-New York with passengers, then to Quebec via Scatarie Island, 59–60; painting of, 235; raging fire and loss of, 142–144, 148, 176, 237, 244; voyages, routes, days at sea and nautical miles travelled, 159*t.*
Massachusetts ship building (Briggs Brothers), 160–161
Massereene, Viscount, 91
master mariners: Barrett, John Alfred (*Princess Alexandra*), 187; Bond (*Genghis Khan*), 81; Bowen, Clement (*Sterling*), 169–170, 172, 185, 197; Croad (*Futteh Salaam*), 124; Darlington (*Miles Barton*), 99; Darroch, Archibald (*Princess Alexandra*), 187, 197; Davis, Alexander (*Dumfriesshire*), 46; Denny (*Camperdown*), 127–128; Eaton, J. D. (*Strathclyde*), 283n190; Ewing (*Dalriada*), 123–124; Findley (*Flora*), 136;

Fitzsimons (*Lord Seaton*), 22; Forbes, James "Bully" (captain), 77, 240–241, 242; Gaggs (*Star of the East*), 113, 116; Grove, (brig *Grove*), 70; Hall (*Sterling*), 161; Hayes (*Jessica*), 57; Heasley (*Epaminondas*), 136; Hicks (*Helen*), 50; Hollywood (*Princess Alexandra*), 238; Hughes (*Petona*), 57; Hunter (*Milicate*), 57; Johnson (*St. Clair*), 57; Johnston (*De Soto*), 131; Jones, Daniel (*Mary Carson*), 143; Just, William (*Bankfields*), 231; Kain (*Princess Alexandra*), 238; Kellett, Nathan (*Princess Alexandra*), 187, 197, 238; Kelley, Charles William (*Princess Alexandra*), 187; Lambert (*Indiana*), 87; Leary (*Queen*), 50; Lepan (*Arethusa*), 27; Lockhart (*Alice Wilson*), 57; McCauley (*Conqueror*), 29; McCleary (*Hilton*), 137–140; McGonnell, James (*Princess Alexandra*), 238; McIntyre, Peter (*Belinda*), 14, 27–28; McMahon, Robert (*Merrie England*), 174–175, 189, 190, 197; McMahon (*Viceroy*), 57; Mills (*Indian Queen*), 77; Molyneux, Samuel (*Princess Alexandra*), 187, 191; Potter (*Henry Brigham*), 142–144; Proctor, John (*Samuel Knight*), 48; Riggall, Samuel (*Express*), 157–158, 161; Robertson (*Star of the East*), 77; Russell (*Transit*), 57; Savage, Roland (*Express*), 162–164; Seabourne, John Vines (*Merrie England, Sterling, James Beazley*), 167, 198, 220, 221, 231, 242; Shaw, Edward James (*Princess Alexandra*), 187; Shelford, James (*Miles Barton*), 144–147; Skeoch (*Lord Seaton*), 22; Sweeting, J. (*William Herdman*), 22; Teague, George (*Sterling*), 169–172; Underwood (*Blue Jacket*), 91; Williams, John (*Princess Alexandra*), 187; Winteringham (*Alchemist*), 98; Wisnom, Hugh (*Sterling*), 151, 167–169, 197, 279n151

Mauritius hurricanes and ocean currents, 139

*Mauritius Illustrated* (Macmillan), 139

*Melbourne Argus,* 78, 88, 93–94, 116, 272n84, 272n85, 273n91, 274n104, 287n215

Melbourne, Australia: distances from Cape of Good Hope, 271n76; French consul's wife at, 117–118; Gold Rush immigrants to, 64, 240–241; immigrants to, 64, 240–241; *Miles Barton* grounded, 93; passages to Manila, 94–95, 96*fig.*, 97*fig.*; race with *Star of the East* to, 113–114, 116, 147–148. See also *Merrie England; Miles Barton;* Stavely, David

*Mémoires* of Céleste Mogador (Comte de Chabrillan's wife), 117–118

Mercantile Marine Act of 1850, 60

Merchant Seamen's Act (1844), 40

Merchant Shipping Bill (1854), 168, 194–196, 197, 281nn172-174

merchants. *See* shipping companies, agents and merchants

*Merrie England* (ship, W. Kelly Sr. as commander): Beazley's profits from, 110, 274n100; cargoes, 113, 116, 119, 120, 121, 125, 131, 135; crew discipline and desertions, 114–115, 120, 121, 274n109, 275n111; description and launch of, 99, 109–111, 112, 236; voyage 1 Liverpool to Melbourne, Ceylon, India, Hong Kong and Shanghai, 113–121, 122*fig.*; voyages 2 and 3 London to Calcutta trips, 121, 124–125; voyage 4 Liverpool to Calcutta and Demerara with return to New Orleans, 125–128, 132*fig.*; voyage 5 Liverpool to Calcutta again, 135; voyages, routes, days at sea and nautical miles travelled, 159–160*t.*; William and John sailing together on, 106, 112–113, 243

*Merrie England* (W. Kelly Sr. as owner): Calcutta cyclone wreck of, 166, 175; cargoes, 166, 174; S. Walters's painting of, 6, 235, 286n209; sinking and loss of, 173, 174–176, 184, 186, 193, 196–198, 219, 237, 280nn156-157; W. Kelly Jr. as third mate on, 173; W. Kelly Sr.'s acquisition of, 83, 165–166

Mersey River (England), 19, 53, 60, 67, 89, 91, 98, 125, 151, 231

Methodism, 206–207, 208

*Miles Barton* passengers: births and deaths at sea, 75–76, 94; passenger letters to families and friends, 69–70, 87; fighting and drunkenness onboard, 72, 73–74; naming of newborn child after the ship, 72; Rev. Buck's farewell religious services, 67–70, 83–87; steerage revolt, 70–71; successful first voyage, 77–80

Miles Barton Reef, 146*fig.*, 147, 277n133

*Miles Barton* (ship, commanded by W. Kelly Sr.): cargoes on, 71, 78, 94, 95, 98; description, naming and launch of, 64–68, 65*fig.*; J. Heard painting of, 83, 101–105, 235, 272n83; Liverpool to Melbourne run-times of, 76, 77, 78, 87–88; shipping company affiliations with, 91, 99; voyages, routes, days at sea and nautical miles travelled, 159*t.*; wooden model of, 64–65, 65*fig.*, 103, 269n67. *See also* Kelly, William Sr., career at sea; Stavely, David

*Miles Barton*, voyage 1: from Liverpool to the Cape of Good Hope, 71–73; from the Cape of Good Hope to Melbourne, 73–76; Melbourne-Calcutta-Ceylon-Bombay voyage, 80–81; from Bombay to

Liverpool, 81–82
*Miles Barton*, voyage 2: from Liverpool to Melbourne and Calcutta, 83–89; from Calcutta to Liverpool, 89–91
*Miles Barton*, voyage 3: Liverpool to Melbourne, Manila, Anjer and Rotterdam round-trip, 91–100; 96–97*figs*.; clergyman's death on wharf at Liverpool, 91–92; running aground at Port Phillip Heads, 93
*Miles Barton* (commanded by James Shelford): with John Kelly (W. Kelly Sr.'s son) serving as ship's boy, 147, 151; and wreck at Cape of Good Hope with 3rd Buffs, 144–148, 146*fig*., 276nn129-131, 277n133, 176, 237, 244
Milford Haven (Welsh port), 136
"milky sea" phenomenon, 152–153, 242, 277n137
Milky Way, 246, 248
Miller, Charles (problematic seaman), 189–190, 191
Millers and Thompson Golden Line of Packets (shipping agents), 66, 70–71, 85, 91
*Miss Powel* (novel by Céleste de Chabrillan), 117
Mississippi River and the Passes, 17, 129, 264n23
Mobile, Alabama, 2, 3, 18, 25, 134, 158*t*.
monsoon winds: encountered by Kelly ships, 1, 62, 80–81, 94, 139, 152; Sumatras and Nor'westers in the Malacca Strait, 118–120

Moore Bros. (John and William), ship brokers and agents, 230–231, 238
Moore, Edith Mary (daughter of Fanny and John Moore), 235
Moore, Fanny (*née* Kelly, daughter of Martha and W. Kelly Sr.): family relations of, 82, 133, 200, 230, 234; inheritance of *Miles Barton* painting, 102, 272n83; in Martha Kelly's will, 235; move with husband into Bella Vista residence, 193; in W. Kelly Sr.'s will, 222
Moore, James Kelly (son of Fanny and John Moore), 272n83
Moore, John, (Belfast ship and insurance broker who married Fanny Kelly), 83, 102, 230–231, 272n83
Moore, John Patrick (son of Fanny and John Moore), 272n83
Moore, Martha Florence (daughter of Fanny and John Moore), 235
Moore, William (Belfast ship and insurance broker, brother of John Moore), 222, 231, 238
Moore, William Gourley (son of Fanny and John Moore, grandson of W. Kelly Sr.), 82–83, 101–102, 272n83
Morin, Francis, Lady Mary and Adeline (passengers), 53
*Morning Chronicle* (London), 113–114
Morrow, Thomas Magee, Rev. (new Presbyterian Church,

Dunadry), 25
Mountain, Armine Wale (son of George Jehoshaphat Mountain), 266n45
Mountain, George Jehoshaphat (Anglican bishop of Quebec), 266n45
Muckamore graveyard and Kelly monument, 3–4, 26, 138–139, 140, 141*figs.*, 148, 229, 230*fig.*, 261nn1,4, 263n21
Mullen, Margaret (domestic in Sam and Maria Rainey household), 130
Mustang aircraft (Royal Australian Airforce), 232

Napoleon/Napoleonic wars, 5–6
Natalias, R. (seaman), 205
National Maritime Museum (Greenwich), 100, 101*fig.*, 273n94
Nepkin (Neptune in *crossing the line* ceremony), 72–73
Nesbitt, John James (Saint-Roch shipyard Quebec), 26–27
New Brunswick, ships built in, 3, 12, 22–23, 24, 58, 63, 64, 66, 165, 186–187, 269n64, 269n66
New Orleans: and *Ambassador* cargo and passengers, 19–21; and *Arethusa* cargo and passengers, 51; and *Belinda* cargo and passengers, 31–32; cotton industry trade, 19–20; and *Dalriada* cargo and passengers, 55–56; and *Mary Carson* cargo and passengers, 58–59; *Merrie England* and the Louisiana Ordinance of Secession, 128–131, 133–134; reconstruction era complexities of the Boyd brothers' trials, 179–180, 181–185; William and Martha Kelly's relocation to and shipping in and out of, 17–18. *See also* Rainey, Sam; Boyd, John; Boyd, Sam; Boyd William
New Orleans (as Crescent City), 17, 31, 57, 58, 128
*New Orleans as It Was* (book by H. Castellanos), 179
*New Orleans Bee*, 59, 129
*New Orleans Commercial Bulletin*, 20–21, 31
New Orleans National Bank, 178, 182
*New Orleans Picayune*, 56
*New York Commercial Advertiser*, 23
*New York Herald*, 23
New Zealand Shipping Company, 165
Newfoundland, 29, 47, 241
Nielsen, Carl (seaman/cook), 203
*North China Herald*, 120
Northern Steam Towing Company, 230. *See also* Moore Bros.
*Northern Whig*, 207
Nova Scotia, 13, 15, 22, 30, 187, 188; Scatarie Island, 44–46, 45*fig.*, 59, 267nn50,52

O'Brien, James (deceased child passenger), 56
*Ocean Passages for the World* (Jackson), xvi, 139, 258

O'Donnell, Judge (pilfered geraniums), 224
Old Bailey Criminal Court, 41–43, 198, 224, 267n49
Orr, James, of Folly, Antrim (father of Sarah Orr), 24, 257, 264n26, 269n60
Orr, John (grandfather of Sarah Orr), xv, 257
Orr, Sarah (married John Kelly, brother of W. Kelly Sr.), xv, 23–24, 257, 264n26
Osborne, Graham & Co. (North Hylton shipbuilders), 220

Pabellón de Pica and Huanillas (Chile guano deposits), 205
Pacific Steam Navigation Company, 205, 211
packet ships, 2, 15*fig.*, 66, 91, 99
paintings and marine art: The Great Gale of 1846, 47–48, 48*fig.*; of *Margaret Johnson* by J. Heard, 14, 15*fig.*; of *Mary Carson*, 235; of *Merrie England* by S. Walters, 235, 286n209; of *Miles Barton* in a heavy sea by J. Heard, 83, 101–105, 235, 272n83; of *Sterling* (unknown artist), 186, 235; wooden model of *Miles Barton*, 64–65, 65*fig.*, 103, 269n67
Parke, George Holmes (Quebec shipbuilder and merchant), 26–27, 28, 54, 136, 264n31. *See also* Grainger, David
Parry, John (lackadaisical seaman), 121
passengers: on *Ambassador*, Liverpool-New Orleans trips, 19–20; on *Arethusa*, 51-52; on *Belinda*, 29–31, 32–38, 43–44, 242; on *Dalriada* Liverpool to New Orleans, 56; on *Dumfriesshire* Belfast to Quebec, 25–26; letters of commendation from, 29, 51–52, 268n56; on *Mary Carson*, 59
passengers: on *Merrie England*, 110–111, 113–114; and Indian immigrants to Demerara, 125–128; and soldiers of the 3rd Buffs, 144–147, 276nn129,131
passengers: on *Miles Barton*, and cabin passengers, 78; clergyman's death on the wharf, 91–92; "crossing the line" ceremony, 72–73; first voyage, 66–70; letters of commendation from, 78-80, 88-89; one fatality on maiden voyage, 75; passengers recruited to supplement crew, 76; revolt in steerage, 70–71; and sending letters from mid-Atlantic, 73
Pasteur, Richard Mason (witness during Boyd trials), 179
Paterson, John (early Methodist), 207
Patterson, William (ship's boy, *Express*), 151
Penobscot Maritime Museum (PMM), 14, 15*fig.*
*Perth Daily News*, 233, 234*fig.*
Peru. *See* Callao, Peru
Peterson, John (seaman/boatswain), 150, 197

Philippines (Manila), 2, 94, 95, 96–97*figs.*/*maps*, 98
Phillips, James (property agent), 91
Pilkington and Wilson (White Star "packet" clipper ships), 99, 111
Planetary Society, The, 246, 247*fig.*, 287n218
Plimsoll marks/lines, 196, 281n173
Plimsoll, Samuel, 194–196, 212–213
Point de Galle, Ceylon, 113, 118, 119, 120, 122*fig.*, 155
Poor Law Unions and Commissioners (Ireland), 33–35, 34*t*.
Port Phillip Heads (bay and channel, Melbourne), 74–75, 89, 93
*Portland Daily Press*, 186
*Portland Evening Star*, 164
Prince's Dock (Belfast), 137
*Princess Alexandra* (ship, owned by W. Kelly Sr.): Cardiff-to Rio de Janeiro, Calcutta, Bombay and Dundee voyage, 189–191; cargoes, 187, 205; lost in a hurricane, 238; murder of J. Christian on, 204–206, 210, 211–212, 215–219, 285n195; previous owners and captains of, 187, 280n165; and W. Kelly Jr., 203–204, 280n167, 282n179; W. Kelly Sr.'s acquisition and ownership of, 186–188, 188*fig.*, 193, 194; in W. Kelly Sr.'s will, 222–223, 225–226
Proctor, John (captain in Great Gale of 1846), 48, 48*fig.*

Psalm 107 (inscription on Kelly monument), 2–3, 148
Public Record Office of Northern Ireland (PRONI), 4–5, 261n2, 263n19, 285n199, 286n208

Quebec: and *Arethusa*, 47–51; and *Belinda*, 26–30, 32–39, 44–45, 158–159*t*., 242, 265n37, 266nn41,45, 271n75; and *Clio*, 22; and *Dalriada*, 54–55, 159*t*; and *Dumfriesshire*, 24–26, 158*t*.; and *Epaminondas*, 136–137; and George H. Parke, 264n31, 265n34; immigration authorities, 32; the Kelly brothers and, 2, 3, 12, 18, 22, 24; and Margaret Johnson, 262–263n13; and Mary Carson, 58–60, 159*t*.; and *Princess Alexandra*, 238; and *Rowena*, 15; winter freezes, 6, 25. *See also* Grainger, David; Parke, George Holmes
*Quebec Gazette*, 27, 29, 47
"Queen of Antrim Town" (acrostic poem), 7–8. *See also* Kelly, Fanny (sister of W. Kelly Sr.)

Raffles, Mr. (judge, Liverpool police court), 212, 216
Rainey, Agnes (mother of Martha Kelly), 131, 133*t*.
Rainey, Catherine (wife of James Kelly/sister-in-law of Martha Kelly), 129–130
Rainey, Emma (daughter of Maria and Sam Rainey), 130, 177

Rainey, Eva (daughter of Maria and Sam Rainey), 177
Rainey, James (older brother of Martha Kelly), 17, 19–20, 129–130, 183
Rainey, John of Ballydunmaul (father of Martha Kelly), 16, 263n18
Rainey, Maria Louise (*née* Hawes, wife of Sam Rainey), 59, 130, 177, 182
Rainey, [name unknown], (stillborn child of Maria and Sam Rainey), 177
Rainey, Sam (younger brother of Martha Kelly): business ventures with William and John Boyd, 177–178, 182–183; Letters Patent and business ventures of, 177; marriage to Maria Louise Hawes, 59; murder of, 20, 177–178, 183; personal relationship with Boyd brothers, 19–20, 181–182; relationship with Martha and W. Kelly Sr., 129–130, 182–183
Rainey, William Kelly (son of Maria and Sam Rainey), 130, 177
Rea, William R. (purchaser of *Princess Alexandra*), 238
Read, Charles, Lieutenant (Confederate naval raider), 171–172
"Red Duster" (Red Ensign), 104, 188
"Relic of *Miles Barton*" (silver snuff box), 82–83
revolver, percussion, of W. Kelly Sr., 100–101, 273n94

Richmond, Charles (seaman who stole mattress), 41–43
Riley, Mary Ann (domestic in Martha and W. Kelly Sr.'s household), 133
River Lagan, 25, 208
Roaring Forties, 73–74, 77, 114
Rotterdam, 2, 91, 98, 159
Rottnest Island, 232, 257, 286n205
*Rowena* (barque, W. Kelly Sr. advertised as captain), 15, 16
Royal Australian Air Force, 232
Royal Navy, 40
Ruddock, Francis and Joseph (New Brunswick ship builders), 186–187. See also *Princess Alexandra*

*sailing on sunlight*, (LightSail 2), wind and ocean currents compared with, 246–248, 247*fig.*, 287n219. See also Planetary Society
sailor superstitions: will not die before smelling land, 127–128; unlucky to commence voyage on a Friday, 137; renaming ship brings bad luck, 232
Saint George's Channel, 62
Saint Lawrence County, New York, 282n178, 283n185
Saint Lawrence River, 25, 27, 28, 30, 59
Saint Peter and Saint Paul Rocks, 62
Salt Pond, Ghana, 186
Salthouse Dock (Liverpool), 71, 91–92

# Index

Samuel Wakeham & Sons (Liverpool), 232
Sankey, Ira D. (American gospel singer/composer), 198, 200
Savage, Mrs. Roland, 162, 163, 227
Savage, Roland (captain of *Express* on ship's last voyage), 162–165
Savannah, Georgia, 3, 23, 47, 142–144
*Savannah Republican*, 23
Scatarie Island, 44–46, 45*fig.*, 52, 54, 59, 159*t.*, 164, 267n50,52
schooners, 18, 23, 48, 49, 75, 164, 171–172, 228. See also vessels mentioned in passing
Scott, Thomas, of Sydenham, Belfast (W. Kelly Sr.'s business associate), 222
scurvy prevention for crew, 114
*Sea Breezes* magazine, W. G. Moore's letter to the editor in, xiii, 82–83, 101–102, 272n83
*Sea Kayaking in Nova Scotia* (Cunningham), 44, 256, 267n50
Sea Ranch, The, 6, 251*fig.*
Seabourne, John Vines (captain on Kelly ships), 167, 198, 220, 221, 231, 242
secessionism in New Orleans, 129–130, 133–134
Semmes, Raphael (Confederate Navy officer), 179
Semmes, Thomas Jenkins (New Orleans lawyer and Confederate senator), 179
Shanghai, 2, 113, 119–121, 122*fig.*, 159*t.*
Shaw, Savill & Albion shipping company, 165
Shelford, James (*Miles Barton* captain, post-Kelly), 144–147
ship building and builders: Albert White & Co. (Waterford—*Merrie England* ), 99, 109–110; Briggs Brothers shipyard (South Boston—*Sterling* ), 160–161; Christopher Boultenhouse (Sackville, New Brunswick—*Mary Carson*), 58, 269n64; Francis and Joseph Ruddock (St. John, New Brunswick—*Princess Alexandra* ), 186–187; George H. Parke & Company (Quebec), 26–27, 28, 54, 136, 264n31; Harland and Wolff shipyard (Belfast), 237; industry cycle and prices of, per W. Kelly Sr., 181, 184; John James Nesbitt (Saint-Roch shipyard, Quebec—*Arethusa* and *Belinda* ), 26–27; Osborne, Graham & Co. (North Hylton, near Sunderland—*James Beazley*), 220; Pierre Brunelle shipyard (Quebec—*Dalriada*), 54; William and Richard Wright shipyard (Marsh Creek, New Brunswick—*Miles Barton*), 64, 269n66; woods used in ship construction, 12
ship collisions and close calls, 72, 213, 215, 283n190
ship operations: first mate's and master's duties, 112–113; getting *Miles Barton* passengers to the Melbourne pier, 75; salvaging wrecks, 45–46,

146–147; Tiller Orders and steering, 213–215; and underwriters, 98, 137–138, 274n101, 277n133

ship owners and ownership: H.C. Bowden and Bowden & Quinn (Belfast), 22, 51; and the Merchant Shipping Bill, 168, 195, 213; ship shareholders and risk distribution, 150; and the Unseaworthy Vessels Bill, 194–196, 212–213, 281n172. *See also* Beazley, James; Grainger, David; William Kelly Sr., as a ship owner

shipping companies, agents and merchants: Atkinson, Usborne & Co. (Quebec), 48–50; Beazley Line (Liverpool), 60; Black Ball Line (New York), 77; Burnet, D. (Quebec), 51; Cook & Smith (Liverpool), 52; Fox Line (of Henry Fox), 91; Gardiner, Sager & Co. (New Orleans), 51; Golden Line (Millers and Thompson, Liverpool), 66, 70–71, 85, 91; Harper & Stuart (Savannah, consignment company of wrecked *Clio*), 23; Moore Bros. (John & William Moore, Belfast), 230, 238; Pilkington and Wilson (White Star Line, Liverpool), 99, 111; Turner & Co. (Shanghai), 120; Wildes, Pickersgill & Co. (Liverpool), 47, 268n53

shipping regulations, certifications, and the Board of Trade, 55, 60, 61*fig.*, 106–108, 107*fig.*, 108*fig.*, 140, 196

shipping routes: *Belinda*, Belfast to New Orleans, 31; *Belinda*, Belfast to Quebec, 26–31; *Belinda*, Liverpool to Callao, Peru and Chincha Islands, 39–40; *Belinda*, London to Bremerhaven to New York and wrecked off Scatarie Island, 43–44; *Express*, Liverpool to Aden, 151–152; *Express,* to Akyab and Singapore, 155; *Mary Carson*, Liverpool to Calcutta, 62–63; *Mary Carson*, Liverpool to New Orleans, 58; *Merrie England*, Liverpool to Calcutta, Demerara and New Orleans, 125–128, 132*fig.*; *Merrie England*, Liverpool to Melbourne to Ceylon, India, Hong Kong and Shanghai, 113–121, 122*fig.*; *Miles Barton*, Liverpool to Melbourne and on to Calcutta and Bombay, 71–75, 80–81; *Miles Barton*, Liverpool to Melbourne and on to Manila, 93–98, 96*fig.*, 97*fig.*

"Ships' Graveyard" near Rottnest Island, 232, 257, 286n205

shipwrecks and disasters: of *Belinda*, 43–46, 237; of *Clio*, 23; of *Dalriada*, 123–124, 237; of *Express*, 162–165, 196–197, 237; fishing fleet in "Great Gale of 1846," 47–48; of *Hilton,* 137–140, 141*figs.*, 148, 237; of *Mary Carson*, 142–144, 237; of *Merrie England,* 174–176, 237; of *Miles*

*Barton*, 145–147, 237; possibly foreshadowing change for W. Kelly Sr., 148; of *Star of the East*, 147–148
signal codes and flags: Marryat's Commercial Code of Signals, 104, 188; the Red Ensign, 104; Watson's Code of Signals, 14
silver snuffbox and *Sea Breezes* letter, 82–83
Singapore, 2, 119, 150, 155, 160
*Singapore Straits Times*, 155
Skinner, Thomas (seaman/first mate), 223
Slavery Abolition Act, 126
Smith, Frank (seaman), 216, 285n195
Smith, W.S., Rev. (Irish clergyman and author), 12
Soeurs de France (nursing organization), 118
South Africa, 144, 146*fig*., 147–148, 232, 245; and the sons of Fanny and John Moore, 272n83
South Indian Ocean, trade currents, hurricanes and hazards of, 139–140
spontaneous combustion at sea (*Dalriada*), 123–124
"standing over," defined, 192
*Star of the East* (ship): compared with *Merrie England*, 77, 110, 113–114, 116, 118, 148, 269n66; compared with *Miles Barton*, 77; destruction of, 147–148; passengers and cargo on Liverpool-Melbourne trip, 113–114
Stavely, David: biography of, 270n71; description of *Miles Barton* passage from Liverpool to Melbourne, 71–77; description of passenger loading and protest, 67, 70–71
Stavely, Patricia (Baird), xvi, 270n71
steering systems and Tiller Orders (standardization of), 213–215
*Sterling* (ship): and the attempted murder of Captain Teague, 169, 170–172; captains and voyages of, 167–169, 173, 185–186, 198, 279n149; importance to W. Kelly Sr. and undetermined fate of, 186; and *Merrie England* as "incubators" for W. Kelly Sr.'s sons, 166; oil painting of, 186, 235; in UK Lloyd's Register of Shipping, 167; W. Kelly Jr.'s service on, 187, 189; W. Kelly Sr.'s ownership of, 160–161, 165–166, 173–174, 194, 221, 278n143
Strait of Belle Isle, 29
Sumatra (island in western Indonesia), 62, 98, 119
Sumatras (monsoon squalls), 119
Sunderland, George H. (seaman/mate on *Express*), 157
Sunderland, port of, 22, 156–158, 160t., 220, 221
"sunkers" (hazardous shoals), 44
"swallowing the anchor," defined, 148, 149
*Sydney Morning Herald*, 110

Tait, Mr. (misspelling in letter). *See* Tate, Mr.

Tasman Sea, 80, 94
Tate, Mr. (first mate on *Miles Barton*), 68, 85, 88, 270n72
Taylor, Robert (constable, East and West India Docks), 42–43
Teague, George Edward (captain), 169–172
Tennyson, Alfred, Lord (*Crossing the Bar* and *The Lotos Eaters*), 227–228, 249
Tezzia, Ferdinand (seaman), 205, 216
Tiller Orders, 213–215
timber trade: and *Arethusa*, 47, 48, 50–51; and Atkinson and Usborne's practice of overloading lumber ships, 49–50; and *Belinda*, 27, 30–31, 44; and *Express*, 164; an important commodity for Britain, xii, 1, 15, 24, 27, 263n13, 284n191; and *Mary Carson*, 59–60; and *Merrie England* as a tramp trader, 166; and *Princess Alexandra*, 187, 280n165; and staves, 31–32, 47, 51, 54, 56; and wood used in ship construction, 12, 262n10
Torres Strait Passage, 80, 95, 97*fig*.

UK Mercantile Navy List, 149
UK Register of Deaths at sea, 140
Union blockade of Southern ports, 129, 134, 171
Union Maritime Insurance Company, 82
Unseaworthy Vessels Bill, 194–196, 197, 281nn172-174. *See also* Merchant Shipping Bill; Plimsoll, Samuel

Vénard, Elizabeth-Céleste (Céleste Mogador), 117–118
Venus, Thomas (first captain of the *Bankfields*), 231
vessels mentioned in passing: *Africa* (ship), 133; *Alchymist* (ship), 98; *Alice Wilson* (ship), 57; *Alnwick Castle* (ship), 127; *Amazon* (schooner), 18; *Amiral Jurien de la Gravière* (barque), 175; *Amyone* (ship), 223, 237; *Anglo Saxon* (towboat), 128; *Apollo* of Warren (ship), 43; *Asia* (ship), 67, 70; *Balaret* (ship), 89; *Baltimore* (brig), 18; *Bangor Castle* (steamship), 230; *Berry* (schooner), 18; *Black Eagle* (tug paddle steamer), 93; *Black Witch* (ship), 43; *Blazer* (steam tug), 111; *Blue Jacket* (ship), 91; *Boyne* (ship), 228, 237; *British Crown* (steamship), 237; *British King* (steamship), 237; *Camperdown* (ship), 127–128; *Carpentaria* (ship), 89; *Childe Harold* (ship), 89; *Clarence* (CSS privateer), 171, 172; *Clarion* (steam barque), 20; *Coalition* (schooner), 164; *Collins* (ship), 47; *Conqueror* (ship), 29; *Cyclops* (steamship), 146–147; *De Soto* (steamship), 131; *Drusilla* (schooner), 18;

*Elizabeth George* (ship), 73; *Elizabeth Hamilton* (ship), 43; *Emeline* (schooner), 18; *Equal Rights* (ship), 138; *Erin* (steamship), 230; *Fair Wind* (ship), 161; *Flora* (ship), 136, 275n121; *Franconia* (steamship), 283n190; *Futteh Salaam* (ship), 124; *Genghis Khan* (ship), 81; *Golden Light* (ship), 161; *Goshawk* (ship), 191; *Grampus*, HMS (navy cruiser), 40, 259, 267n48; *Helen* (ship), 50; *Henry Brigham* (ship), 142–144; *Hillsborough* (ship), 13, 262n12; *Horatius* (steamship), 237; *Hudson* (steamship), 237–238; *Iberia* (steamship), 205, 211–212, 285n195; *Indiana* (steamship), 87; *Indian Queen* (ship), 77; *Inglewood* (barque), 237; *Janet* (ship), 89; *Jessica* (ship), 57; *Jessie* (brig), 21, 106; *John George* (ship), 74; *Joseph* (schooner), 23; *Juliet* (ship), 89; *Kate Stewart* (schooner), 171–172; *Koh-i-Noor* (paddle steamer), 237; *Lightning* (ship), 240; *Loodiana* (ship), 127; *Lord Seaton* (ship), 22, 106; *M.A. Schindler* (schooner), 171; *Marco Polo* (ship), 240; *Marmaluke* (ship), 161; *Mary* (steamship), 170; *Mermaid* (ship), 99; *Meteor* (ship), 161; *Milicate* (ship), 57; *Nantucket* (ship), 138; *North America* (steamship), 30; *Northern Light* (ship), 160–161; *Petona* (ship), 57; *Prince Albert* (barque), 30; *Queen* (ship), 50; *Red Jacket* (ship), 85; *Rowena* (barque), 15, 16; *R.W. Brown* (brig), 18; *St. Clair* (ship), 57; *Samuel Knight* (schooner), 48; *Saracen* (ship), 161; *Schomberg* (ship), 240; *Sea King* (ship), 30; *Sir Henry Pottinger* (barque), 30, 265n35; *South Stockton* (ship), 14; *Star of the East* (ship), 77, 110, 113–114, 116, 118, 147, 148, 269n66; *Strathclyde* (steamship), 283n190; *Success* (ship), 13, 262n12; *Swan* (steam tug), 20; *Tacony* (barque), 171, 172; *Tiptree* (ship), 99; *Tom Moore* (ship), 30; *Transit* (ship), 57; *Twin Sisters* (schooner), 228; *Tyrian* (steamship), 237; *Ulysses* (ship), 127; *Viceroy* (ship), 57; *White Star* (ship), 99, 113; *William Archer* (schooner), 18; *William Herdman* (barque), 22, 106

Villiers, Alan, xix, 77, 244, 245, 260, 272n79, 287n217

Walcott, G. (Secretary of Colonial Land and Emigration Commission), 33–34, 260, 265n40

Wallace, Frederick William (Canadian journalist and historian), 12, 260, 262n10

Wallace, John Orr (husband of

Mary McConnel Kelly), 226, 285n200
Wallace, Mary McConnel (*née* Kelly, daughter of Martha and W. Kelly Sr.), 82, 133, 200, 220, 222, 226, 230, 235, 286n209
Wallace, William Kelly (son of Mary and John Wallace, grandson of W. Kelly Sr.), 100, 273n94
Walters, Samuel (maritime artist): painting of *Merrie England*, 6, 104–105, 235, 286n209
Ward, James (seaman), 32
Warde, Michael (Irish commercial traveler), 59
Waterford, Ireland, 99, 106, 109, 110, 111, 176, 236, 260, 262n10
Watson's Code of Signals, 14
Webb, Thomas (seaman), 174
*Weekly Advertiser,* 24
Wellington Wharf, Quebec, 47
Wesley, John (a founder of Methodism), 207, 208
West India Dock, London, 40, 41, 42, 43
White, Albert (ship builder, Ferry-bank Waterford), 99, 109
Whiting, William (hymnist), 148
Wildes, Pickersgill & Co. (Anglo-American merchant bank), 47, 268n53
Wilkinson, George (seaman), 171
Wilks, Samuel (M.D.) on paraplegia, 209
William and Richard Wright (shipbuilder, New Brunswick), 64, 269n66
Williams, Charles (seaman), 151
Williams, Thomas (seaman, sole survivor, wreck of *Express*), 163–164
Wisnom, Hugh, 151, 167–169, 197, 279n150
Wisnom, Jane (wife of Hugh Wisnom, *née* McAlpine), 167, 168
Wisnom, John McLain (seaman, son of Jane and Hugh Wisnom), 168–169
Wolfendens of Lambeg, 207, 208
"wonders in the deep," 3. *See also* "milky sea" phenomenon
woods used in ship construction, 12
workhouse emigrants on *Belinda*, 32–38, 34*t.*, 242
Workington, Samuel (geranium thief), 223–224

*yellow dust* (guano), 39–41
yellow fever, 18, 22, 263n21
*yellow meal* (Indian corn) rations, 35–37

Zangwill, Israel (British writer), 243, 287n216

## About the Author

Born in Ottawa, Ontario, Harold Bradley now lives in the San Francisco Bay Area where he has worked as a writer in the telecommunications, aerospace, industrial safety systems, energy, and scientific software industries. He is a family historian with two generations of nineteenth-century master mariners in his family tree. With the publication of *Seaward*, he has moved from writing in industry to researching and recounting his family's first generation of wind-jamming seafarers.

www.ingramcontent.com/pod-product-compliance
Lightning Source LLC
LaVergne TN
LVHW021651060526
838200LV00050B/2305